Advanced Data Streaming with Apache NiFi
Engineering Real-Time Data Pipelines for Professionals

Contents

1 **Introduction to Apache NiFi**   **11**

  1.1   What is Apache NiFi? 11

  1.2   History and Evolution of Apache NiFi 13

  1.3   Key Features of Apache NiFi 15

  1.4   Core Components of Apache NiFi 16

  1.5   How Apache NiFi Works: A High-Level Overview 19

  1.6   Understanding the NiFi User Interface 21

  1.7   Basic Concepts: FlowFiles, Processors, Connections, and
Flow Controllers 23

  1.8   Apache NiFi vs Other Data Integration Tools 24

  1.9   Use Cases for Apache NiFi 26

  1.10 Getting Started: Setting Up a Basic NiFi Environment . . 28

2 **Apache NiFi Architecture and Core Concepts**   **31**

  2.1   Overview of NiFi Architecture 31

  2.2   The Role of the Flow Controller 33

  2.3   Understanding Processors and Processor Groups 35

  2.4   Exploring Connections and FlowFiles 36

  2.5   The Functionality of Controller Services 38

  2.6   Backpressure and FlowFile Prioritization 40

  2.7   Data Provenance in Apache NiFi 41

2.8 Apache NiFi's Pluggable Components and Custom Processors 43

2.9 FlowFile Repository, Content Repository, and Provenance Repository 45

2.10 High Availability and Fault Tolerance in NiFi 47

2.11 Integrating NiFi with External Systems 49

2.12 Best Practices for Apache NiFi Architecture Design . . . 51

3 Working with Processors in NiFi   **55**

3.1 Introduction to Processors in NiFi 55

3.2 Commonly Used Processors for Data Ingestion 57

3.3 Data Extraction and Transformation Processors 59

3.4 Processors for Data Routing and Distribution 61

3.5 Understanding Processor Configuration 63

3.6 Utilizing Processor Properties and Relationships 65

3.7 Managing Processor Scheduling and Concurrency 67

3.8 Error Handling and Retry Mechanisms in Processors . . 69

3.9 Custom Processors Development 71

3.10 Optimizing Processor Performance 73

3.11 Using Processors for Data Enrichment 75

3.12 Debugging and Troubleshooting Processors 77

4 Data Flow Management and Routing   **81**

4.1 Overview of Data Flow Management in NiFi 81

4.2 Designing Data Flows: Best Practices 83

4.3 Routing Data Based on Content and Attributes 85

4.4 Utilizing Process Groups for Organized Data Flow 87

4.5 Handling Backpressure and Data Prioritization 89

4.6 Data Partitioning and Multiple FlowFile Processing . . . 90

4.7 FlowFile Queues and Load Balancing Strategies 92

4.8 Splitting and Aggregating FlowFiles 94

4.9 Data Flow Monitoring and Real-time Feedback 95

4.10 Implementing Advanced Routing Techniques 97

4.11 Error Handling and Failure Recovery in Data Flows . . . 99

4.12 Automating Data Flow Management with Templates and Parameters 101

5 NiFi Expression Language and Attributes   105

5.1 Introduction to NiFi Expression Language 105

5.2 Understanding Attributes in NiFi 107

5.3 Basic Syntax and Functions of NiFi Expression Language 109

5.4 Dynamic Property Setting Using Expression Language . 110

5.5 Manipulating Attributes with Expression Language . . . 112

5.6 Using Expression Language for Routing and Filtering . . 114

5.7 Date and Time Handling in Expression Language 116

5.8 Accessing External Properties and Environment Variables 118

5.9 Advanced Techniques: Regular Expressions in Expression Language 120

5.10 Debugging and Troubleshooting Expression Language Expressions 122

5.11 Performance Considerations When Using Expression Language 124

5.12 Real-world Use Cases for Expression Language 126

6 Advanced NiFi Techniques and Best Practices   129

6.1 Advanced Data Flow Design Patterns 129

6.2 Optimizing NiFi for Large Data Volumes 132

6.3 Securing Sensitive Data within Flows 134

6.4 Leveraging Scripting Processors for Custom Logic 135

6.5 Integration with Big Data Tools and Systems 137

6.6 Automating NiFi Processes with REST API 139

6.7 Version Control and Deployment Strategies 141

6.8 Cluster-Wide Configuration and Management 143

6.9   Troubleshooting Complex Flows 145

6.10 Monitoring NiFi Performance and Health 147

6.11 NiFi Extensions: Custom Processors and Controller Services 149

6.12 Best Practices for Scalability and Maintenance 151

7 Securing Data Flows in Apache NiFi   **155**

7.1   Understanding Security in Apache NiFi 155

7.2   Configuring SSL/TLS for Secure Data Transfer 157

7.3   User Authentication and Authorization Mechanisms . . 159

7.4   Managing Sensitive Properties and Passwords 161

7.5   Data Encryption Techniques within NiFi 163

7.6   Using Access Policies for Securing Data Flains in Apache NiFi 165

7.7   Audit Logging and Data Provenance for Security 167

7.8   Securing NiFi in Multi-tenant Environments 169

7.9   Integrating NiFi with External Security Systems 171

7.10 Securing NiFi REST API and UI 173

7.11 Common Security Pitfalls and How to Avoid Them . . . 174

7.12 Security Best Practices for Apache NiFi Deployment . . . 176

8 Monitoring, Logging, and Troubleshooting NiFi   **179**

8.1   Overview of NiFi Monitoring Capabilities 179

8.2   Configuring and Reading NiFi Logs 181

8.3   Monitoring NiFi Performance and Health 182

8.4   Utilizing NiFi's Built-in Reporting Tasks 185

8.5   Custom Monitoring and Alerting with NiFi 186

8.6   Understanding and Managing Backpressure 188

8.7   Diagnosing Common Issues in NiFi Flows 190

8.8   Troubleshooting Processor Failures 192

8.9   Recovering from Data Flow Interruptions 194

8.10 Performance Tuning for NiFi 196

8.11 Using the NiFi Bulletin Board for System Messages . . . 198

8.12 Best Practices for Logging and Monitoring in NiFi 200

9 Building Real-Time Data Pipelines with Apache NiFi   203

9.1 Introduction to Real-Time Data Pipelines 203

9.2 Designing Data Pipelines with Apache NiFi 205

9.3 Ingesting Data from Various Sources 207

9.4 Processing and Transforming Data in Real-Time 209

9.5 Routing Data to Multiple Destinations 211

9.6 Integrating with External Systems and Databases 213

9.7 Ensuring Data Quality and Consistency 215

9.8 Scaling NiFi for High Volume Data Processing 217

9.9 Monitoring and Managing Pipeline Performance 219

9.10 Handling Failures and Ensuring Data Recovery 221

9.11 Securing Real-Time Data Pipelines 223

9.12 Case Studies: Real-World Data Pipeline Scenarios 225

10 NiFi Cluster Configuration and Management   229

10.1 Introduction to NiFi Clustering 229

10.2 Setting Up a NiFi Cluster 231

10.3 NiFi Cluster Architecture and Concepts 232

10.4 Configuring NiFi Nodes and Cluster Properties 234

10.5 Load Balancing in a NiFi Cluster 236

10.6 Data Synchronization and State Management 238

10.7 Securing a NiFi Cluster 240

10.8 Monitoring and Managing Cluster Health 241

10.9 Cluster Scaling and Capacity Planning 243

10.10 Troubleshooting Common Cluster Issues 245

10.11 Best Practices for Cluster Configuration and Management 247

10.12Migrating and Upgrading NiFi Clusters 249

Preface

This book, titled *Advanced Data Streaming with Apache NiFi: Engineering Real-Time Data Pipelines for Professionals*, is designed to provide readers with a comprehensive guide to mastering Apache NiFi, a powerful and versatile open-source software for automating the flow of data between systems. With the proliferation of data in today's digital world, the ability to manage, process, and analyze data in real-time has become crucial for organizations across various industries. Apache NiFi offers a flexible and scalable solution to data streaming challenges, making it an indispensable tool for data engineers, IT professionals, and system administrators seeking to optimize their data workflows.

The objective of this book is threefold. First, it aims to introduce readers to the foundational concepts and architecture of Apache NiFi, equipping them with the necessary knowledge to understand how NiFi processes and moves data. Second, it seeks to provide a practical, hands-on approach to using Apache NiFi, with detailed explanations and examples on configuring and deploying data pipelines, managing data flow, securing data, and troubleshooting common issues. Finally, the book endeavors to share advanced techniques and best practices for designing and managing complex data integration scenarios, ensuring readers are well-prepared to tackle real-world data streaming challenges.

The substance of the book is structured into meticulously organized chapters, each focusing on a distinct aspect of Apache NiFi, from its architecture and core concepts to securing data flows and building real-time data pipelines. The content is presented in a logical sequence, allowing readers to build their knowledge incrementally, with later chapters building upon the concepts introduced in earlier ones. Throughout the book, emphasis is placed on real-world applications and practical scenarios to highlight how NiFi can be leveraged to solve complex data streaming problems.

This book is intended for a broad audience, including data engineers, system administrators, software developers, and IT professionals involved in data management and integration. Whether you are new to Apache NiFi or looking to deepen your existing knowledge, this book offers valuable insights and guidance on leveraging NiFi to its full potential. By focusing on practical applications and real-world scenarios, it aims to empower readers to effectively design, implement, and manage robust data streaming solutions using Apache NiFi.

In addition to foundational topics, the book delves into advanced features and extensions of Apache NiFi, such as custom processor development, integrating NiFi with various big data ecosystems, and optimizing performance for large-scale data flows. Readers are also guided through case studies and best practices accumulated from industry expertise, offering a rich context and deeper understanding of how to tackle specific challenges they might encounter in professional settings.

Whether your goal is to streamline data ingestion and processing, ensure compliance with data governance policies, or architect a highly resilient data pipeline, this book serves as a complete guide to mastering these objectives using Apache NiFi. Through a blend of theoretical insights and practical guidance, it ensures that readers are not only able to implement effective data solutions but also innovate and adapt as the data landscape continues to evolve.

Chapter 1

Introduction to Apache NiFi

Apache NiFi is an open-source project designed to automate the flow of data between software systems. Originally developed by the National Security Agency (NSA) and later contributed to the Apache Software Foundation, NiFi provides a highly configurable and flexible platform that supports scalable data routing, transformation, and system mediation logic. It is built to facilitate easy and rapid data ingestion, processing, and distribution across various data sources and destinations, offering a user-friendly interface for managing data flows. With its robust framework and extensive features, NiFi caters to the complex requirements of data streaming and processing, making it a critical tool for modern data-driven organizations.

1.1   What is Apache NiFi?

Apache NiFi is an integrated data logistics platform for automating the movement of data between disparate systems. It is distinguished by its scalable, visual, and configurable design that facilitates the rapid development of data flows. At its core, NiFi was developed to automate the flow of data between systems, a process crucial for today's data-driven environments where data latency and bottlenecks can have significant impacts.

11

NiFi operates on a fundamental concept known as "Flow-Based Programming" (FBP), which emphasizes the movement of data through a network of processors, each dedicated to a specific operation. This approach allows for high degrees of customization and flexibility in handling data of varying formats and sizes across different protocols and services, from simple file transfer protocols to complex distributed systems like Kafka and HDFS.

One of the remarkable features of Apache NiFi is its user-friendly web-based user interface (UI), which allows for drag-and-drop configuration of data flows. This interface provides real-time visualization of data flows, including the state of each component and the movement of data between components, allowing for immediate feedback and adjustments. The UI is not just for monitoring; it is an integral part of the system that provides detailed configuration options for every aspect of the data flow, ensuring that components are properly connected and configured according to the requirements of the data management task.

At the heart of NiFi's architecture are several key concepts and components:

- `FlowFiles` represent each piece of data as it traverses through a data flow.

- `Processors` perform operations on FlowFiles, such as reading, writing, transforming, routing, or any custom logic.

- `Connections` link processors together, creating a path for Flow-Files to follow.

- `Flow Controllers` manage the overall data flow, ensuring resources are allocated correctly and that system-wide settings are enforced.

These elements work in concert to provide a robust framework for data routing, transformation, and mediation between systems.

Moreover, NiFi is designed with a strong emphasis on security and governance. It supports secure data transmission protocols, fine-grained access control, data provenance, and is compliant with various regulatory requirements. This makes it suitable for enterprises that handle sensitive or regulated data.

In terms of scalability, NiFi can be run on both standalone servers and on clusters to support large-scale, high-throughput data flows. Its architecture is designed to scale horizontally, allowing for additional nodes to be added to a cluster as data demand grows. This scalability, combined with its fault tolerance and load-balancing capabilities, ensures that NiFi can meet the demands of complex, high-volume data processing tasks.

Comparatively, NiFi offers a unique proposition in the realm of data integration and processing tools. Unlike traditional ETL (extract, transform, load) tools that are batch-focused, NiFi supports both event-driven and batch processing paradigms, making it ideal for real-time data processing needs. Its comprehensive list of processors, extensive connectivity options, and dynamic prioritization of data flows allow for flexibility not commonly found in other tools of its kind.

Ultimately, Apache NiFi stands out as a powerful tool for building complex data pipelines. Its ability to efficiently process and route data in real time, combined with its ease of use and flexibility, makes it an essential component of modern data architectures. Whether for simple data transfers, complex event processing, or integration with big data ecosystems, NiFi provides a scalable solution to meet the evolving needs of data-driven organizations.

1.2 History and Evolution of Apache NiFi

Apache NiFi originated as a high-scale data routing and transformation system project developed by the National Security Agency (NSA) of the United States. Named as "Niagarafiles" or NiFi, it was designed to automate and improve the flow of data between disparate and distributed data systems regardless of their data formats or schemas. The NSA built NiFi to address specific challenges in dataflow management, such as system failure recovery, data prioritization, and ensuring that data delivery is guaranteed.

In 2014, the NSA opted to contribute the Niagarafiles project to the Apache Software Foundation (ASF), aiming to leverage the expertise and contributions of the global development community to enhance and evolve NiFi further. This strategic decision marked a pivotal turn in the project's lifecycle, transitioning from a government-only tool to an open-source platform available to the public. Shortly after its contribution to ASF, Niagarafiles was renamed to Apache NiFi, and it became part of the Apache incubator.

During its incubation period, Apache NiFi quickly garnered attention and gained contributors from a diverse range of industries, which enriched the project with a variety of perspectives and use cases. This collaborative effort led to significant improvements in NiFi's usability, scalability, and reliability. Contributors worked diligently to enhance its core features, as well as to increase its extensibility through the development of additional processors and services. The community focus was on creating a robust platform that could cater to the complex and evolving needs of data-driven enterprises.

Apache NiFi graduated from the incubator in July 2015, becoming a top-level project within the ASF. This graduation was a testament to its vibrant community, solid governance processes, and its alignment with the ASF's model of open-source development. Since becoming a top-level project, Apache NiFi has seen rapid evolution and adoption. The community has consistently delivered updates that introduce new features, improve performance, and strengthen security measures. One notable advancement of NiFi is the introduction of the NiFi Registry, a sub-project that simplifies the flow development and management process, allowing for versioning and sharing of flows.

The design of Apache NiFi is driven by its foundational concepts such as FlowFiles, Processors, Connections, and Flow Controllers, contributing to its flexibility and ease-of-use. The platform's architecture supports backpressure and prioritization of dataflows, ensuring efficient use of network and system resources. Moreover, Apache NiFi utilizes a highly configurable and user-friendly interface, making it accessible to users with various levels of technical expertise.

Today, Apache NiFi is considered a critical component in modern data architecture, supporting data ingestion, processing, and analytics pipelines across diverse sectors such as finance, healthcare, telecommunications, and government. Its evolution reflects an ongoing commitment to meet the high demands of real-time data processing and integration in an era where data volume, variety, and velocity continue to grow exponentially.

The history and evolution of Apache NiFi underscore the importance of community-driven development in advancing technology that addresses complex data management challenges. Through continuous contributions and improvements, Apache NiFi remains at the forefront of dataflow management solutions, enabling organizations to harness the full potential of their data assets in real time.

1.3 Key Features of Apache NiFi

Apache NiFi stands out in the realm of data streaming and processing tools due to its unique and powerful set of features. These features are designed to provide comprehensive capabilities for data routing, transformation, and systemic mediation. This section will discuss the key attributes that contribute to the robustness and flexibility of Apache NiFi, making it a preferred choice for various data integration and processing needs.

- **Data Provenance:** One of the paramount features of Apache NiFi is its support for detailed data provenance. It maintains a comprehensive record of every data byte that flows through the system, including where it originated from, how it was processed, and where it was sent to. This capability is crucial for auditing, compliance, and troubleshooting purposes, allowing users to track the lifecycle of the data through the system with precision and ease.

- **User-friendly Interface:** Apache NiFi offers a highly intuitive web-based user interface that simplifies the design, control, feedback, and monitoring of data flows. Users can effortlessly drag and drop components onto a canvas, configure them, and connect them to create complex data pipelines. This graphical user interface is accessible from any web browser, enabling the visualization of real-time data flows and facilitating an agile development process.

- **Scalability:** The architecture of Apache NiFi supports both horizontal and vertical scaling. This means it can scale out across many nodes in a cluster to handle high volumes of data, as well as scale up to make efficient use of the nodes it runs on by processing multiple tasks concurrently. Such scalability ensures that NiFi can meet the demands of large-scale data processing tasks without sacrificing performance.

- **Flexible and Configurable Data Routing:** Apache NiFi allows for flexible and dynamic routing of data. Processors can be configured to route data flows based on content and metadata, enabling complex processing logic and decision-making capabilities within the data flow. This feature ensures that data can be dynamically directed to different paths and destinations based on real-time processing results or external triggers.

- **Extensive Connectivity:** With over 300 pre-built processors and numerous controllers and services, Apache NiFi can connect to a wide array of data sources and destinations. These include but are not limited to, major databases, cloud services, file systems, and messaging systems. This extensive connectivity makes it a highly versatile tool for integrating diverse systems and bridging the gap between disparate data sources.

- **Guaranteed Delivery:** NiFi guarantees that data is not lost during transfer, even in the event of system failure. This is achieved through its use of a reliable and robust flow-based architecture, along with checkpoints and content repositories for recoverability. Such features ensure that every piece of data that enters the NiFi system is persisted until it is safely delivered to its destination.

- **Fine-grained Control over Back Pressure and Prioritization:** NiFi provides mechanisms for managing back pressure and setting priority queues to efficiently handle data under various network conditions and system loads. This allows for granular control over how data flows are managed, ensuring that resources are used optimally and high-priority tasks are executed with precedence.

These features collectively make Apache NiFi an immensely powerful tool for data ingestion, processing, and distribution. Its design emphasizes ease of use, scalability, and robustness, catering to the needs of modern, data-intensive applications. By providing detailed data provenance, a user-friendly interface, and versatile connectivity options, among other advanced capabilities, Apache NiFi equips organizations with the means to build comprehensive and reliable data pipelines that support complex data processing workflows and integrations.

1.4   Core Components of Apache NiFi

Apache NiFi consists of several core components that together facilitate the management, processing, and distribution of data. Understanding these components is crucial for designing and implementing effective data flow strategies. This segment delineates the fundamental elements that constitute Apache NiFi's architecture and operational framework.

First among NiFi's components is the `FlowFile`. A `FlowFile` represents a single piece of data within NiFi, which not only contains the data itself but also metadata describing attributes of the data. This dual nature facilitates both the movement and transformation of data through various processors. The structure of a `FlowFile` can be visualized as follows:

```
+-----------------------+
| FlowFile Attributes   |
+-----------------------+
| FlowFile Content      |
+-----------------------+
```

This composition allows `FlowFiles` to be highly flexible and supportive of diverse data processing tasks.

The next foundational component is the `Processor`. Processors are the workhorses of Apache NiFi, tasked with executing specific operations on `FlowFiles`. Operations can range from data ingestion, routing, transformation, to delivery. Apache NiFi comes equipped with a large library of processors, each designed for specific tasks such as retrieving data from a source, converting data formats, or writing data to a destination.

```
1  <processor>
2    <id>generate-flowfile</id>
3    <class>org.apache.nifi.processors.standard.GenerateFlowFile</class>
4    <properties>
5      <property name="File Size">1024</property>
6    </properties>
7  </processor>
```

The configuration above creates a simple processor that generates `FlowFiles` of a specified size.

Connections within Apache NiFi serve as conduits between processors, enabling the flow of `FlowFiles`. These connections not only transport data but also apply back pressure and prioritize data flow, ensuring efficient processing even under heavy loads. The definition of connections is integral to designing a data flow strategy, as it dictates the path `FlowFiles` will take through the processing pipeline.

```
1  <connection>
2    <source>processor-id-1</source>
3    <destination>processor-id-2</destination>
4  </connection>
```

This snippet establishes a connection between two processors, thereby defining a simple data flow path.

17

The Flow Controller orchestrates the overall data flow, managing the scheduling of processors and the allocation of resources. It ensures that processors execute according to the designed flow and that system resources are efficiently used. The Flow Controller thus plays a pivotal role in maintaining the performance and reliability of the NiFi system.

Process Groups are organizational units within NiFi that encapsulate a collection of processors, connections, and other components. They allow for modular development of data flows, enabling reuse and simplification of complex data processing tasks. Process groups can be nested, offering hierarchical organization of data flows that reflect organizational or functional structures.

```
1   <processGroup>
2     <id>process-group-1</id>
3     <name>Data Ingestion Group</name>
4     <processors>
5       <!-- List of processors -->
6     </processors>
7     <connections>
8       <!-- List of connections -->
9     </connections>
10  </processGroup>
```

Through Process Groups, developers can modularize and manage data flows with ease, enhancing maintainability and scalability.

The Controller Services are shared services that provide functionality to processors. Examples include database connections, SSL contexts, and third-party client services. By abstracting these services, NiFi allows processors to share resources efficiently, reducing redundancy and facilitating easier configuration management.

```
1   <controllerService>
2     <id>db-connection-pooling-service</id>
3     <class>org.apache.nifi.dbcp.DBCPConnectionPool</class>
4     <!-- Additional configuration -->
5   </controllerService>
```

Here, a Controller Service is defined for managing database connections, which processors can utilize as needed.

In summary, Apache NiFi's architecture is built around these core components: FlowFiles that encapsulate data, Processors that perform operations, Connections that define data paths, the Flow Controller that orchestrates processing, Process Groups that organize components, and Controller Services that offer shared functionalities. Together, these elements enable NiFi to efficiently and flexibly manage complex data flows, catering to the diverse and dynamic needs of data-driven enterprises.

1.5 How Apache NiFi Works: A High-Level Overview

Apache NiFi operates on the fundamental principle of dataflow management. It is designed to automate the movement of data between disparate data sources and systems in real-time, providing a streamlined and efficient means to ingest, process, and distribute data. To understand how Apache NiFi achieves this, it is essential to become familiar with several core elements of its architecture: the dataflow manager, flowfiles, processors, and connections.

At the heart of NiFi's architecture is the concept of a flowfile. A flowfile in Apache NiFi represents a single piece of data moving through the system. It contains not only the content of the information being transferred but also metadata about the data, including attributes that are used to manage and route the data as it moves through a data pipeline.

Flowfiles are processed and routed through the system by entities known as processors. Processors are the workhorses of NiFi, capable of performing a vast array of data processing tasks such as reading from and writing to various data sources, transforming data, routing data based on conditions, and more. Processors are highly configurable, allowing for the customization of their behavior to fit a wide range of data processing needs.

Connections in NiFi are responsible for linking processors together to form a data pipeline. These connections determine the path that flowfiles take as they move from one processor to another. They can also be configured to manage how data is prioritized, queued, and distributed among different paths within the flow.

To manage these components and the dataflow, Apache NiFi employs a dataflow manager. This component oversees the orchestration of data movement through the system, managing the execution of processors and the routing of flowfiles based on a designed flow. The dataflow manager ensures that data movement is efficient, reliable, and resilient to failures, leveraging back pressure and prioritization mechanisms to handle varying loads and conditions in the data pipeline.

Let's illustrate the movement of a flowfile through a simple NiFi data pipeline with the following activities:

- A flowfile is created by a processor that ingests data into NiFi from an external source, such as a file system or a web service.

- The flowfile, containing the ingested data, is then routed to another processor designed to transform the data, for example, encoding the content or enriching the data with additional information.

- Once the transformation is complete, the flowfile is sent to another processor that may filter or route the data based on specific conditions defined within the flow.

- Finally, the processed flowfile is directed to a processor that exports the data out of NiFi to a destination system, such as a database or a cloud storage service.

Each step in this process is managed carefully by NiFi's dataflow manager, ensuring that the movement of data is executed according to the designed pipeline, with full consideration of operational aspects such as error handling, load balancing, and system monitoring.

To encapsulate the operation of a NiFi pipeline in its entirety, one can view it as a dynamically managed, continuous loop of data ingestion, processing, and distribution, facilitated by a network of processors interconnected through precisely configured connections. This model allows NiFi to support a broad spectrum of data processing activities, from simple data movement tasks to complex dataflows involving multiple sources, destinations, and processing steps.

Understanding the high-level workings of Apache NiFi provides a foundation for delving into more specific features and capabilities of the platform. The flexibility, scalability, and robustness of NiFi's architecture make it an invaluable tool for modern data-driven organizations, enabling the automation of dataflows in a way that is both powerful and accessible.

1.6   Understanding the NiFi User Interface

Apache NiFi's user interface (UI) is designed for simplicity and efficiency, enabling users to manage data flows visually. It operates within a web browser, offering a convenient platform for users to interact directly with their data flow components. The UI is segmented into several key areas, each serving a distinct purpose in the management and operation of data flows.

The main components of the NiFi UI are as follows:

- The Operate Palette

- The Components Toolbar

- The Global Menu

- The Status Bar

- The Canvas

The Operate Palette is situated on the left side of the UI and consists of controls for managing the data flow. These controls include starting or stopping all processors, enabling or disabling controllers, and refreshing the flow's status.

The Components Toolbar, located at the top of the UI, provides the tools needed to design data flows. This includes adding processors, input ports, output ports, process groups, and remote process groups. Users can drag and drop these components onto the canvas to start constructing their data flow.

The Global Menu, found in the upper right corner, encompasses several options for configuring and controlling the NiFi environment. Options within the Global Menu allow users to manage controller services, reporting tasks, templates, and access the NiFi flow configuration history.

The Status Bar, positioned at the bottom of the UI, displays key information about the current state of the NiFi system. This includes the number of active threads, the time the system has been up, and the system's overall health and performance metrics.

The Canvas is the central area of the NiFi UI where data flows are visually constructed and monitored. Users can arrange components, connect them with flow lines, and configure their settings all from within the canvas.

Data flow management within the NiFi UI involves creating and configuring process groups and processors. Processors are the building blocks of NiFi's data flows, each designed to perform a specific function, such as data ingestion, transformation, or routing. Users can double-click on any processor to configure its properties, define its relationships, and adjust its scheduling settings.

Every data flow component on the canvas exhibits a context menu, accessed by right-clicking on the component, which offers various actions such as starting, stopping, copying, pasting, and deleting. This context menu provides quick access to managing individual components without needing to navigate through the UI.

NiFi's UI also offers a detailed component view for in-depth configuration and monitoring. This view includes tabs for settings, scheduling, properties, and comments, allowing users to fine-tune the behavior of their processors and connections thoroughly.

One of NiFi's standout UI features is the data provenance tool. This tool tracks data flow through the system, providing users with the ability to audit, review, and troubleshoot the movement and transformation of data. Accessible through the Global Menu, the data provenance interface shows the lineage and attributes of data as it progresses through the flow, enabling comprehensive oversight.

To illustrate the layout and interaction within the NiFi UI, consider the following simple example:

```
1    // Adding a processor to the canvas
2    Drag the "GenerateFlowFile" processor from the Components Toolbar onto the canvas.
3
4    // Configuring the processor
5    Double-click the "GenerateFlowFile" processor to open its configuration dialogue.
6    Set the "File Size" property to 100 KB to specify the size of the generated files.
7
8    // Connecting processors
9    Drag a "LogAttribute" processor onto the canvas and use the mouse to draw a
             connection from the "GenerateFlowFile" processor to the "LogAttribute"
             processor. This routes the generated flow files for logging.
10
11   // Starting the data flow
12   Right-click the "GenerateFlowFile" processor and select "Start" from the context
             menu to commence the generation and logging of flow files.
```

The design and organization of the NiFi UI underscore its focus on providing a user-friendly environment for data flow management. By enabling users to create and monitor data flows graphically, Apache NiFi demystifies the complexities of data processing and makes it accessible to users with varying levels of expertise.

1.7 Basic Concepts: FlowFiles, Processors, Connections, and Flow Controllers

In the context of Apache NiFi, understanding the foundational elements such as FlowFiles, Processors, Connections, and Flow Controllers is crucial for harnessing the full potential of data streaming and processing. These concepts represent the building blocks of any data flow in NiFi, enabling the design and execution of complex data pipelines with ease and precision.

FlowFiles are the heart of Apache NiFi's data processing capabilities. They represent a single piece of data moving through the system, encapsulating the data itself or a pointer to the data, along with metadata and attributes associated with the data. Attributes are key-value pairs that provide contextual information about the data, such as its origin, type, or processing history. This abstraction allows NiFi to handle diverse data types and sizes, from bytes to gigabytes, uniformly across various processors without necessitating changes to the data itself.

```
1   // Example of a FlowFile attribute modification
2   UpdateAttribute processor {
3       // Adds or updates an attribute named 'dataOrigin' with the value 'sensorA'
4       Add/Update Attribute: dataOrigin = sensorA
5   }
```

Processors are the workhorses of Apache NiFi, responsible for receiving, processing, and sending FlowFiles to the next destination in the data pipeline. NiFi comes with a vast library of processors, each designed for specific tasks such as reading from or writing to a file system, transforming data formats, routing FlowFiles based on conditions, or invoking external web services. Processors are highly configurable, enabling fine-tuned control over their behavior and the data processing logic.

```
1   // Example of using a processor to convert JSON to Avro format
2   ConvertRecord processor {
3       // Configuration to specify record readers and writers
4       Record Reader: JSONTreeReader
5       Record Writer: AvroRecordSetWriter
6   }
```

Connections link processors together, forming a directed graph that represents the data flow. They are responsible for queueing FlowFiles as they move from one processor to another, ensuring that downstream processors have a steady supply of data to process. Connections also enable back pressure and prioritization, mechanisms that control the flow of data to prevent system overload and ensure that critical data is processed first.

Flow Controllers orchestrate the overall data flow, managing the scheduling of processors and the allocation of system resources. The Flow Controller is responsible for initiating the execution of processors according to the designed data pipeline, handling processor threading, and ensuring that resources are utilized efficiently without causing bottlenecks or resource contention.

In a NiFi cluster environment, the Flow Controller also plays a critical role in managing the cluster's nodes, balancing load, and ensuring data is processed reliably across the distributed architecture. This enables NiFi to scale out to handle larger volumes of data and more complex processing scenarios.

Understanding these core concepts is pivotal for designing effective data pipelines in Apache NiFi. FlowFiles provide the data abstraction needed to handle a wide variety of data types flexibly. Processors perform the data transformations and processing. Connections enable the flow of data between processors, and the Flow Controller ensures the entire process is executed efficiently and reliably. Together, these elements form the foundation of Apache NiFi's power and versatility in data streaming and processing.

1.8   Apache NiFi vs Other Data Integration Tools

When considering Apache NiFi in the landscape of data integration tools, it's essential to understand its distinctive features compared to other competitors in the market. This comparison will include popular data integration software such as Apache Kafka, Talend, and Informatica.

Apache NiFi, with its origin in the National Security Agency (NSA) and its subsequent handover to the Apache Software Foundation, was specifically designed to automate the movement of data between systems with a keen emphasis on flow management and data processing. One of its core strengths lies in its user-friendly, web-based user interface, which allows for the dynamic management of data flows.

Moreover, NiFi's component-based architecture promotes reusability and easy configuration, components such as processors, connections, flow controllers, and flow files. This design approach facilitates rapid development and deployment of data flow systems.

Apache Kafka, in contrast, is a distributed streaming platform, focusing on high-throughput, fault-tolerant messaging systems. Kafka is exceptionally well-suited for building real-time streaming data pipelines that reliably move data between systems or applications. Unlike NiFi, Kafka operates primarily as a publish-subscribe messaging system, with strong capabilities in back-pressure and real-time data streaming but lacks the comprehensive data routing, transformation, and mediation logic inherent in NiFi.

Talend, another significant player in the data integration arena, offers a more extensive suite of tools for data integration, quality, management, and cloud storage. Talend's approach to data integration is heavily oriented towards ETL (Extract, Transform, Load) processes, and it shines in scenarios where complex data transformation and data quality are the main concerns. While Talend provides excellent data processing capabilities, it does not offer the same level of intuitive and real-time data flow management as NiFi.

Informatica, known for its cloud data management and integration solutions, provides powerful tools for ETL processes, data quality, and big data management. Informatica's products are designed for large enterprises with complex data landscapes, offering deep capabilities in data integration and data governance. While Informatica delivers a comprehensive suite of data integration tools, its learning curve and cost may be steep compared to NiFi, particularly for organizations looking for a flexible and scalable solution capable of real-time data flow management with less overhead.

- Apache NiFi's emphasis is on easy-to-configure data routing, transformation, and system mediation logic, with a user-friendly, web-based interface.

- Apache Kafka excels in high-throughput, real-time messaging and streaming data applications, but does not natively provide data transformation and routing.

- Talend focuses on ETL processes and data quality, offering a wide range of data integration solutions but with less emphasis on real-time data flow management.

25

- Informatica offers a comprehensive suite for enterprise data integration and governance, targeting complex and large-scale data ecosystems, but with higher complexity and cost.

When selecting a data integration tool, it's crucial to consider the specific needs of the organization, including the complexity of data flows, real-time processing requirements, user interface preferences, and overall system scalability. Apache NiFi stands out for its robust data flow management capabilities, ease of use, and flexibility, making it an optimal choice for organizations looking to streamline their data integration processes with a focus on real-time data processing and flow management.

1.9   Use Cases for Apache NiFi

Apache NiFi is a versatile platform designed for data routing, transformation, and mediation processes. Its usage spans various domains and applications. This section will discuss several key use cases that demonstrate NiFi's capabilities and flexibility in addressing complex data integration and management tasks.

- **Data Ingestion and Distribution**: One of the primary use cases for Apache NiFi is to facilitate the ingestion of data from multiple sources, such as databases, logs, external APIs, and sensor data. NiFi supports real-time data ingestion, enabling organizations to collect, process, and distribute data across systems efficiently. For instance, NiFi can consume messages from a Kafka topic, perform transformations like format conversion or enrichment, and then distribute the data to HDFS or another data storage system for further analysis.

- **Log and Event Data Processing**: Companies generate vast amounts of log and event data that must be collected, aggregated, and analyzed to gain insights into user behavior, system performance, and potential security threats. NiFi can streamline the collection and processing of log data from various sources, apply filters or transformations, and deliver processed data to centralized logging platforms or storage solutions. This enables quicker anomaly detection and facilitates operational intelligence.

- **IoT Data Management**: With the explosion of Internet of Things (IoT) devices, managing the data generated by these devices has become increasingly complex. NiFi excels in scenarios that require the collection, processing, and analysis of IoT data. It can handle high volumes of data generated by sensors, perform preprocessing tasks like aggregation or normalization, and route the processed data to appropriate analytics or storage systems, enabling real-time monitoring and decision-making.

- **Data Lake Integration**: As organizations move towards adopting data lakes for centralized data storage and analysis, NiFi serves as a critical component in integrating disparate data sources into a data lake. It supports pulling data from various sources, applying necessary conversions or transformations, and loading the refined data into a data lake, ensuring that the data lake contains high-quality, consistent data for analytics purposes.

- **Stream Processing**: Apache NiFi is well-suited for stateless stream processing applications where data flows constantly and needs to be processed in real-time. NiFi's processors can filter, modify, and route streaming data, allowing organizations to create dynamic, scalable data pipelines that support real-time analytics and decision-making.

Each of these use cases showcases NiFi's ability to handle diverse data types, volumes, and processing requirements, making it an indispensable tool for modern data-driven environments. Its low latency, high throughput, and flexible data routing capabilities ensure that NiFi can be tailored to specific operational needs, further underlining its utility in a wide array of data integration and processing tasks.

1.10 Getting Started: Setting Up a Basic NiFi Environment

Setting up a basic environment for Apache NiFi involves several critical steps that ensure a proper foundation for deploying and testing data flows. This section will discuss the prerequisites, installation process, initial configuration, and the verification of a successful setup.

Prerequisites: Before installing NiFi, ensure that your system meets the minimum hardware and software requirements. Apache NiFi requires Java 8 or 11, and it is compatible with operating systems that support these Java versions. Additionally, a minimum of 4GB RAM and a dual-core processor is recommended for basic usage. However, for processing large volumes of data or for production environments, more powerful hardware specifications may be necessary.

Installation: Apache NiFi is distributed as a standard ZIP file containing all necessary binaries and documentation. To install NiFi, perform the following steps:

- Download the latest version of Apache NiFi from the official Apache NiFi website.

- Extract the ZIP file to a directory of your choice, which will be referred to as the `NiFi_home` directory.

- Ensure that the JAVA_HOME environment variable is set to the path of your Java installation.

Starting NiFi: To start NiFi, navigate to the `NiFi_home` directory and execute the appropriate script:

- On Windows, run the `run-nifi.bat` script.

- On Unix/Linux/Mac OS X, run the `./nifi.sh start` command.

Upon starting, NiFi initializes its components and begins listening for incoming connections on its web interface.

Accessing the NiFi Web Interface: By default, the NiFi web interface is accessible at `http://localhost:8080/nifi`. Open this URL in a web browser to view the NiFi user interface, which provides access to all features and allows for the design, control, feedback, and monitoring of data flows.

Verifying the Installation: To verify that NiFi has been successfully installed and is running correctly, perform the following checks:

- Ensure that the NiFi web interface is accessible and responsive.

- Check the `logs/nifi-app.log` file in the `NiFi_home` directory for any errors during startup. A successful start should not contain error messages indicating critical failures.

- Review the list of available processors by dragging a new processor onto the canvas. If the installation is successful, a wide range of processors will be available for selection.

Basic Configuration: Apache NiFi's default configuration is sufficient for exploring its features and building simple data flows. However, for enhanced performance and security, consider the following basic configuration steps:

- Increase the Java heap size based on available system memory. This can be done by adjusting the '-Xms' and '-Xmx' parameters in the nifi-bootstrap.conf file.

- Configure security settings, including HTTPS protocol, user authentication, and authorization. This ensures that sensitive data managed within NiFi is protected against unauthorized access. Security configuration details can be found in the NiFi System Administrator's Guide.

- Tune performance settings such as flowfile repository, component status repository, and content repository configurations to match the specifics of your data flow requirements and system capabilities.

With Apache NiFi installed and configured, you are now ready to develop powerful data flows for routing, transformation, and system mediation. As you become more familiar with NiFi, you may explore more advanced configurations and optimizations to tailor the environment to your specific workload requirements. The flexibility and robustness of Apache NiFi make it an indispensable tool for building real-time data pipelines in various operating environments.

Chapter 2

Apache NiFi Architecture and Core Concepts

The architecture of Apache NiFi is designed to accommodate the demands of data flow management through a highly concurrent model and distributed computing environment. At the heart of NiFi lies its flow-based programming model, encapsulated within a series of components such as Processors, FlowFiles, Connections, Process Groups, and Controller Services. These core concepts enable NiFi to efficiently process and route data across different systems, regardless of the data's source, format, or size. Understanding these foundational elements is crucial for effectively leveraging NiFi's capabilities to design, deploy, and manage data pipelines that are both resilient and scalable.

2.1 Overview of NiFi Architecture

Apache NiFi, a versatile and powerful data processing and distribution system, is built upon a unique architecture that emphasizes flexibility, scalability, and ease of use. This architecture is fundamentally designed to support the efficient movement, transformation, and management of data in real-time. At the core of NiFi's architecture is the concept of flow-based programming, which facilitates the design of data flows in a highly visual and configurable manner. This approach enables users to create complex data processing pipelines that can be easily monitored and adjusted in response to changing requirements.

The primary component of Apache NiFi's architecture is the Flow Controller, which acts as the brain of the operation. It is responsible for orchestrating the execution of data flows, managing system resources, and ensuring that data is processed reliably. The Flow Controller manages a series of interconnected processors, each of which performs a specific data processing task. Processors in NiFi are highly configurable components that can route, transform, and process data in various ways. They are the building blocks of any data flow and can be connected together to form complex processing pipelines.

Data flows in NiFi are represented as directed graphs, where the nodes are processors and the edges are connections that define the flow of data between these processors. This graphical representation not only makes it straightforward to design and understand complex data flows but also allows for real-time monitoring and modifications. The connections between processors facilitate the movement of data in the form of FlowFiles. A FlowFile in NiFi represents a piece of information moving through the system, encapsulating the data and its associated metadata.

A distinctive feature of NiFi's architecture is its use of FlowFiles to abstract the details of the underlying data format and structure. This abstraction allows NiFi to process and route any type of data, from various sources and formats, through a unified framework. FlowFiles move through the data pipeline, being transformed and routed by processors, until they reach their destination or are otherwise processed as required by the data flow design.

To further enhance its capabilities, NiFi includes the concept of Process Groups, enabling the organization of processors into reusable, modular components. Process Groups can encapsulate a part of a flow for specific functions or processing patterns, making it easier to design and manage complex data flows. This modularity is complemented by Controller Services, which provide shared services or resources that processors within a data flow can use. Controller Services might include database connections, SSL contexts, or any other shared resource that needs to be centrally managed and distributed across the data flow.

NiFi's design also focuses on operational flexibility and resilience. It incorporates features such as backpressure and prioritization to manage data flow dynamically, ensuring that the system can handle varying volumes of incoming data without becoming overwhelmed. Additionally, NiFi supports data provenance, allowing users to track and audit the movement and transformation of data through the system.

The architecture of Apache NiFi supports highly available and distributed deployments. Its clustered design ensures that data flows can be executed across multiple nodes, providing fault tolerance and allowing for scalable processing capacity. This distributed nature of NiFi makes it well-suited for building robust, large-scale data processing and distribution systems.

In essence, the architecture of Apache NiFi is built to provide a comprehensive, yet flexible, framework for data flow management. Its component-based design, coupled with the abstraction of FlowFiles and the graphical representation of data flows, enables users to efficiently design, deploy, and manage complex data pipelines. This foundation allows Apache NiFi to meet the challenges of modern data processing needs, making it a valuable tool in the ecosystem of big data technologies.

2.2 The Role of the Flow Controller

The Flow Controller is a central component in Apache NiFi's architecture that oversees the creation, scheduling, and coordination of tasks across the entire data flow. It is primarily responsible for managing the life cycle of Processors and other core components, such as Controller Services and Process Groups. This ensures that data flow processes are executed efficiently, maintaining the system's overall performance and reliability.

The Flow Controller operates at the heart of Apache NiFi, orchestrating the movement of FlowFiles through various processors and managing the system resources to optimize data processing. It employs a sophisticated scheduling mechanism that determines when and how often Processors should be executed, based on configurable strategies that may include event-driven triggers or scheduled intervals. This flexibility allows for the fine-tuning of data flows to meet specific performance and throughput requirements.

Under the management of the Flow Controller, processors are executed within threads that are handled by a thread pool. This design facilitates a highly concurrent processing environment, enabling multiple data flow tasks to be performed simultaneously. The concurrency model is a key aspect of NiFi's architecture, allowing it to process high volumes of data with minimal latency.

The Flow Controller also plays a crucial role in handling backpressure and prioritizing FlowFiles. Backpressure is a mechanism that prevents system overload by controlling the flow of FlowFiles based on configurable thresholds. When these thresholds are reached, the Flow Controller temporarily suspends the input of additional FlowFiles until the system can catch up. This ensures that NiFi can maintain stable performance under varying loads.

In addition to managing backpressure, the Flow Controller is responsible for implementing FlowFile prioritization strategies. These strategies determine the order in which FlowFiles are processed, allowing for the prioritization of certain data flows over others. This is particularly useful in scenarios where certain data is more time-sensitive or requires higher priority processing.

The Flow Controller's responsibilities extend to the management of Controller Services, which are shared resources that provide functionality to Processors across the data flow. By managing these services, the Flow Controller enables the reuse of common functionalities such as database connections, clients for external systems, and data conversion services, thereby reducing redundancy and simplifying the data flow design.

Furthermore, the Flow Controller is integral to NiFi's provenance data collection, which records the history and lineage of each FlowFile. This capability is essential for tracking the movement of data through the system, auditing data processing activities, and troubleshooting issues within the data flow.

The architecture of the Flow Controller is designed to ensure high availability and fault tolerance. It supports clustering, allowing multiple instances of NiFi to work together and maintain data flow operations even in the event of node failure. This is achieved through the distribution of processing tasks across the cluster and the replication of flow configuration across nodes, ensuring that the system can continue to operate with minimal disruption.

The Flow Controller is a cornerstone of Apache NiFi's architecture, playing a vital role in managing the complex logistics of data flow processes. Its capabilities in scheduling, resource management, backpressure handling, FlowFile prioritization, service management, and provenance data collection are essential for orchestrating efficient, reliable, and scalable data pipelines. Understanding the intricacies of the Flow Controller's functionality and leveraging its features is key to designing and deploying effective data flow systems with Apache NiFi.

2.3 Understanding Processors and Processor Groups

Apache NiFi's architectural robustness is significantly attributed to its modular design, where processors play a pivotal role. Processors are the primary elements that facilitate the data flow, supporting a vast array of data processing functions such as ingestion, routing, transformation, and delivery of data. Each processor is designed to perform a specific task, enabling developers to construct flexible and powerful data pipelines by configuring and connecting these processors in a flow.

Processors in NiFi are inherently versatile. They can handle different types of data sources and formats, making NiFi a highly adaptable tool for real-time data processing. To utilize a processor, one must configure its properties and relationships. The properties dictate how the processor operates, such as specifying the source of data or the criteria for data filtering. Relationships determine how processors connect to each other, defining the path of the data flow based on the outcome of the processing (e.g., success, failure).

```
1   // Example of a simple NiFi processor configuration in Java
2   public class MyProcessor extends AbstractProcessor {
3       @Override
4       public void onTrigger(ProcessContext context, ProcessSession session) throws
            ProcessException {
5           FlowFile flowFile = session.get();
6           if ( flowFile == null ) {
7               return;
8           }
9           // Perform processing here
10      }
11  }
```

In a complex data flow, managing a large number of processors and their interactions could become cumbersome. To address this, NiFi introduces the concept of Processor Groups. Processor Groups are containers that encapsulate a group of processors, along with their connections, controller services, and remote process groups. They serve not only as organizational units that simplify the design of data flows by grouping related processors but also as a means to logically separate different functional areas of a data pipeline for better manageability.

Processor Groups are also pivotal in scaling and distributing NiFi's data processing capabilities. They can be deployed across different nodes in a NiFi cluster, enabling distributed data processing and enhancing the fault tolerance and reliability of the data pipeline. This distributed nature allows NiFi to efficiently process large volumes of data by leveraging the computational resources of multiple nodes.

Moreover, Processor Groups facilitate the development of reusable components. Once a Processor Group is defined, it can be exported as a template, which can then be imported and reused in other data flows. This encourages the sharing of best practices and significantly speeds up the development of new data pipelines.

NiFi's architecture thus supports a high degree of customization and flexibility through the use of Processors and Processor Groups. This design facilitates the rapid development of data flows that can scale from handling simple data transformations to managing complex data processing pipelines across distributed computing environments. Through careful planning and organization of processors into groups, NiFi users can achieve efficient data flow management, making Apache NiFi a powerful tool for real-time data processing and analytics.

2.4 Exploring Connections and FlowFiles

In this section we will discuss the fundamental elements within Apache NiFi's architecture that are pivotal for managing data flow: Connections and FlowFiles. These components are essential in the orchestration of data movement and transformation across the data pipeline.

Connections in NiFi are responsible for the data flow between Processors, Process Groups, and external systems. They serve as the conduits through which FlowFiles move within the system. A Connection is more than merely a link; it carries important configuration details such as the following:

- Prioritization: Determines the order in which FlowFiles are sent through the Connection.

- Backpressure settings: Controls the maximum size or count of FlowFiles that can queue up in the Connection, preventing system overload.

- Load balancing: Distributes the data load across the cluster, optimizing resource utilization and performance.

The configuration of Connections is crucial for ensuring that data flows efficiently and reliably from source to destination, taking into account the system's performance and fault tolerance requirements.

FlowFiles are the heart of NiFi's data flow model. They encapsulate the information moving through the system, but it's important to distinguish that a FlowFile consists of two major components: attributes and content. The content is the data payload, while the attributes are key-value pairs that store metadata about the data. This design allows NiFi to efficiently manage and route data based on its attributes without necessarily having to inspect the content directly.

The structure of a FlowFile can be represented as follows:

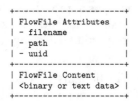

```
+-----------------------+
| FlowFile Attributes   |
| - filename            |
| - path                |
| - uuid                |
+-----------------------+
| FlowFile Content      |
| <binary or text data> |
+-----------------------+
```

Manipulating a FlowFile typically involves processors that either change its attributes, alter its content, or both. For example, a processor might compress the content of a FlowFile, add or update attributes to reflect the compression, and pass the modified FlowFile along to the next stage of processing.

To exemplify how processors interact with FlowFiles, consider the following code snippet:

```
1   # Processor that adds an attribute to each incoming FlowFile
2   def addAttribute(flowFile, session):
3       if flowFile != None:
4           # Add or update an attribute
5           flowFile = session.putAttribute(flowFile, "newAttribute", "newValue")
6           # Transfer the FlowFile to the next relationship
7           session.transfer(flowFile, REL_SUCCESS)
```

The code demonstrates the simplicity with which processors can manipulate the flow of data by augmenting FlowFiles with new attributes. This flexibility allows data flows to be dynamically adjusted based on the attributes of the FlowFiles moving through the system.

Connections and FlowFiles are foundational to constructing data pipelines in Apache NiFi. By understanding how to configure Connections to manage data flow effectively and how to manipulate FlowFiles to transform and route data, developers and data engineers can build complex, efficient, and scalable data processing workflows. As we delve further into the architecture and core concepts of Apache NiFi, the importance of these elements in designing resilient and performant data pipelines will become increasingly apparent.

2.5   The Functionality of Controller Services

Controller Services in Apache NiFi play a pivotal role in managing shared resources and functionality across various components of a dataflow. These services are designed to provide a centralized mechanism for components, such as processors and other controller services, to access shared capabilities or configurations. This approach ensures that common functions are abstractly managed and efficiently utilized, eliminating the need for duplicate configurations and facilitating ease of maintenance.

A Controller Service typically encapsulates functionality that is common across multiple types of Processors or other components within NiFi. This can include, but is not limited to, database connection pooling, SSL context settings, and third-party service clients (e.g., AWS S3, Apache Kafka). By leveraging Controller Services, developers can significantly streamline the configuration process and improve the robustness of dataflows.

Understanding the lifecycle of a Controller Service is crucial for effective utilization. The lifecycle includes several states: enabling, enabled, disabling, and disabled. Transition between these states allows for safe modifications of configurations and ensures that dependent components can adjust accordingly without causing data loss or corruption.

To configure a Controller Service, one navigates to the NiFi UI, accesses the Controller Settings pane, and creates a new service by selecting the desired service type. The configuration parameters vary depending on the type of service being set up. For instance, a database connection pooling service would require parameters such as database URL, username, password, and driver class name. Once configured, the service can be enabled, making it available for Processors and other services to reference.

An example of configuring and using a database connection pooling service is illustrated below:

```
1  // Example of configuring a DBCPConnectionPool Controller Service in Apache NiFi
2  ControllerService dbcpService = new DBCPConnectionPool();
3  dbcpService.setDatabaseURL("jdbc:mysql://localhost:3306/nifi");
4  dbcpService.setUsername("nifiuser");
5  dbcpService.setPassword("nifipassword");
6  dbcpService.setDriverClassName("com.mysql.jdbc.Driver");
7  dbcpService.create();
8  dbcpService.enable();
```

Once enabled, Processors can reference the Controller Service by its identifier, facilitating operations that require database connections without handling connection pooling logic directly. This abstraction layer not only simplifies processor configuration but also enhances pipeline efficiency by centralized management of critical resources.

Controller Services are also instrumental in implementing advanced features like secure data transformations and interactions with external systems. For example, a Processor that fetches data from an S3 bucket can use an AWS credentials Controller Service. This setup allows for centralized management of AWS credentials, which can be updated or rotated without modifying each processor configuration individually.

In the context of scaling and managing complex dataflows, Controller Services offer significant advantages. They provide a mechanism for sharing configurations and services across a cluster, ensuring consistent operations and configurations across the entire NiFi instance. This is particularly beneficial in distributed environments where consistency and efficiency are paramount.

Controller Services are a fundamental aspect of Apache NiFi's architecture, offering a flexible and efficient way to share resources and configurations across various components of a dataflow. By centralizing common functionality, NiFi allows for smoother operation, reduces duplication of configurations, and enhances overall efficiency and maintainability of data pipelines. Understanding and effectively leveraging Controller Services is a critical skill for architects and developers working with Apache NiFi to ensure the development of robust, scalable, and efficient dataflows.

2.6   Backpressure and FlowFile Prioritization

Backpressure and FlowFile prioritization are two fundamental concepts in Apache NiFi that directly impact the performance and reliability of data flows. These mechanisms are designed to manage data flow dynamically, ensuring system stability and efficiency even under high load conditions. This section will discuss the mechanisms of backpressure and FlowFile prioritization in detail, elucidating their importance in the management of data pipelines.

Backpressure is a flow control mechanism that prevents the overwhelming of any component within a NiFi data flow. As data flows from one processor to another, there exists the potential for a bottleneck to occur at any point in the pipeline, especially if a downstream processor is slower than its upstream counterpart. Backpressure acts to mitigate such situations by temporarily halting the flow of data, thus preventing the possible accumulation and eventual loss of data at any bottleneck point.

The implementation of backpressure in Apache NiFi is handled through two primary settings on a connection: `BackPressure Data Size Threshold` and `BackPressure Object Threshold`. The `BackPressure Data Size Threshold` limits the total size of data allowed to be queued on a connection before backpressure is applied, whereas the `BackPressure Object Threshold` limits the number of FlowFiles allowed to be queued. When either of these thresholds is exceeded, NiFi temporarily stops the flow of data to prevent overwhelming the system. Using these thresholds, administrators can fine-tune the flow of data to match the processing capabilities of their system, ensuring smooth and efficient data processing.

FlowFile prioritization, on the other hand, is a mechanism that allows the prioritization of data packets (FlowFiles) within a queue based on specific criteria. This ensures that more critical data can be processed and passed through the system more quickly than less critical data. In Apache NiFi, prioritization is achieved by assigning prioritizers to the queues that hold FlowFiles. NiFi comes with several built-in prioritizers, including:

- First In, First Out (FIFO) - Processes FlowFiles in the order they were received.

- Last In, First Out (LIFO) - Prioritizes the processing of the most recently received FlowFiles.

- Priority Attribute Prioritizer - Uses FlowFile attributes to determine prioritization.

- Newest FlowFile First - Prioritizes the processing of the newest FlowFiles over older ones.

- Oldest FlowFile First - Ensures that the oldest FlowFiles in the queue are processed first.

Custom FlowFile prioritizers can also be developed and integrated into NiFi, allowing for highly tailored data flow management based on the specific needs of a project.

Integrating backpressure and FlowFile prioritization into NiFi data flows allows administrators to effectively manage the flow of data through the system, ensuring that resources are allocated efficiently and that high priority data is processed in a timely manner. This not only increases the performance of data pipelines but also contributes significantly to their reliability and fault tolerance.

Implementing these mechanisms requires a deep understanding of the data flow requirements of a given project, as well as the processing capabilities of the deployed NiFi system. Through careful configuration of backpressure thresholds and FlowFile prioritizers, NiFi administrators can create robust, efficient, and reliable data pipelines capable of managing diverse and dynamic data sets.

2.7 Data Provenance in Apache NiFi

Data provenance in Apache NiFi refers to the ability to track and document the lifecycle of a FlowFile within a data flow. This includes comprehensive details about where data originated from, how it moved and transformed through the system, and where it was sent. Apache NiFi provides this capability through its Data Provenance feature, enabling users to audit, review, and diagnose the behavior of data in their flows with precision and granularity.

In NiFi, each action performed on a FlowFile is recorded as a provenance event. These events capture various types of information, such as the event type (e.g., create, modify, route, clone, join, fork), the components involved (processors, controller services, etc.), timestamps, and attributes changes. This data forms a detailed audit trail for each piece of data that flows through the system.

The Provenance Repository is where these events are stored. NiFi allows for the configuration of the repository's storage capacity and location, providing flexibility in how provenance data is managed. The implementation of the repository is pluggable, with the default being a high-performance local disk storage mechanism. This design supports fast write operations and efficient querying capabilities, crucial for minimal impact on NiFi's performance.

Querying data provenance is facilitated through NiFi's Provenance UI, a graphical interface that lets users conduct searches based on numerous criteria like processor IDs, FlowFile UUIDs, and keywords. The UI presents a timeline view of events, detailed information about selected events, and the ability to replay a FlowFile through the flow. Replaying a FlowFile is a particularly valuable feature for debugging and error handling, as it allows users to send a copy of the FlowFile back through the data flow for analysis without altering the original flow's state.

Security considerations are integral to the management of data provenance. NiFi ensures that access to provenance information is controlled through its fine-grained policies and user authentication mechanisms. Users can be restricted to viewing only the provenance events related to the data they have permissions to interact with, thereby safeguarding sensitive data from unauthorized access.

The importance of data provenance in Apache NiFi cannot be understated, especially in environments where data governance and compliance are critical. The ability to trace every piece of data through its entire lifecycle provides not just troubleshooting capabilities but also supports audit requirements, compliance with regulations, and verification of data integrity.

However, managing the volume of provenance data generated in a large-scale NiFi deployment can be challenging. The space used by the Provenance Repository can grow significantly, requiring strategies for pruning and archiving old provenance events without losing the ability to audit historical data flows. NiFi offers configurable data retention policies for managing repository size, allowing users to balance between detailed audit trails and system performance.

Data provenance in Apache NiFi delivers a powerful set of features for monitoring, auditing, and troubleshooting data flows. By providing detailed insight into the journey of each FlowFile, NiFi empowers users with the capability to ensure data integrity, comply with governance standards, and optimize their data flow processes for high reliability and performance.

2.8 Apache NiFi's Pluggable Components and Custom Processors

Apache NiFi offers a comprehensive framework to facilitate the flow of data between systems. A pivotal aspect of this framework is its support for pluggable components and the ability to extend its capabilities with custom processors. This flexibility is crucial for adapting to the unique requirements of various data flow scenarios, enabling the development of highly customizable and scalable data pipelines.

At its core, NiFi's architecture is built to be extensible. It defines a set of APIs that developers can implement to create custom processors, controller services, and reporting tasks. These components are dynamically loadable at runtime, allowing users to enhance their data flows without significant disruptions.

Pluggable Components: NiFi's out-of-the-box processors cover a wide range of functionality, from data ingestion, transformation, and routing to system-to-system data transfers. However, specific use cases may require operations that are not supported by the existing processors. This is where pluggable components come into play. Developers can build upon the existing framework to create new processors, controller services, or reporting tasks that fit their precise needs. Once developed, these components can be shared across the NiFi community, bolstering the tool's versatility and utility.

To implement a custom processor, one must understand the Processor API. The lifecycle of a processor in NiFi involves several key methods: onScheduled, onTrigger, and onStopped. The onTrigger method, in

43

particular, is where the bulk of the processor's logic resides. It is responsible for reading and writing FlowFiles, NiFi's data objects, through the processor's input and output relationships.

```
1  @Override
2  public void onTrigger(ProcessContext context, ProcessSessionFactory sessionFactory)
        throws ProcessException {
3      ProcessSession session = sessionFactory.createSession();
4      FlowFile flowFile = session.get();
5      if ( flowFile == null ) {
6          return;
7      }
8      // Processor logic here
9  }
```

Developing a custom processor also involves defining properties and relationships. Properties are configurable parameters that dictate the processor's behavior, while relationships determine how FlowFiles are routed upon completion of the processor's execution.

```
1   @Override
2   protected List<PropertyDescriptor> getSupportedPropertyDescriptors() {
3       final List<PropertyDescriptor> properties = new ArrayList<>();
4       properties.add(new PropertyDescriptor.Builder()
5           .name("Example Property")
6           .description("An example property for the custom processor.")
7           .required(true)
8           .addValidator(StandardValidators.NON_EMPTY_VALIDATOR)
9           .build());
10      return properties;
11  }
12
13  @Override
14  public Set<Relationship> getRelationships() {
15      final Set<Relationship> relationships = new HashSet<>();
16      relationships.add(new Relationship.Builder()
17          .name("SUCCESS")
18          .description("Successful execution relationship")
19          .build());
20      return relationships;
21  }
```

NiFi's pluggable nature doesn't end with processors. Controller Services provide shared functionality to processors, such as database connections or client services for external systems. By developing custom Controller Services, users ensure that processors remain lightweight and focused on their specific tasks, promoting a separation of concerns that is crucial for maintaining clean and manageable code.

```
1   public class CustomControllerService extends AbstractControllerService implements
        MyServiceInterface {
2       @Override
3       public void executeMyService() {
4           // Implementation of service logic
5       }
6   }
```

Equally important is the ability to test custom components. NiFi offers a comprehensive testing framework that simulates the runtime behavior of processors and controller services, allowing developers to verify their logic under different scenarios and configurations. This framework ensures that custom components meet the desired specifications and behave as expected within NiFi's execution environment.

The flexibility provided by Apache NiFi's support for pluggable components and custom processors is a cornerstone of its design philosophy. This extensibility empowers developers to tailor data flow solutions to their specific needs, fostering innovation and collaboration within the NiFi community. By leveraging the provided APIs and adhering to best practices in component development, users can enhance NiFi's functionality and address a broad spectrum of data processing challenges.

2.9 FlowFile Repository, Content Repository, and Provenance Repository

Apache NiFi's ability to handle vast volumes of data across multiple nodes with fault tolerance and data lineage features is encapsulated within its repository structures: the FlowFile Repository, the Content Repository, and the Provenance Repository. These repositories are central to NiFi's robust data management capabilities, providing persistence, reliability, and scalability for data streaming applications.

The FlowFile Repository is primarily responsible for storing FlowFile metadata. A FlowFile in NiFi is an abstraction that represents each piece of information flowing through the system. However, the actual data content of the FlowFile is not stored within this repository. Instead, the repository tracks the state of every FlowFile as it traverses through the NiFi dataflows, including its attributes and lineage. The persistence of FlowFile metadata allows NiFi to resume operations transparently after a restart, mitigating data loss risks. It is important to understand that the repository does not persist the content but rather the attributes and information required to reconstruct the journey of the FlowFile through the flow.

The actual data content of a FlowFile is stored in the Content Repository. This separation of concerns allows for efficient data processing and storage management. The Content Repository holds the binary content of the data as it moves through NiFi, enabling the system to perform content-based routing, filtering, and transformation without having to read data from an external source repeatedly. For high-volume dataflows, the Content Repository can be configured to use various storage backends to balance performance and storage capacity needs.

The Provenance Repository plays a critical role in data auditing and lineage tracking. It records the complete history of each `FlowFile`, including all the processing steps it has undergone, such as transformations, routing decisions, and external system interactions. This comprehensive data lineage is invaluable for debugging, regulatory compliance, and optimization tasks. The Provenance Repository can handle an immense amount of event data, enabling users to trace dataflows back to their source and understand how data was processed and transformed over time. Queries against the Provenance Repository allow users to efficiently audit and review dataflows, facilitating greater transparency and accountability in data processing operations.

Configuring these repositories to meet the demands of specific data streaming applications requires careful consideration of factors such as disk space, I/O performance, and data retention policies. The FlowFile and Content Repositories, being heavily write-oriented, benefit from fast storage media such as SSDs, especially in high-throughput environments. Conversely, the Provenance Repository, given its extensive write and read operations, may require a balanced approach to storage configuration to support efficient querying without compromising on write performance.

To illustrate, consider a scenario where a NiFi instance is configured with a Content Repository on high-performance SSDs while utilizing a network-attached storage (NAS) for the Provenance Repository to take advantage of larger storage capacity for lineage data. Such a configuration ensures that the high-speed processing of data is maintained without sacrificing the ability to store extensive lineage information for auditing and debugging purposes.

In summary, the integrated management of `FlowFile` metadata, content, and provenance information through these repositories enables Apache NiFi to provide a resilient, scalable, and transparent platform for building complex data pipelines. By carefully configuring these repositories according to the specific needs of a dataflow, developers can optimize NiFi deployments for performance, reliability, and compliance with data governance requirements.

2.10 High Availability and Fault Tolerance in NiFi

Apache NiFi is designed with robust mechanisms to ensure high availability (HA) and fault tolerance (FT) within dataflows. These capabilities are essential for creating resilient systems that can tolerate failures and maintain continuous operation without data loss. This exploration into NiFi's HA and FT features reveals the inherent design principles, configurations, and strategies that underpin its operational resilience.

At the core of NiFi's high availability strategy is the cluster architecture. A NiFi cluster is composed of multiple nodes connected together, where each node operates an independent NiFi instance. The clustering model is designed to support scalability and provide redundancy, whereby data processing tasks can be distributed across nodes, and the failure of one node does not lead to system-wide failure or data loss. The coordination among nodes within a cluster is facilitated by a primary node and a cluster coordinator. The primary node is responsible for tasks that can only be executed by a single node at a time, such as data ingestion from sources that do not naturally support parallel operations. The cluster coordinator, on the other hand, manages the distribution of tasks among nodes and handles node status, ensuring that workload is appropriately balanced and that node failures are detected and managed.

To configure a NiFi cluster, one must ensure that the 'nifi.properties' file on each node is correctly set to reflect the cluster's settings, including the addresses of the zookeeper instances being used for cluster coordination. This setup enables NiFi to maintain a consistent state across the cluster, facilitating seamless failover capabilities in the event of a node failure.

Fault tolerance in NiFi is achieved through several mechanisms, including the use of persistent storage for critical operational data and the replication of FlowFiles across cluster nodes. NiFi uses three repositories for storing various types of data: the FlowFile Repository, the Content Repository, and the Provenance Repository. These repositories can be configured to use disk partitions that are resilient to failures, such as redundant array of independent disks (RAID) configurations, to prevent data loss. Additionally, NiFi allows for the configuration of FlowFile replication across the cluster, ensuring that data is not lost even if a node fails. This is complemented by the automatic rebalancing of FlowFiles across the cluster when nodes are added or removed, further increasing the resilience of the system.

Apache NiFi also supports backpressure and prioritization mechanisms that enhance its fault tolerance capabilities. Backpressure prevents data overload on nodes or connections by temporarily halting data ingestion or processing when predefined thresholds are met, thus preventing system crashes due to resource exhaustion. This is an essential feature for maintaining operational stability, especially in scenarios with highly variable data volumes. Prioritization, on the other hand, ensures that critical data is processed first, which is particularly useful in failover situations to maintain the integrity and timeliness of high-priority data processing.

In data provenance, NiFi offers comprehensive tracking of dataflow, which is crucial for diagnosing issues in a system's operation and ensuring data integrity. The Provenance Repository captures detailed records of all events related to data processing, including send, receive, clone, and content modification actions. These records are invaluable for auditing and tracing data lineage, which is a critical component of fault-tolerant systems, enabling quick identification and resolution of data-related issues.

Lastly, integrating NiFi with external systems for monitoring and alerting can further enhance its high availability and fault tolerance. By leveraging external tools to monitor the health and performance of NiFi clusters, administrators can be alerted to potential issues before they lead to system failure. This proactive approach to system management allows for timely interventions that prevent downtime and ensure continuous operation.

In summary, Apache NiFi's architecture and core features are meticulously designed to support high availability and fault tolerance. Through its clustering model, persistent storage mechanisms, backpressure, prioritization, and comprehensive data provenance, NiFi ensures that dataflows are robust, resilient, and capable of sustaining operational continuity even in the face of failures. These features, combined with proper configuration and integration with monitoring tools, make NiFi an ideal platform for managing critical dataflows requiring uninterrupted operation and maximum data integrity.

2.11 Integrating NiFi with External Systems

Integrating Apache NiFi with external systems is a crucial component in designing effective real-time data pipelines. This integration enables data ingestion from and export to various sources and sinks, such as databases, cloud services, and file systems, thereby facilitating a seamless flow of information. The capacity of NiFi to connect with external systems is underpinned by its vast library of processors and controller services, designed specifically for this purpose.

Processors for External Integration

The primary mechanism through which NiFi interacts with external systems is through its processors. There are numerous built-in processors for a wide variety of systems, including but not limited to SQL databases, NoSQL databases, message queues, file systems, and web services. Each of these processors is designed to either ingest data from or deliver data to the external systems they are associated with.

For instance, to fetch data from a relational database, one might use the ExecuteSQL processor, which executes a provided SQL select query. Conversely, to send data to a relational database, the PutSQL processor is used, executing insert or update SQL commands with the data contained in FlowFiles.

Custom Processors

While NiFi offers a comprehensive set of processors for interacting with external systems, specific use cases may require the development of custom processors. NiFi's extensible architecture allows for the creation of such processors, providing the flexibility to meet unique requirements. The process of creating a custom processor involves implementing the necessary Java interfaces and extending base classes provided by the NiFi API. A thorough understanding of the NiFi Processor API and the target system's API or protocol is required to accomplish this.

Controller Services for External Integration

Controller Services in NiFi provide shared services or configurations that can be used by processors. For external integration, controller services are particularly useful for managing connections to external systems, such as database connection pooling or credentials for accessing a web service. By centralizing these configurations in controller services, changes can be made in a single location without the need to edit each processor configuration individually, thus enhancing maintainability and scalability of the data pipeline.

For example, the DBCPConnectionPool controller service is used to manage a pool of database connections that can be shared among several database-related processors. This not only optimizes connection utilization but also centralizes the database connection configuration, simplifying management and adjustments over time.

Handling Different Data Formats

In the course of integrating with external systems, Apache NiFi often encounters a wide variety of data formats. Processors such as ConvertJSONtoSQL and ConvertAvroToOrc are examples of how NiFi provides capabilities to seamlessly transform data between formats to ensure compatibility with the target external system. Additionally, the Record oriented processors allow for the processing of data in various formats using a common schema approach, making it easier to work with heterogeneous data.

Secure Data Exchange

Security is paramount when integrating with external systems, particularly when sensitive data is being transferred. NiFi supports secure data exchange with external systems through processors that are capable of TLS/SSL encryption, SSH, and other secure protocols. Alongside this, it provides features such as encrypted provenance repositories and FlowFile content encryption. Moreover, for authentication and access control with external systems, NiFi can be integrated with enterprise security systems using processors that support OAuth, Kerberos, and other mechanisms.

Best Practices on Error Handling and Retry Mechanisms

Integrating with external systems can sometimes lead to connectivity issues or data transmission errors. NiFi addresses these challenges by allowing the configuration of retry mechanisms and error handling policies. Processors in NiFi typically have properties to configure retry attempts and back-off periods, enabling robust error resilience. Furthermore, NiFi's queue prioritization and backpressure capabilities ensure that system failures or delays do not compromise the stability of the entire data flow.

Integrating Apache NiFi with external systems is facilitated through a variety of built-in processors, customizable processor capabilities, and controller services. These integrations are bolstered by comprehensive support for different data formats, secure data exchange mechanisms, and robust error handling features. With these tools, Apache NiFi is equipped to be a central component of any data pipeline, capable of connecting disparate systems in a secure, efficient, and manageable manner.

2.12 Best Practices for Apache NiFi Architecture Design

Designing an architecture with Apache NiFi requires a strategic approach to ensure the scalability, reliability, and efficiency of data flows. This section will discuss best practices for Apache NiFi architecture design, focusing on structuring NiFi flows, managing resources, monitoring performance, securing the data pipeline, and maintaining the overall health of the system.

Strategic Partitioning of Process Groups: Organizing flow designs into modular components enhances maintainability and scalability. Process groups should encapsulate specific functionalities or business logic, allowing for easier management and potential reuse. Proper partitioning aids in isolating issues and making incremental changes without affecting the entirety of the data flow.

Efficient Processor Configuration: Each processor in NiFi is designed for distinct tasks with various configurations. It is imperative to understand the processor's purpose and configure it to optimize performance. For instance, adjusting the Concurrent Tasks settings can significantly impact data throughput by allowing parallel execution of tasks where applicable.

Utilization of Controller Services: Controller Services offer shared functionalities such as database connections or SSL contexts that can be reused by multiple components. Leveraging these services avoids redundant configurations and promotes a cleaner flow design. It is advisable to centralize configuration parameters within Controller Services to streamline updates and maintenance.

- Implement caching where possible to reduce load on external services and databases.

- Use the DBCPConnectionPool for database connections to manage pool sizes and connection lifecycles efficiently.

Backpressure and FlowFile Prioritization Strategies: Backpressure mechanisms prevent system overload by pausing data flow when specific thresholds are met. Designing with backpressure in mind ensures that NiFi can handle surges in data without loss or system instability. Alongside, prioritizing FlowFiles ensures critical data is processed first, enhancing the flow's responsiveness to business needs.

Data Provenance and Monitoring: Apache NiFi provides detailed data provenance that tracks data flow through the system. It is essential to utilize this feature to monitor data flow health, troubleshoot issues, and audit data processing activities. Configuring appropriate logging and employing NiFi's reporting tasks can furnish real-time insights into system performance and anomalies.

Security Considerations: Ensuring the security of data as it flows through NiFi is paramount. Utilize NiFi's built-in mechanisms for user authentication, authorization, and encryption to protect sensitive information. Configure HTTPS protocols for web interfaces and apply encryption for data at rest and in motion.

Repository Management: NiFi's FlowFile, Content, and Provenance Repositories are critical components that store state, attributes, content, and the history of FlowFiles, respectively. It is crucial to allocate sufficient storage resources, regularly monitor repository sizes, and configure appropriate backup and data retention policies to prevent data loss and ensure operational continuity.

High Availability and Fault Tolerance: Implementing a clustered NiFi environment can provide high availability and fault tolerance. This setup distributes data flows across multiple nodes, ensuring no single point of failure. Techniques such as load balancing and failover strategies further enhance the resilience of the data pipeline.

Integration with External Systems: When designing NiFi flows that interact with external systems, it is important to consider the impact on those systems. Rate limiting, batching requests, and understanding the throughput capacities of external systems can mitigate the risk of overwhelming these resources.

Documentation and Version Control: Documenting the NiFi flow design and maintaining version control are vital best practices. This facilitates knowledge sharing, enables collaborative development, and simplifies rollback in case of issues. Utilizing NiFi's Version Control feature can manage changes effectively, providing a mechanism for reviewing, auditing, and deploying flow changes systematically.

Designing an effective Apache NiFi architecture necessitates a comprehensive understanding of NiFi's components and features. By adhering to these best practices, architects and developers can leverage NiFi to build robust, efficient, and secure data pipelines capable of managing complex data flow scenarios.

Chapter 3

Working with Processors in NiFi

Processors are the primary components within Apache NiFi responsible for data ingestion, routing, transformation, and delivery. They act as the building blocks of data flow management, enabling users to create complex data processing pipelines tailored to specific needs. Each processor is designed to perform a unique task, ranging from reading data from a file system to transforming data formats or even interacting with external systems. With over 280 processors available, understanding how to configure and connect these processors is fundamental to harnessing the power of NiFi for efficient data streaming and manipulation.

3.1   Introduction to Processors in NiFi

Processors in Apache NiFi form the backbone of data flow within the NiFi ecosystem. These vital components are responsible for the execution of a myriad of tasks essential for data processing, such as ingestion, routing, transformation, and eventual delivery of data. Understanding the functionality and application of processors is pivotal for leveraging Apache NiFi's capabilities in streamlining real-time data pipelines.

At its core, a processor is designed to operate on a set of data, referred to as FlowFiles within the NiFi context. Each FlowFile represents a single piece of data, which could be as simple as a line of text or as complex as a multi-gigabyte video file. The power of NiFi lies in its ability to handle these data elements with flexibility and scalability, allowing for the management of vast quantities of information seamlessly.

A typical processor in NiFi follows a straightforward life cycle: receiving data, performing a designated operation on that data, and then transferring the processed data to the next stage of the pipeline. This operation could range from modifying the content of data, such as converting formats (e.g., from CSV to JSON), to altering its state or metadata, or even interacting with external systems like databases and web services.

To navigate the extensive catalog of over 280 processors available in Apache NiFi, it is essential to understand the categorization of these processors. They are broadly divided based on their primary function:

- Data Ingestion: Processors that are designed to read data from various sources, including file systems, web services, databases, and messaging systems.

- Data Extraction and Transformation: These processors focus on extracting meaningful information from data or converting data from one format to another.

- Data Routing and Distribution: Processors that route data to different destinations based on certain criteria or distribute data to multiple destinations in parallel.

- Interaction with External Systems: Processors that communicate with external systems, either by pulling data from or pushing data to such systems.

Configuring a processor involves setting various properties that dictate its behavior. These properties can range from specifying the location from which to read data, to defining rules for data transformation, or to setting up criteria for routing data. Furthermore, each processor also defines a set of relationships that determine the next course of action. For example, a processor might route data to a 'Success' relationship if processed successfully, or to a 'Failure' relationship if an error occurs.

To effectively utilize processors, understanding of scheduling and concurrency settings is also necessary. These settings allow users to tune the performance of each processor according to the specific demands of their data flows. For instance, increasing the concurrent tasks of a processor can enhance throughput but may also lead to higher resource consumption.

In summary, processors are the building blocks of data pipelines in Apache NiFi, enabling the construction of sophisticated data flow mechanisms. Mastery over the selection, configuration, and optimization of these processors is crucial for anyone looking to harness the full potential of Apache NiFi in data streaming and manipulation tasks. By understanding the fundamentals of processors, as outlined in this introduction, users can embark on creating efficient, scalable, and reliable data pipelines tailored to their unique requirements.

3.2 Commonly Used Processors for Data Ingestion

Data ingestion is the preliminary step in data processing pipelines, where data from various sources is collected and brought into Apache NiFi for further processing. This section will discuss various processors in NiFi that are commonly used for data ingestion purposes.

- **GetFile**: This processor is used to ingest data from the local file system. It polls a specified directory for files and ingests them into NiFi. The processor is highly configurable, allowing users to specify file filtering criteria, polling intervals, and whether or not to delete the files after ingestion. The GetFile processor is suitable for scenarios where data is batched into files and requires periodic ingestion into NiFi for processing.

- **ListenHTTP**: The ListenHTTP processor enables NiFi to act as an HTTP server to ingest data. It listens on a specified port for HTTP requests and ingests the content of these requests. This processor is versatile and can be used to ingest data from a variety of sources that can send HTTP requests, including sensors, mobile devices, and other web services.

- **ConsumeKafka**: Apache Kafka is a popular distributed streaming platform, and the ConsumeKafka processor allows NiFi to ingest data from Kafka topics. It supports both the 0.9.x and newer versions of the Kafka client, making it a flexible option for real-time data ingestion from Kafka. This processor can handle high volumes of data and supports configurable consumer group settings, enabling efficient parallel data ingestion.

- **FetchSFTP**: For ingesting data from remote systems securely, the FetchSFTP processor is used. It connects to a remote SFTP server, downloads files based on specified criteria, and ingests them into NiFi. This processor is essential for workflows that require secure file transfer from remote systems for processing in NiFi.

- **GetSQL**: The GetSQL processor is used for ingesting data from relational databases. It executes a specified SQL query, retrieves data from the database, and ingests it into NiFi as flowfiles. This processor simplifies the process of ingesting data from databases, enabling SQL queries to be used as a data source for NiFi workflows.

For demonstration purposes, the following example illustrates the configuration of the `GetFile` processor to ingest CSV files from a local directory.

```
1  <property name="Input Directory">/path/to/input/directory</property>
2  <property name="File Filter">[regex for matching CSV files]</property>
3  <property name="Polling Interval">5 mins</property>
4  <property name="Keep Source File">false</property>
```

Upon successful ingestion, a flowfile is created for each file, which can then be routed to other processors for further processing. The output below shows an example of a log entry indicating successful file ingestion.

```
2019-07-25 10:23:45,123 INFO [NiFi logging component]
processor.GetFile GetFile[id=12345678-1234-1234-1234-123456789abc]
Successfully ingested file /path/to/input/directory/data.csv
```

Given the diversity of data ingestion needs, selecting the right processor is critical for efficient data pipeline creation. Factors to consider include the data source type, security requirements, data volume, and ingestion frequency. By understanding the capabilities and configurations of these commonly used processors, users can effectively design and implement robust data ingestion workflows in Apache NiFi. This foundational step sets the stage for subsequent data extraction, transformation, and processing tasks, enabling the construction of comprehensive data pipelines tailored to specific processing requirements.

3.3 Data Extraction and Transformation Processors

Data extraction and transformation are critical operations in the construction of efficient and effective data processing pipelines. In Apache NiFi, a rite of processors is dedicated to performing these tasks, allowing users to ingest raw data from various sources, manipulate and enrich it, then format it appropriately for consumption by downstream systems or storage solutions. This section will discuss several key processors in NiFi that facilitate data extraction and transformation, including ExtractText, ReplaceText, TransformXML, JoltTransformJSON, and EvaluateJsonPath.

The ExtractText processor is often the first step in data extraction, especially when dealing with text-based data like logs, XML, or JSON files. It allows users to apply regular expressions to extract specific sections of the data. For example, extracting timestamps, error codes, or user IDs from logs can be accomplished using the ExtractText processor.

```
1  <ExtractText>
2      <Properties>
3          <Property>
4              <Name>Error Code</Name>
5              <Value>\b\d{3}\b</Value>
6              <Description>Extracts three-digit error codes</Description>
7          </Property>
8      </Properties>
9  </ExtractText>
```

The ReplaceText processor complements ExtractText by allowing users to modify extracted data. It can replace the text in incoming flow files with either a static value or a dynamically generated string using regular expression capturing groups. This is particularly useful for masking sensitive information or correcting known errors in the data.

When working with XML data, the TransformXML processor enables the transformation of XML structures using XSLT (eXtensible Stylesheet Language Transformations). This is useful for converting XML documents into a different XML format or even into other data formats like HTML for reporting purposes.

```
1  <TransformXML>
2      <Properties>
3          <Property>
4              <Name>XSLT File</Name>
5              <Value>/path/to/transformation.xslt</Value>
6              <Description>Path to XSLT file for transformation</Description>
```

```
7        </Property>
8      </Properties>
9  </TransformXML>
```

For JSON data, JoltTransformJSON and EvaluateJsonPath processors are particularly notable. JoltTransformJSON applies a JOLT specification to transform JSON data structure in a way that's more suitable for the intended use. This is instrumental when dealing with JSON from diverse sources and it's required to normalize or enrich the data.

```
1  <JoltTransformJSON>
2      <Specifications>
3          {
4              "operation": "shift",
5              "spec": {
6                  "timestamp": "ts",
7                  "user": "usr",
8                  "message": "msg"
9              }
10         }
11     </Specifications>
12 </JoltTransformJSON>
```

EvaluateJsonPath allows for the extraction of specific data from a JSON structure using JSONPath expressions. This is useful for parsing JSON data to extract particular values without needing to transform the entire document.

```
1  <EvaluateJsonPath>
2      <Properties>
3          <Property>
4              <Name>Timestamp</Name>
5              <Value>$.timestamp</Value>
6          </Property>
7      </Properties>
8  </EvaluateJsonPath>
```

Utilizing these processors effectively requires a good understanding of the data's format and structure and the end goal of the extraction and transformation operations. Configuring processors with the appropriate settings, including regular expressions, XSLT paths, JSONPath expressions, and JOLT specifications, is crucial to achieving desired outcomes. Moreover, chaining these processors together in a NiFi dataflow allows for complex data manipulations that can extract value from raw data and transform it into a valuable asset for an organization.

In practice, combining these processors forms the backbone of most NiFi dataflows, enabling the handling of diverse datasets and the fulfillment of specific business logic requirements. Through the judicious

application of these processors, NiFi users can construct highly customized data processing pipelines that are both flexible and powerful,
catering to a wide array of data extraction and transformation needs.

3.4 Processors for Data Routing and Distribution

In this section, we will discuss the critical role processors play in data
routing and distribution within Apache NiFi, focusing on how these
processors enable the dynamic routing of data flows based on content
or attributes and the distribution of data across various destinations for
efficient processing and storage. Apache NiFi offers a suite of processors specifically designed for these tasks, aiding in the development of
flexible and robust data pipelines.

The importance of data routing and distribution cannot be overstated
in a data-centric environment. Proper routing ensures that data reaches
the correct destination, adhering to business logic and operational
requirements, while distribution strategies can improve system scalability and reliability by balancing load and segregating data appropriately.

RouteOnAttribute Processor

The `RouteOnAttribute` processor is a pivotal component in Apache
NiFi for routing data based on its attributes. This processor evaluates
expressions set by the user against the attributes of FlowFiles and
routes them to the corresponding relationship.

```
1  <property name="RouteToSpain">
2  ${country:equals('Spain')}
3  </property>
```

In the above example, FlowFiles with an attribute country equal to
'Spain' will be routed to the relationship RouteToSpain. This flexible
routing based on dynamically assessed conditions allows for complex
decision-making processes in data flows.

PartitionRecord Processor

The `PartitionRecord` processor is utilized for dividing a single Flow-File containing multiple records into multiple FlowFiles, each containing a subset of records based on a specified partitioning strategy. This is particularly useful for distributing load across systems or organizing data into more manageable segments.

```
1  <property name="partitioningField">
2  country
3  </property>
```

Specifying country as the partitioning field, the processor will generate separate FlowFiles for each unique country value found in the records, enabling tailored processing or storage.

MergeContent Processor

To optimize network utilization and reduce the overhead of processing numerous small files, the `MergeContent` processor can be employed to aggregate multiple FlowFiles into a single, larger FlowFile. Configuration options offer control over how and when to merge FlowFiles, based on size, count, or a defined timeout.

```
1  <property name="Merge Strategy">
2  Bin-Packing Algorithm
3  </property>
4
5  <property name="Maximum number of Bins">
6  5
7  </property>
```

This example demonstrates setting the processor to use a bin-packing algorithm to merge FlowFiles efficiently until the maximum number of bins is achieved. This strategy is advantageous for reducing input/output operations and improving downstream processing efficiency.

DistributeLoad Processor

Although not a specific processor in Apache NiFi, the concept of load distribution can be realized through various processors, including custom ones, or by employing NiFi's built-in capabilities like prioritizers and load-balanced connections. Configuring connections with load balancing (e.g., round-robin, random, partitioned) ensures that data is evenly distributed among available paths, fostering efficient utilization of resources and redundancy.

```
Connection Configuration:
Load Balancing Strategy: Round Robin
```

This configuration directs NiFi to evenly distribute FlowFiles across all outgoing connections, enhancing throughput and avoiding bottlenecks.

Processors dedicated to data routing and distribution play an indispensable role in Apache NiFi. They provide the mechanisms required to ensure data is efficiently and accurately directed through data pipelines, enhancing both performance and reliability. By leveraging these processors, developers can design data flow systems that are both dynamic and robust, capable of handling complex routing, load balancing, and data segmentation needs.

3.5 Understanding Processor Configuration

Let's start with the foundation of configuring processors in Apache NiFi to ensure effective data flow management. Each processor in NiFi comes with a set of configurable properties and scheduling strategies that dictate how data is processed and managed as it moves through the system. The configuration of these properties is key to optimizing performance, managing resource allocation, and achieving desired outcomes in data processing pipelines.

The first step in processor configuration is understanding the Processor Properties. These are the parameters that control the behavior of the processor. With NiFi's graphical user interface, users can easily configure these properties to suit their specific requirements. The properties range from essential settings, such as the input directory for a 'GetFile' processor, to more advanced configurations, like character encoding or cryptographic algorithms in processors that handle data transformation and security.

```
1  Example of Setting Processor Property:
2  Name: Input Directory
3  Value: /path/to/input/directory
```

It is crucial for users to understand the implications of these settings. For example, incorrect setup of cryptographic properties might lead to data being processed in an insecure manner, which could compromise data security. As a result, thorough testing and validation of processor configurations in development environments is highly recommended before deploying to production.

Following the configuration of processor properties, scheduling settings play a critical role in defining how processors execute over time. NiFi provides a flexible scheduling strategy that includes:

- Timer-Driven: Executes a processor at a defined interval.

- Event-Driven: Triggers execution based on specific events, useful for real-time data processing.

- Cron-Driven: Uses cron expressions to schedule processor execution, allowing for complex timing patterns.

```
1   Example of a Timer-Driven Scheduling Configuration:
2   Run Schedule: 30 sec
3   This configuration executes the processor every 30 seconds.
```

Another essential aspect is Understanding Processor Relationships. After a processor completes its task, it transfers the flowfiles to one or more predefined relationships. Configuring these relationships is vital as it determines the path data takes through a NiFi flow. Misconfigurations can lead to data being sent to incorrect destinations or even data loss if not properly managed.

```
1   Example of Processor Relationship Configuration:
2   Name: success
3   Description: FlowFiles processed successfully are transferred to this relationship.
```

Concurrency settings are also a significant part of processor configuration. They determine the number of tasks that can run concurrently for a given processor, which directly impacts data throughput and system resource utilization. Apache NiFi allows users to adjust these settings based on the performance characteristics of their environment and the specific requirements of their data flow.

```
1   Example of Concurrency Configuration:
2   Concurrent Tasks: 5
3   This configuration allows up to 5 instances of the processor to run in parallel.
```

In addition to these configurations, error handling and retry mechanisms are critical to ensuring robust data flow operations. Processors in NiFi are designed to handle errors gracefully, allowing users to configure retry intervals and penalties for failures. This ensures that transient errors do not cause a data pipeline to halt abruptly but are rather retried according to the configured policies.

Lastly, monitoring and debugging are integral to the processor configuration process. NiFi provides extensive logging capabilities, allowing users to troubleshoot issues and understand the behavior of processors within their flows. Effective logging and monitoring strategies can significantly reduce the time required to diagnose and resolve issues, leading to more reliable and maintainable data pipelines.

```
Example of Processor Log Message:
2023-01-01 12:00:00,123 INFO [Processor Name]: Processor successfully processed
 10 FlowFiles.
```

Understanding and appropriately configuring processor settings in Apache NiFi represents a substantive layer of knowledge essential for building efficient, scalable, and reliable data processing pipelines. Through meticulous attention to detail and an understanding of the underlying mechanisms of each processor, users can significantly enhance the performance and functionality of their data flows.

3.6 Utilizing Processor Properties and Relationships

In Apache NiFi, processors are the fundamental building blocks used to define specific tasks within a data flow. Each processor has a set of configurable properties and relationships that determine its behavior and how it interacts with the flow. Understanding how to utilize these properties and relationships is crucial for designing efficient and effective data pipelines.

Processor Properties are key-value pairs that configure the behavior of a processor. These properties can include file paths, database connection strings, data formats, and other processor-specific settings. To effectively utilize processor properties, it is essential to comprehend the role and impact of each property on the processor's functionality.

For instance, consider the GetFile processor, which retrieves files from a specified directory. Its critical properties include:

- Input Directory: Specifies the directory from which files should be fetched.

- `Keep Source File`: Determines whether the original file should be kept or deleted after being fetched.

Configuring these properties appropriately ensures that the processor accurately performs its intended task.

On the other hand, **Processor Relationships** define the path data will take after being processed. Processors can have multiple relationships, each labeled to describe the nature of the data flow (e.g., `success`, `failure`). It is through these relationships that processors are linked together, forming a coherent and functional data processing pipeline.

The routing of flow files between processors based on these relationships is demonstrated in handling different data processing outcomes. For example, a processor designed to validate data formats might have two relationships: `valid` for successfully validated data and `invalid` for data that fails validation checks. This allows for the segregation of data based on its validity and ensures that downstream processing is based on this categorization.

To illustrate the practical application of processor properties and relationships, let's examine a typical NiFi data flow setup:

```
1   # Configure GetFile Processor
2   GetFile Input Directory = '/data/input'
3   GetFile Keep Source File = 'false'
4
5   # Setup relationships
6   RouteOnAttribute {
7       success -> TransformData
8       failure -> LogError
9   }
```

In this setup, the `GetFile` processor is configured to pull files from '/data/input' and delete them after processing. Depending on the attributes of the flow files, they are then routed to either a data transformation processor (`TransformData`) on `success` relationship or an error logging processor (`LogError`) on `failure`.

To efficiently manage these processor properties and relationships, NiFi offers a user-friendly interface that allows for the drag-and-drop configuration of processors and their connections. Additionally, by right-clicking on a processor, users can access the settings to adjust properties and manage relationships. It is through meticulous configuration of these settings that one can harness the full potential of Apache NiFi's processors to build robust, flexible, and high-performing data pipelines.

The key to leveraging Apache NiFi's capabilities lies in the detailed understanding and effective utilization of processor properties and their relationships. By carefully configuring these components, developers and data engineers can create intricate data flows that meet specific processing requirements, thereby enabling the realization of comprehensive data management and analysis solutions.

3.7 Managing Processor Scheduling and Concurrency

Managing processor scheduling and concurrency in Apache NiFi allows users to maximize data processing efficiency and control over how and when data flows through the system. Each processor in NiFi has settings to manage its scheduling strategy, run duration, concurrent tasks, and penalization period. These settings collectively determine how processors are executed in a NiFi flow and how they manage tasks in parallel.

Scheduling Strategy: NiFi offers two primary scheduling strategies for processors: Timer Driven and Event Driven. The Timer Driven scheduling strategy triggers the processor to run at regular intervals, specified in terms of time. This is useful for operations that need to run periodically, such as polling a file directory or querying a database for updates. The Event Driven strategy, on the other hand, executes the processor in response to an event, such as the arrival of new data in a queue. This strategy is ideal for processors that need to react promptly to incoming data.

```
1  // Example of setting a scheduling strategy in NiFi
2  processor.setSchedulingStrategy(SchedulingStrategy.TIMER_DRIVEN);
3  processor.setSchedulingPeriod("5 mins");
```

Run Duration: The run duration setting controls how long a processor runs each time it is executed, allowing for a balance between task granularity and throughput. A longer run duration means the processor can execute more work in each scheduled execution, but this may also lead to less responsive system behavior if the processor monopolizes threads for extended periods.

Concurrent Tasks: This setting determines the number of instances of the processor that can run simultaneously. Increasing the number of concurrent tasks for a processor can significantly enhance throughput, particularly for processors that are handling independent pieces of work in parallel and are not bottlenecked by shared resources such as disk or network I/O.

```
Concurrent Tasks: 4
```

Penalization Period: NiFi allows processors to penalize flow files that need to be retried or require special handling, delaying their re-processing for a specified period. This mechanism helps manage workload and system resources by preventing problematic flow files from overwhelming the system with continuous processing attempts.

```
1  // Example of setting a penalization period in NiFi
2  processor.setPenalizationPeriod("30 sec");
```

When configuring these parameters, it is crucial to consider the overall objectives of the data flow and the characteristics of the work being performed by each processor. For example, a processor that performs a quick transformation of incoming data may benefit from a shorter run duration and a higher number of concurrent tasks, allowing it to efficiently handle high volumes of data with minimal latency. Conversely, a processor that makes network calls to external systems may need to be throttled back using a lower number of concurrent tasks or a longer penalization period to prevent overwhelming the external system or running into rate limits.

In addition to these settings, NiFi provides advanced scheduling options that allow users to further fine-tune processor execution according to the specific demands of their data flow. These options include custom cron scheduling for timer-driven processors, allowing precise control over execution times, and priority scheduling strategies that determine how processor tasks are prioritized relative to other tasks in the system.

Understanding and effectively managing processor scheduling and concurrency is essential for building efficient and responsive data flows in NiFi. By carefully configuring these settings, users can optimize the performance of their processors and ensure that data is processed in a timely and resource-efficient manner.

- Take advantage of the Event Driven scheduling strategy for processors that need to respond quickly to dynamic data conditions.

68

- Adjust the Run Duration to balance task granularity with throughput, taking into account the nature of the tasks being performed.

- Increase the number of Concurrent Tasks for processors handling independent pieces of work to enhance throughput.

- Use the Penalization Period setting to manage problematic flow files and control system resource utilization.

- Consider the overall data flow objectives and processor work characteristics when configuring these settings.

By mastering the management of processor scheduling and concurrency in NiFi, users gain the ability to fine-tune their data flows for optimal performance, ensuring that data is processed efficiently, accurately, and promptly.

3.8 Error Handling and Retry Mechanisms in Processors

In this section, we will discuss the strategies and mechanisms Apache NiFi provides for handling errors and implementing retry logic in processors. Error handling and retry mechanisms are crucial in designing resilient and fault-tolerant data flows that can gracefully recover from transient failures or data anomalies.

Apache NiFi's built-in support for error handling is primarily based on routing data to appropriate relationships. Each processor is designed to emit FlowFiles (the unit of data within NiFi) to different relationships based on the outcome of its processing task. Typically, processors have at least two relationships: `success` and `failure`. FlowFiles processed without any issues are routed to the `success` relationship, whereas those that encounter problems are routed to the `failure` relationship. Managing these relationships allows the data flow designer to specify how errors should be handled, such as retrying the operation, logging the error, or rerouting the problematic data for inspection.

To facilitate error handling and enable retry mechanisms, several key processor properties and NiFi features can be leveraged:

- **Backpressure Settings:** NiFi allows configuring backpressure settings on connections. By adjusting these settings, NiFi can be configured to hold back data at certain points in the flow, preventing overloading downstream processors or systems. This is particularly useful when intermittent issues occur that temporarily block or slow down processing. Adjusting backpressure can effectively act as a throttle during errors, giving systems time to recover before attempting to process the data again.

- **Penalization:** When a processor fails to process a FlowFile correctly, the FlowFile can be penalized. Penalization is a mechanism that temporarily removes the failed FlowFile from processing, allowing other files to proceed. The penalization period is configurable on a per-processor basis. This feature prevents a single problematic FlowFile from continuously failing and hogging resources, thus acting as a simple retry mechanism by allowing the processor to attempt processing the FlowFile again after the penalization period has expired.

- **Retry FlowFiles:** Some processors offer specific properties to handle retries automatically. For example, properties like `Retry Count` and `Retry Interval` can be configured to determine how many times and how frequently NiFi should attempt to reprocess a FlowFile before considering it a failure. This built-in retry logic is crucial for handling transient issues such as temporary network outages or overloaded external systems.

- **Retry Processors:** In some cases, the retry logic needs to be explicitly defined in the data flow. This can be achieved by using processors like `RetryFlowFile` and `ExecuteScript` to create custom retry logic. These processors can inspect attributes of a FlowFile, such as a retry counter, and make decisions on whether to retry the operation, escalate the error, or perform other actions. Custom scripts or flow logic can increment retry counters, delay processing, and ultimately route FlowFiles based on the outcome of retry attempts.

It is essential to note that while retries can help in overcoming temporary issues, they should be used judiciously to avoid creating endless loops of retry attempts for errors that require manual intervention or changes in configuration to resolve. Therefore, implementing error handling and retry mechanisms should also include setting sensible limits on retries and ensuring there are clear strategies for dealing with FlowFiles that cannot be processed successfully after all retry attempts have been exhausted. This might include routing them to a

DeadLetterQueue or a similar strategy for manual review or alternative processing.

Apache NiFi equips users with robust error handling and retry mechanisms to build resilient data flows. By appropriately configuring processors and leveraging the strategies outlined above, NiFi users can ensure that data flows can tolerate temporary errors and recover gracefully, thereby maintaining the integrity and reliability of the data streaming process.

3.9 Custom Processors Development

Developing custom processors in Apache NiFi allows for extending its capabilities beyond the provided set of processors. This is crucial for addressing unique data processing requirements that cannot be met by existing processors. The development of a custom processor involves a comprehensive understanding of NiFi's API, Java programming language, and the specific data handling requirements of the application.

To create a custom processor, the following steps are generally involved:

1. Setting up a development environment with necessary tools and dependencies, including Apache Maven for project management and build processes, and an Integrated Development Environment (IDE) such as Eclipse or IntelliJ IDEA.

2. Creating a Maven project that adheres to the NiFi Processor API dependencies to ensure compatibility with NiFi.

3. Implementing the Processor interface provided by the NiFi API, which involves overriding essential methods such as onTrigger, init, and getRelationships.

The onTrigger method is particularly important as it defines the custom processor's core logic. This method is where the processor reads from, and writes to, the flowfile content, and interacts with NiFi's ProcessSession and ProcessContext, enabling the processor to perform its intended function.

Let's illustrate with a simple example of developing a custom processor:

```
1   package org.apache.nifi.processors.custom;
2
3   import org.apache.nifi.processor.AbstractProcessor;
4   import org.apache.nifi.processor.ProcessContext;
5   import org.apache.nifi.processor.ProcessSession;
6   import org.apache.nifi.processor.ProcessorInitializationContext;
7   import org.apache.nifi.processor.Relationship;
8   import org.apache.nifi.processor.exception.ProcessException;
9
10  import java.util.Collections;
11  import java.util.HashSet;
12  import java.util.Set;
13
14  public class MyCustomProcessor extends AbstractProcessor {
15
16      private Set<Relationship> relationships;
17
18      @Override
19      protected void init(final ProcessorInitializationContext context) {
20          final Set<Relationship> relationships = new HashSet<>();
21          relationships.add(new Relationship.Builder().name("success").description("
                Successfully processed data").build());
22          this.relationships = Collections.unmodifiableSet(relationships);
23      }
24
25      @Override
26      public Set<Relationship> getRelationships() {
27          return relationships;
28      }
29
30      @Override
31      public void onTrigger(final ProcessContext context, final ProcessSession
                session) throws ProcessException {
32          // Core processing logic here
33      }
34  }
```

After implementing the custom processor, the next steps involve com-
piling the project, packaging it into a NAR (NiFi Archive) file, and
deploying the NAR to the NiFi library directory. Upon restarting NiFi,
the custom processor will be available for use within the NiFi user
interface.

```
mvn clean install
```

The output of running the above Maven command will be a NAR file
located in the target directory of your project. This NAR file contains
the compiled custom processor code and any dependencies required
by the processor.

It is also essential to consider error handling within the custom processor. NiFi offers mechanisms for handling processing errors, including
routing flowfiles to a failure relationship. Implementing comprehensive error handling ensures that the processor can gracefully manage

unexpected conditions, maintaining the stability and reliability of the data flow.

Testing plays a critical role in developing custom processors. It involves unit testing individual methods and integration testing within a NiFi environment. Apache NiFi provides a testing toolkit designed to facilitate the testing of custom processors. This toolkit allows developers to simulate the NiFi environment and verify the behavior of their processors under various conditions.

Developing custom processors in NiFi requires a solid understanding of NiFi's API, Java programming, and the specific data processing needs. By following the outlined steps and adhering to best practices for error handling and testing, developers can extend NiFi's capabilities, enabling bespoke solutions for advanced data processing challenges.

3.10 Optimizing Processor Performance

Optimizing the performance of processors in Apache NiFi is essential for building efficient real-time data pipelines. Performance optimization not only ensures maximum throughput but also helps in minimizing the resource utilization, leading to cost-effective and scalable deployments. This section will discuss strategies for enhancing the performance of processors, involving configuration adjustments, efficient data flow design, and the use of advanced NiFi features.

Firstly, it is crucial to understand the key factors affecting processor performance. These include the volume of data being processed, the complexity of the data transformations, the speed of external systems interacting with the pipeline, and the hardware resources available. Given these variables, performance optimization is often a balance between processing speed and resource consumption.

To begin with, configuring processor properties effectively plays a significant role. Each processor in NiFi comes with a set of configurable properties that determine its behavior. Adjusting these properties to suit the specific requirements of your data flow can lead to significant performance gains. For example, the Concurrent Tasks property allows multiple threads to concurrently execute a single processor. Increasing this value can dramatically improve the throughput of a processor, especially for IO-bound tasks, but it requires careful consideration of the hardware resources available to avoid overwhelming the system.

```
1  <property name="Concurrent Tasks">
2      <value>5</value>
3  </property>
```

Additionally, the Back Pressure settings are pivotal in managing data flow between processors. Properly configured back pressure prevents data queues from becoming bottlenecks, ensuring a smooth and efficient flow of data. Adjusting the back pressure criteria based on throughput and data size can prevent processors from becoming overwhelmed, thus maintaining optimal performance.

Another vital aspect is the design of the data flow itself. Efficient pipeline design involves minimizing the number of processors used and selecting the most efficient processor for a given task. This could mean preferring processors that perform multiple transformations in a single step over chaining several processors together, or utilizing processors that filter out unnecessary data early in the flow to reduce the volume of data processed downstream.

Employing batching techniques where possible can also yield significant performance improvements. Many processors support batching, which allows them to process multiple flow files or records in a single execution. This reduces the overhead associated with processing each item individually and can greatly increase throughput.

```
Processed 1000 records in one batch. Execution time: 2 seconds.
```

Monitoring and fine-tuning are continuous processes in the optimization journey. NiFi provides detailed metrics for each processor, including execution time, queue size, and throughput. Regularly reviewing these metrics allows for identifying bottlenecks and understanding the effects of any configuration changes.

- Review processor metrics regularly.

- Identify and address bottlenecks promptly.

- Continuously refine processor configurations based on performance data.

Finally, leveraging the power of custom processors and scripted processors can address specific performance bottlenecks. While developing custom processors requires a deep understanding of NiFi's API and Java, they offer unparalleled flexibility to optimize performance for specialized tasks. Scripted processors, on the other hand, provide a quicker way to implement custom logic with languages like Groovy or Python but may not offer the same level of performance as custom Java processors.

Optimizing processor performance in Apache NiFi is a multifaceted process that requires a thorough understanding of both the processors and the data being handled. Through careful configuration, efficient data flow design, continuous monitoring, and, when necessary, custom processor development, it is possible to achieve highly efficient and performant data pipelines.

3.11 Using Processors for Data Enrichment

Data enrichment is a critical phase in data processing where the value of data is enhanced through the integration of additional information from internal or external sources. Apache NiFi provides a versatile suite of processors capable of enriching data as it flows through the system. This allows for more informed decision-making and deeper insights into the processed information. The objective of this section is to discuss the configuration and application of specific NiFi processors for data enrichment purposes.

Data enrichment involves augmenting or refining raw data with relevant context to increase its value and utility before it is stored or further processed. This can include appending metadata, merging data streams, enhancing data with information from databases or APIs, and more. In the context of Apache NiFi, various processors facilitate these actions seamlessly.

The `LookupAttribute` and `LookupRecord` processors are among the most commonly used for data enrichment in NiFi. These processors allow for the lookup of data from several different sources, including simple key-value stores, databases, or even RESTful APIs. The enrichment process involves fetching additional information based on keys or identifiers present in the flow files being processed.

```
1  <processor>
2    <class>org.apache.nifi.processors.standard.LookupAttribute</class>
3    <properties>
4      <property>
5        <name>Lookup Service</name>
```

```
6            <value>SimpleKeyValueLookupService</value>
7        </property>
8    </properties>
9 </processor>
```

Enrichment with `LookupAttribute`, for instance, involves specifying the lookup service which might be a simple CSV file acting as a key-value store or a more complex database service. Configuring such processors involves understanding the nature of the data source and the data itself to map the inputs to outputs effectively.

Joining disparate data streams is another form of enrichment effectively handled by the `MergeContent` and `MergeRecord` processors. These processors can combine flow files based on criteria or attributes, effectively stitching together data from different sources into a single, enriched dataset.

```
1 <processor>
2    <class>org.apache.nifi.processors.standard.MergeContent</class>
3    <properties>
4        <property>
5            <name>Merge Strategy</name>
6            <value>Defragment</value>
7        </property>
8    </properties>
9 </processor>
```

The configuration of the `MergeContent` processor, as shown above, necessitates defining a merge strategy that aligns with the objectives of the data enrichment process—whether it's combining fragments of a larger dataset or aggregating related but distinct datasets into a cohesive whole.

Furthermore, invoking external services for data enrichment involves processors like `InvokeHTTP` for accessing REST APIs or `ExecuteSQL` for retrieving information from a database. These processors fetch additional data required for enriching the original dataset being processed.

```
1 <processor>
2    <class>org.apache.nifi.processors.standard.InvokeHTTP</class>
3    <properties>
4        <property>
5            <name>HTTP Method</name>
6            <value>GET</value>
7        </property>
8    </properties>
9 </processor>
```

This example demonstrates configuring the `InvokeHTTP` processor to perform a GET request to a specified URL where the response is expected to contain data that can be used to enrich the original flow file.

Efficiency and accuracy in data enrichment require a carefully planned strategy that considers the data's source, format, and the target enrichment. This entails a thorough analysis of the data at hand, clear identification of the enrichment goals, and a detailed configuration of the NiFi processors to ensure that the enrichment adds value without introducing errors or inconsistencies.

Data enrichment with Apache NiFi is a powerful capability that enhances data utility and supports more sophisticated analytics and decision-making. By configuring and employing a variety of processors, such as LookupAttribute, MergeContent, and InvokeHTTP, users can enrich their data streams effectively, making NiFi an indispensable tool in modern data architectures. Understanding these processors and their configurations is essential for leveraging NiFi's full potential in data enrichment scenarios.

3.12 Debugging and Troubleshooting Processors

Debugging and troubleshooting processors in Apache NiFi involves a systematic examination of the data flow to identify and resolve issues that prevent the processors from operating as intended. Despite the robust nature of NiFi processors, challenges such as data flow bottlenecks, processor misconfigurations, and external system integration problems can arise. This section will discuss practical strategies for debugging and troubleshooting these issues to ensure the smooth operation of data pipelines.

Firstly, monitoring the NiFi dataflow is crucial for effective troubleshooting. NiFi provides a rich set of tools and metrics for monitoring processor performance, including queue lengths, processor status, and connection metrics. By observing these metrics, users can quickly identify underperforming processors or congested dataflows. For instance, a processor with a consistently full incoming queue might indicate a need for adjustment in scheduling or an increase in task concurrency.

```
1  // Example of a command to view processor status
2  nifi.sh status processor --processorId <processor-id>
```

```
Processor Status:
- ID           : <processor-id>
- Name         : <processor-name>
- Type         : <processor-type>
```

```
- Run Status    : Running
- Health        : Healthy
- Input         : 1000 (5 MB)
- Output        : 950 (4.9 MB)
- Tasks/Time    : 100 tasks, 0:00:05.123
```

Secondly, effective use of log files cannot be overstated. NiFi logs detailed information about each processor's activities, errors, and warnings which are invaluable for diagnosing issues. By default, logging is configured to provide a balanced level of detail that aids in identifying problems without overwhelming the user with information. However, it can be adjusted for more verbose output if detailed analysis is necessary. For example, to troubleshoot a processor that is failing to route data as expected, increasing the logging level for that processor can provide insights into the decision-making process within the processor.

```
1  // Example of adjusting logging levels via logback.xml
2  <logger name="org.apache.nifi.processors" level="DEBUG"/>
```

Effective problem-solving also involves understanding the data processed by NiFi. Tools like the 'Data Provenance' feature allow users to track the life cycle of a dataflow, providing visibility into how data is modified and routed through the system. This feature can be particularly helpful in identifying where data is being lost, duplicated, or incorrectly modified.

```
1  // Accessing data provenance information via NiFi UI
2  Click on 'Data Provenance' in the Operate panel
```

Furthermore, configuration missteps are a common source of issues within NiFi processors. Each processor has a set of configurable properties and relationships that dictate its behavior. Misconfiguration can lead to unforeseen errors or suboptimal performance. Therefore, verifying property settings and ensuring that all required properties are correctly configured is essential. Additionally, thoroughly understanding the role of each processor relationship and ensuring data is correctly routed based on these relationships is fundamental.

```
1  // Example of a common configuration check
2  Ensure that all required processor properties are filled
3  Review relationship configurations to prevent data loss
```

Concurrent execution is another aspect that requires attention during troubleshooting. Processors in NiFi can be configured to run multiple concurrent tasks. While this can significantly improve data processing efficiency, it can also lead to resource contention or race conditions if not managed carefully. It is advisable to gradually adjust concurrency settings while monitoring system performance to find the optimal configuration.

Lastly, external system interactions often introduce complexity into the debugging process. Processors that interact with external systems, such as databases or APIs, may fail due to external service unavailability or network issues. Diagnosing these problems requires a combination of monitoring the NiFi application logs, checking the availability of the external service, and possibly increasing logging verbosity for the processor to capture more detailed error information.

Debugging and troubleshooting NiFi processors demand a multifaceted approach, leveraging NiFi's monitoring and logging capabilities, understanding processor configuration, and being vigilant about external system interactions. Through careful observation and methodical analysis, most processor-related issues can be resolved, ensuring the reliability and effectiveness of dataflow processing within Apache NiFi.

Chapter 4

Data Flow Management and Routing

Effective data flow management and routing are crucial to ensuring that data moves seamlessly and efficiently through various stages of processing within Apache NiFi. This encompasses the design and execution of data workflows that include the ingestion, processing, and distribution of data. By utilizing NiFi's robust routing capabilities, users can manage data flows dynamically, directing data to different paths based on attributes, content, or other criteria. This enables organizations to implement complex data integration and transformation scenarios, addressing the challenges of handling diverse data types and formats across disparate systems.

4.1 Overview of Data Flow Management in NiFi

Apache NiFi, a robust, scalable, and flexible platform, provides comprehensive solutions for data flow management, designed to automate the flow of data between systems. Unlike traditional data handling tools, NiFi emphasizes key principles such as secure data routing, transformation, and system mediation logic. At its core, NiFi allows for the design, control, feedback, and monitoring of data flows, thus enabling real-time data processing and analytics.

The architecture of Apache NiFi is built around the fundamental concept of Flow-Based Programming (FBP), where data flows through a network of processes, each dedicated to a specific task such as data ingestion, transformation, or routing. This section will discuss the critical aspects of data flow management within the NiFi ecosystem, highlighting essential components such as Processors, Connections, FlowFiles, and Process Groups.

- Processors are the building blocks of NiFi data flows. Each processor is designed to perform a single, specific task such as fetching data from a source, transforming data, routing data based on certain conditions, or sending data to a destination.

- Connections link processors together, forming a directed graph that represents the data flow. Connections also manage data queueing between processors, ensuring smooth data transfer and handling backpressure.

- FlowFiles represent a single piece of data moving through the flow. Each FlowFile has attributes (key-value pairs) and the data content itself. Attributes can be used to make routing decisions or transform data.

- Process Groups allow for encapsulation and modularization of data flows. They enable users to organize a set of components into a higher-level group, simplifying complex data flows and promoting reuse.

Building an effective NiFi data flow involves configuring these elements to work together seamlessly, forming a coherent process that meets specific data processing requirements. The Flow Controller, the brain of the operation, manages the scheduling of all tasks and threading within NiFi. One of the critical tasks in data flow management is the efficient routing of data. Routing can be based on various criteria, such as attributes extracted from the data itself, metadata, or external signals.

A powerful feature of NiFi is its ability to dynamically adapt data flows. Through user interaction with the NiFi UI or via automated control mechanisms, data flows can be altered in real-time to accommodate changing data sources, formats, and processing requirements. This dynamic adaptability makes NiFi particularly suited for scenarios where data is non-uniform, the schema is evolving, or the sources are intermittent.

Furthermore, the design of NiFi's data flow management system emphasizes security, provenance, and auditability. Each component in the data flow ensures data integrity, authenticity, and traceability, allowing for comprehensive monitoring and reporting on data movement and transformation. NiFi's fine-grained data tracking capabilities enable developers and data engineers to gain insights into the data flow's performance, quickly identify bottlenecks or errors, and make informed decisions to optimize the data handling process.

In summary, data flow management in Apache NiFi is a multifaceted process that involves the consideration of numerous factors such as data routing, system scalability, flexibility, and security. By leveraging NiFi's comprehensive toolset and adhering to best practices in data flow design and management, organizations can build efficient, reliable, and secure data pipelines capable of handling complex data integration and processing scenarios.

4.2 Designing Data Flows: Best Practices

Designing efficient and robust data flows within Apache NiFi requires a strategic approach that accounts for the complexity of data processing tasks and the dynamism of real-world data. This segment elucidates several best practices that, when adhered to, can significantly enhance the efficiency, maintainability, and scalability of NiFi data flows.

Let's start with the principle of simplicity. The design of data flows should commence with the simplest configuration that meets the functional requirements. Complex data flow designs tend to introduce unnecessary complications that can impede performance and make maintenance a daunting task. To uphold simplicity, use a modular approach by encapsulating related processing tasks within separate process groups. This not only eases understanding and management of the data flows but also enhances reusability across different workflows.

Another critical aspect is designing for scalability. Data flows should be designed with future growth in mind, which involves considering both the increase in data volume and the potential need to expand processing logic. Utilizing NiFi's built-in capabilities for load balancing and backpressure ensures that data flows can handle varying loads efficiently. Implementing partitioning of data and parallel processing can further augment scalability. For instance:

```
1   <processor>
```

```
2      <class>org.apache.nifi.processors.standard.PartitionRecord</class>
3      <properties>
4          <property name="partitioning.field.name" value="customerId"/>
5      </properties>
6  </processor>
```

In the above example, the `PartitionRecord` processor is configured to partition records based on `customerId`, enabling parallel processing of data for different customers.

Error handling is another essential component of robust data flow design. NiFi provides various processors and mechanisms to facilitate graceful error handling and recovery. Careful planning of error handling strategies, including specifying backout queues and designing routes for failed processing attempts, ensures data integrity and operational reliability. Configuring processors with appropriate failure relationship links enables data to be routed to specific paths for troubleshooting or reprocessing.

Documentation and naming conventions contribute significantly to the maintainability of NiFi data flows. Each processor, connection, and process group should be named descriptively to reflect its purpose within the workflow. Leveraging NiFi's documentation features to add annotations and usage instructions further aids in understanding and maintaining the data flows.

Adhering to best practices for security and compliance from the onset is imperative. This encompasses enforcing encryption for sensitive data, using processors that support data tokenization and anonymization, and implementing access controls and auditing mechanisms. Compliance with regulatory requirements and organizational policies should be embedded into the design of the data flow, ensuring that data handling proceeds within a secure environment.

Lastly, constant monitoring and feedback are crucial for the iterative improvement of data flows. Apache NiFi's data provenance and monitoring tools offer detailed insights into the performance and behavior of data flows, enabling developers to identify bottlenecks, inefficiencies, and errors. Regular review and refinement of data flows based on real-time feedback lead to continuous optimization.

In summary, designing data flows in Apache NiFi is a meticulous process that demands attention to detail and adherence to best practices. By prioritizing simplicity, scalability, error handling, documentation, security, and continuous improvement, developers can craft efficient, robust, and maintainable data workflows capable of handling the complexities of modern data processing requirements.

4.3 Routing Data Based on Content and Attributes

Routing data based on content and attributes is a pivotal technique within Apache NiFi that facilitates efficient data flow management. This process allows data to be dynamically directed through various paths of a pipeline, contingent upon specific conditions derived from data content or metadata attributes. This capability is paramount for orchestrating complex data processing workflows which can efficiently adapt to the intricacies of data being processed, thereby optimizing the data processing lifecycle.

At the core of Apache NiFi's data routing mechanism are several key processors that enable conditional data flow management. This includes, but is not limited to, RouteOnAttribute, RouteOnContent, and RouteBasedOnLookup. Each of these processors leverages different aspects of the data to make routing decisions, allowing for a multifaceted approach to data flow management.

Routing Based on Attributes: The RouteOnAttribute processor is a versatile tool for making routing decisions based on the evaluation of FlowFile attributes. One can specify conditions using NiFi Expression Language, allowing for the comparison of attribute values or the existence of certain attributes within a FlowFile. An illustrative example is provided below:

```
1  <#-- Example of using RouteOnAttribute processor -->
2  <property>
3      <name>attributeName</name>
4      <value>expression</value>
5  </property>
```

This snippet indicates how a routing condition is specified in NiFi. If the condition evaluates to true, the FlowFile is routed to a corresponding relationship; otherwise, it can be routed to an 'unmatched' relationship.

Routing Based on Content: For scenarios where the data content itself dictates the routing logic, the RouteOnContent processor comes into play. This processor scans the content of each FlowFile against user-defined criteria, which is particularly useful for routing data based on specific patterns, keywords, or sequences present in the data content.

```
1   <#-- Example of using RouteOnContent processor -->
2   <property>
3       <name>contentMatchingRegex</name>
4       <value>regex</value>
5   </property>
```

In the above example, a regular expression (regex) is used to define the content-based routing criterion. FlowFiles whose content matches the regex are routed to a designated path.

Routing Based on External Conditions: With   the `RouteBasedOnLookup` processor, NiFi can route FlowFiles based on conditions external to the data itself, such as lookup tables or external data sources.   This capability enables dynamic routing decisions that can adjust in real time to changes in external conditions or criteria.

`RouteOnAttribute`, `RouteOnContent`, and `RouteBasedOnLookup` processors embody the essence of data routing in Apache NiFi, enabling not merely the flow of data but its intelligent, condition-based redirection. Leveraging these processors effectively requires a deep understanding of the data, the processing requirements, and the desired outcomes of the data pipeline.

The implications of routing data based on content and attributes extend beyond mere data movement. These routing decisions can significantly influence the efficiency and effectiveness of data processing. By directing data along the most appropriate paths, processing resources can be optimally utilized, reducing bottlenecks and enhancing the overall throughput of the system. Furthermore, such routing enables more sophisticated data processing workflows. For instance, data can be dynamically classified, segregated, or aggregated based on its attributes or content, facilitating nuanced processing that is responsive to the data's inherent characteristics.

Routing data based on content and attributes within Apache NiFi is a fundamental aspect of managing complex data flows. Through the judicious application of routing processors, NiFi can orchestrate flexible, dynamic data pipelines. These pipelines not only address the prerequisites of diverse data processing tasks but also contribute to the scalability and robustness of data infrastructure. As data volume, variety, and velocity continue to escalate, the ability to adeptly route data becomes crucial in deriving meaningful insights and achieving operational efficiencies in real-time data processing environments.

4.4 Utilizing Process Groups for Organized Data Flow

Process groups in Apache NiFi serve a fundamental role in organizing the components of a data flow, encapsulating a set of processors, connections, input ports, output ports, and even other process groups. This encapsulation allows for modular data flow design, where each process group can represent a specific function or segment of the overall data processing pipeline. By leveraging process groups, data engineers can achieve a higher level of abstraction, making complex data flows more manageable and easier to maintain.

The inception of a process group begins with the intention to segment a data flow into logical units that can be developed, managed, and monitored independently. This capability is crucial for teams working on large-scale data integration projects, where the complexity of data flows can quickly become unmanageable. In NiFi, creating a process group is as simple as selecting the process group component from the toolbar and dragging it onto the canvas.

Once a process group is created, it acts as a container for any number of processors and other components. The internal structure of a process group can be as simple or as complex as necessary. For instance, a process group could encompass a straightforward sequence of processors performing data enrichment, or it could contain a sophisticated arrangement of nested process groups each handling different stages of data processing such as ingestion, transformation, and distribution.

Isolating functionalities into separate process groups also facilitates the reusability of common data flow patterns. For example, a process group designed to normalize data formats can be reused across multiple data pipelines within an organization, thereby reducing development time and ensuring consistency in data processing routines.

Moreover, process groups contribute to better data flow management through version control. Apache NiFi supports versioning of process groups, enabling data engineers to track changes, roll back to previous versions, and migrate process groups between environments. This feature is particularly beneficial in regulated industries where audit trails and change management are paramount.

Data flow variables are another feature enhanced by the use of process groups. Variables defined at the process group level can be used to parameterize the processors within that group, allowing for dynamic configuration of processor properties. This capability significantly simplifies the management of environment-specific configurations, such as file paths, API endpoints, and database connections.

The conceptual separation achieved through process groups is further bolstered by NiFi's access control mechanisms. Permissions can be set at the process group level, granting or restricting access to different parts of the data flow based on user roles. This allows organizations to enforce the principle of least privilege, ensuring that users only have access to the data and components necessary for their role.

In the context of handling data backpressure and load balancing, process groups offer a granular level of control. Each process group can be configured with specific backpressure settings and load balancing strategies, optimizing the performance and reliability of data flows. For instance, critical data flows can be prioritized with higher throughput settings to ensure timely processing, while less critical flows can be configured to yield under high system load.

To visualize and monitor the performance of data flows, NiFi provides real-time metrics at the process group level. These metrics include data flow throughput, processing speed, and queue sizes. By analyzing these metrics, data engineers can identify bottlenecks, optimize processor configurations, and ensure that data flows are running efficiently.

Utilizing process groups in Apache NiFi is a best practice for designing, implementing, and managing organized data flows. Through encapsulation, abstraction, and modular design, process groups enable the development of scalable and maintainable data pipelines. Their use simplifies complex data processing tasks, enhances reusability and version control, facilitates configuration management, and supports granular access control. As such, process groups are indispensable tools for data engineers seeking to harness the full potential of Apache NiFi in building real-time data pipelines.

4.5 Handling Backpressure and Data Prioritization

Handing backpressure is a critical aspect of managing data flows in Apache NiFi, ensuring that the system can operate smoothly without being overwhelmed by the volume of incoming data. Backpressure occurs when downstream components or processes cannot keep up with the rate at which data is being produced by upstream processes, potentially leading to system instability or data loss. NiFi addresses this challenge through configurable backpressure settings that allow users to define thresholds for queue size and data size. When these thresholds are breached, NiFi automatically pauses data flow in upstream processes, preventing further data from being queued until the congestion is alleviated.

Data prioritization complements backpressure by providing mechanisms to control the order in which data is processed. This is particularly useful in scenarios where certain data items are more urgent or have higher value than others. Apache NiFi allows users to define custom prioritization schemes based on the attributes or content of FlowFiles. By doing so, users can ensure that critical data is processed and passed on with minimal delay.

Backpressure settings in NiFi can be adjusted on a per-connection basis. To configure these settings, users need to access the configuration dialog for a connection and specify the desired thresholds for queue count and data size. For instance, a configuration might specify that backpressure should be applied when a queue reaches 10,000 FlowFiles or 1GB of data. It is worth noting that these settings should be determined judiciously, taking into account the overall capacity of the system and the specific requirements of the data flow.

In terms of data prioritization, NiFi provides several out-of-the-box strategies, such as First In, First Out (FIFO); Last In, First Out (LIFO); and Priority Attribute. The Priority Attribute strategy allows data flow managers to specify which attribute of a FlowFile should be used for prioritization, enabling fine-grained control over how data is processed. To implement custom prioritization, users can develop custom Prioritizer implementations that can be deployed and selected within NiFi.

```
Example of backpressure configuration:
- Queue Count Threshold: 10,000 FlowFiles
- Data Size Threshold: 1GB
```

```
Example of data prioritization configuration:
- Priority Strategy: Priority Attribute
- Priority Attribute Name: urgency
- Priority Levels: High, Medium, Low
```

It is also important to note that backpressure and data prioritization mechanisms need to be monitored and adjusted periodically to adapt to changing data flows and processing capabilities. Overly restrictive backpressure settings may lead to unnecessary delays in data processing, while excessively lenient settings could overwhelm downstream processes. Similarly, the effectiveness of prioritization schemes should be evaluated regularly to ensure that they align with the evolving objectives and requirements of the data flow.

The integration of backpressure and data prioritization into NiFi's design reflects the platform's comprehensive approach to data flow management. By allowing users to dynamically manage data flows based on system capacity and data characteristics, Apache NiFi facilitates the creation of flexible, robust, and efficient data pipelines. Consequently, understanding and effectively configuring these features is essential for NiFi users aiming to optimize their data processing workflows.

Managing backpressure and data prioritization is paramount in creating efficient and reliable data flows in Apache NiFi. Through careful configuration and ongoing oversight, users can harness these features to enhance the performance and resilience of their data processing environments.

4.6   Data Partitioning and Multiple FlowFile Processing

In the context of Apache NiFi, effective data management is not complete without addressing the challenges of data partitioning and multiple FlowFile processing. Data partitioning involves dividing a dataset into smaller, manageable parts, while ensuring that each part can be processed in a way that is both efficient and does not compromise the integrity or accuracy of the data. This is particularly relevant in scenarios where the volume of incoming data exceeds the capacity of a single processing task or where different parts of the dataset require different processing workflows. Multiple FlowFile processing, on the other hand, refers to the capability of handling several FlowFiles simultaneously, leveraging parallel processing to enhance the throughput and efficiency of data flows.

Data partitioning in Apache NiFi can be achieved using various processors, but the `PartitionRecord` processor stands out due to its flexibility and ease of configuration. The `PartitionRecord` processor allows for partitioning incoming FlowFiles based on the content or attributes of the data they contain. This enables the dynamic routing of data segments to different paths within a NiFi dataflow, facilitating specialized processing on each partition.

```
1   <PartitionRecord name="Partition by Region">
2       Property Name: Record Reader
3       Value: CSVReader
4
5       Property Name: Record Writer
6       Value: CSVRecordSetWriter
7
8       Property Name: Partitioning Strategy
9       Value: Expression Language
10
11      Property Name: Partitioning Field Name
12      Value: region
13  </PartitionRecord>
```

In the above example, the `PartitionRecord` processor is configured to partition FlowFiles based on the 'region' field within a CSV file. Each partition can subsequently be directed to different processors or process groups for region-specific processing.

Multiple FlowFile processing is intricately linked with NiFi's scheduling strategies, which allow for concurrent tasks within processors. By adjusting the concurrent tasks setting for a processor, Apache NiFi can process multiple FlowFiles in parallel, significantly increasing the throughput of a dataflow. However, it is essential to balance the number of concurrent tasks with system resources to prevent potential performance bottlenecks.

```
Concurrent Tasks: 4
```

In the code snippet above, setting the concurrent tasks to 4 allows the processor to handle four FlowFiles concurrently. This configuration is beneficial for data-intensive applications, enabling the system to maintain high performance even under significant data load.

FlowFile queues play a crucial role in managing Processed Flows between processors, especially in the context of multiple FlowFile processing. NiFi provides sophisticated mechanisms for queue prioritization and backpressure settings. Through queue configuration, dataflows can be optimized to ensure that high-priority data is processed first, and system stability is maintained by regulating the FlowFile queue size to prevent out-of-memory errors.

Data partitioning and multiple FlowFile processing are pivotal in scaling Apache NiFi dataflows to meet the demands of large-scale and complex data integration tasks. By judiciously segmenting data and exploiting parallel processing capacities, NiFi fosters a highly efficient, flexible, and scalable environment for data flow management. This not only maximizes resource utilization but also enhances the overall performance, making NiFi a powerful tool for comprehensive data management solutions.

4.7 FlowFile Queues and Load Balancing Strategies

In Apache NiFi, the efficient management of FlowFiles through the system is central to performing seamless data processing operations. FlowFile queues play a pivotal role in this management by acting as buffers between processors. These queues enable asynchronous processing across different components, ensuring that the system remains resilient to fluctuations in data volume and processing speeds. This section will delve into the intricacies of FlowFile queues and the strategies for load balancing that can optimize the flow of data through these queues, thereby enhancing the throughput and reliability of data pipelines.

FlowFile queues are more than simple FIFO (First In, First Out) structures. They are sophisticated mechanisms that support priority-based queueing, backpressure, and load balancing. When a processor sends a FlowFile to the next processor in the flow, it does so by placing the FlowFile into a queue. If the receiving processor is busy or slow to process its incoming FlowFiles, the queue acts as a buffer, preventing data loss and allowing the sending processor to continue its work without delay.

The handling of backpressure, which is a critical aspect of FlowFile queues, is configured through two primary settings: Backpressure Object Threshold and Backpressure Data Size Threshold. These settings allow administrators to define the conditions under which backpressure is applied, essentially pausing the upstream processors to prevent the queue from becoming overwhelmed. This mechanism ensures that the system can gracefully handle surges in data, maintaining stability and performance.

```
1  # Example queue configuration snippet in NiFi
2  <queue>
3      <maxQueueSize>1000</maxQueueSize>
4      <backpressureObjectThreshold>10000</backpressureObjectThreshold>
5      <backpressureDataSizeThreshold>1 GB</backpressureDataSizeThreshold>
6  </queue>
```

Load balancing strategies in NiFi provide a means to distribute the workload evenly across a cluster, ensuring that no single node becomes a bottleneck. NiFi supports several load balancing strategies, each tailored for specific scenarios and operational requirements. The most commonly used strategies are:

- Round Robin: Distributes FlowFiles evenly across all available nodes, ensuring that each node processes approximately the same number of FlowFiles over time.

- Random: Assigns FlowFiles to any available node at random. This strategy is useful when the processing load is uniform, and there is no benefit to evenly distributing FlowFiles.

- Partition by Attribute: Routes FlowFiles to nodes based on the value of specified attributes. This strategy is particularly valuable when processing needs to be localized, such as when FlowFiles need to be processed by the same node based on certain criteria.

Determining the appropriate load balancing strategy involves analyzing the data flow's characteristics and processing requirements. Factors such as the size and variability of data, the processing capabilities of nodes, and the need for localized processing should all be considered.

Implementing effective load balancing can significantly impact the performance and reliability of NiFi data flows. It ensures that no single node is overwhelmed with work, which can lead to slower processing times and potential failures. Moreover, it allows for more efficient use of resources, as work is distributed in a way that leverages the full capacity of the cluster.

In summary, FlowFile queues and load balancing strategies are essential components of NiFi's architecture that significantly contribute to the platform's ability to handle complex and high-volume data flows. Proper configuration and utilization of these mechanisms are paramount for achieving optimal performance, reliability, and efficiency in data processing operations.

4.8 Splitting and Aggregating FlowFiles

In Apache NiFi, effectively managing data flow often necessitates the manipulation of FlowFiles to accommodate various processing requirements. Specifically, the operations of splitting and aggregating FlowFiles play a pivotal role in optimizing data flow management. This section will discuss the mechanisms for splitting and aggregating FlowFiles within NiFi, highlighting their importance and providing guidance on their implementation.

Splitting FlowFiles is a process that involves dividing a larger FlowFile into smaller ones. This operation is crucial when individual records within a FlowFile need to be processed independently or in parallel, enhancing processing efficiency. The SplitText and SplitJson processors are common tools used for this purpose. These processors allow for splitting based on specific conditions such as line count in a text file or the structure of a JSON file.

For instance, consider a scenario where a large text file containing multiple records needs to be processed line by line. The SplitText processor can be configured as follows:

```
1   <SplitText>
2       Line Split Count: 1
3   </SplitText>
```

This configuration ensures that each line of the text file is separated into individual FlowFiles, allowing for parallel processing of each record.

On the other hand, aggregating FlowFiles refers to the process of combining multiple smaller FlowFiles into a larger one. This is often necessary when a collective data set needs to be packaged for downstream processing or storage. The MergeContent and MergeRecord processors facilitate this operation. They can be configured to aggregate FlowFiles based on criteria such as size, count, or time, ensuring that data batching meets the requirements of downstream systems or processes.

An example configuration for the MergeContent processor to merge text files based on a total combined size limit could be:

```
1   <MergeContent>
```

```
2    Maximum Number of Bins: 5
3    Max Bin Age: 10 mins
4    Maximum Group Size: 500 MB
5  </MergeContent>
```

This configuration instructs NiFi to aggregate text files into a single FlowFile until the total size reaches 500 MB or the oldest file in the bin reaches 10 minutes in age, whichever comes first.

It is worth noting that the choice between splitting and aggregating FlowFiles significantly impacts data flow performance and efficiency. Splitting enables more granular processing but may increase the overhead of managing a larger number of FlowFiles. Conversely, aggregating can reduce the overhead but may introduce latency if the aggregation criteria are not met promptly.

Furthermore, careful consideration should be given to the downstream processors in the NiFi flow. Processors that are capable of handling multiple records within a single FlowFile efficiently may not require upfront splitting. Similarly, if downstream systems require single, consolidated files for ingestion, proper aggregation settings must be applied to ensure compatibility.

The ability to split and aggregate FlowFiles in Apache NiFi provides users with powerful tools to customize data flows according to specific processing needs. By understanding and applying these techniques appropriately, one can achieve enhanced data processing efficiency, flexibility, and performance. It is recommended to experiment with different configurations in a controlled environment to determine the optimal settings for specific use cases, thereby ensuring that data flows are managed in the most effective manner possible.

4.9 Data Flow Monitoring and Real-time Feedback

Effective data flow monitoring and the provision of real-time feedback are paramount for the successful operation of data pipelines in Apache NiFi. This ensures not only the smooth processing of data through various stages but also enables the quick identification and resolution of issues, thus maintaining the integrity and reliability of data flows. Apache NiFi offers a comprehensive set of tools and features designed to facilitate this, empowering developers and administrators to keep a vigilant eye on the health and performance of their data pipelines.

One of the foundational elements of data flow monitoring in Apache NiFi is the use of the Data Provenance feature. Data Provenance tracks data flow from its inception to its current state, recording every change and traversal it undergoes through different processors and connections. This comprehensive audit trail enables users to perform detailed analysis and troubleshooting, ensuring transparency and accountability in data processing.

```
Example of a Data Provenance record:

Provenance Event ID: 12345
Event Type: ATTRIBUTES_MODIFIED
FlowFile UUID: abcde-fghij-12345-67890
Timestamp: 2023-01-01 12:00:00
Component ID: processor-xyz
Details: size=1024 bytes, mime.type=text/plain
```

The Bulletin Board is another critical feature for real-time feedback. It aggregates and displays warning and error messages generated by processors and other NiFi components. By monitoring the Bulletin Board, operators can quickly identify components that are experiencing difficulties, analyze diagnostic information, and take corrective action to mitigate issues promptly. This instant feedback mechanism is vital for maintaining the operability of data flows, especially in complex environments where issues need to be addressed in real-time to prevent data loss or corruption.

To facilitate fine-grained monitoring, Apache NiFi provides extensive support for metrics and reporting tasks. Users can configure Reporting Tasks to generate metrics related to the performance and health of the NiFi instance, including JVM metrics, Content Repository usage, and FlowFile Processing metrics. These metrics can be sent to external monitoring systems such as Grafana or Prometheus, enabling the visualization and analysis of data pipeline performance over time.

```
1   Example of a Reporting Task configuration:
2
3   Name: MonitorMemory
4   Type: MonitorMemory Reporting Task
5   Properties:
6       Threshold Duration: 5 minutes
7       Reporting Interval: 1 minute
8       Memory Pool: Metaspace
```

The integration of custom scripts and external monitoring solutions like Apache NiFi's Site-to-Site protocol enhances monitoring and feedback capabilities. By using Site-to-Site, metrics and data flow statistics can be securely transmitted between different NiFi instances or to external systems, allowing for centralized monitoring of distributed data flows.

For data flow administrators and developers, the implementation of comprehensive monitoring and real-time feedback mechanisms is not just about maintaining operational stability; it's about gaining insights into performance bottlenecks, optimizing data throughput, and enhancing the efficiency of data processing workflows. Effective monitoring strategies employ a combination of NiFi's built-in features - from Data Provenance and the Bulletin Board to Reporting Tasks and external integrations. By leveraging these tools, users can ensure that their data flows are not only robust and reliable but also adaptive to the changing dynamics of real-time data processing.

Monitoring and real-time feedback play a crucial role in the management of data flows in Apache NiFi. Through diligent application of NiFi's monitoring features and the integration of external tools, organizations can achieve heightened levels of operational visibility, performance optimization, and system reliability, thereby ensuring the seamless processing of data across their pipelines.

4.10 Implementing Advanced Routing Techniques

Implementing advanced routing techniques in Apache NiFi involves utilizing a set of sophisticated features that allow for conditional data routing, dynamic flow adjustments, and enhanced flow control capabilities. These procedures are pivotal for developing complex, adaptable, and efficient data pipelines. In this section, we will discuss the implementation of rule-based routing, attribute-based routing, and content-based routing, along with the use of Expression Language for dynamic routing decisions.

Rule-based routing in NiFi is facilitated through the use of the RouteOnAttribute and RouteOnContent processors. These processors evaluate flow files against user-defined criteria, directing them to different paths within the dataflow based on the results of the evaluation.

```
1  <processors>
2    <processor>
3      <type>RouteOnAttribute</type>
4      <properties>
5        <property name="routing.strategy" value="route.to.property.name"/>
```

```
6        <property name="dynamic.property.name" value="attribute.expression"/>
7      </properties>
8    </processor>
9  </processors>
```

The RouteOnAttribute processor enables the routing of FlowFiles based on their attributes. Here, dynamic property names represent different routing conditions, and their values are specified using NiFi's Expression Language, allowing for a highly flexible routing mechanism. An example attribute expression might look like ${attribute:equals('value')}, which routes FlowFiles where the attribute equals 'value'.

On the other hand, the RouteOnContent processor examines the actual content of FlowFiles, using regular expressions to determine routing paths. This facilitates content-sensitive dataflow decisions, essential for scenarios where data content dynamically influences pipeline behavior.

```
1  <processors>
2    <processor>
3      <type>RouteOnContent</type>
4      <properties>
5        <property name="search.string" value="regular.expression"/>
6      </properties>
7    </processor>
8  </processors>
```

Attribute-based routing is enhanced further by leveraging the Expression Language for dynamic decision-making. This language can access FlowFile attributes and manipulate them through a variety of functions and operators, enabling complex routing conditions to be succinctly expressed and evaluated at runtime.

```
1  <expression>
2    $\{filename:startsWith('log')\}
3  </expression>
```

Content-based routing, facilitated by the RouteOnContent processor, is invaluable for scenarios where the data's substance directly informs its proper destination. Regular expressions or other content-matching mechanisms are utilized to inspect data packets, ensuring that content-specific handling can be dynamically applied.

Advanced routing strategies often employ a combination of these techniques to construct nuanced, conditionally responsive dataflows. The integration of process groups and remote process groups further expands the routing capabilities, allowing for data to be directed not only within a single NiFi instance but also across distributed NiFi environments.

Implementing advanced routing strategies in Apache NiFi necessitates a thorough understanding of how data attributes, content, and dynamic expressions can be leveraged to make informed routing decisions. Through the use of specialized processors and expression language, complex dataflows can be constructed, which react in real-time to the changing landscapes of incoming data streams. These techniques, when applied judiciously, enable the construction of sophisticated, resilient, and efficient data processing pipelines that are capable of addressing a wide array of data ingestion, processing, and distribution scenarios.

4.11 Error Handling and Failure Recovery in Data Flows

Error handling and failure recovery are critical components in managing data flows within Apache NiFi, ensuring robust and resilient data pipelines. This section will discuss strategies to detect, respond, and recover from errors and failures that may occur during data flow execution.

Firstly, understanding and categorizing the types of errors that can occur is essential for effective error handling. In Apache NiFi, errors can be broadly classified into processing errors and system errors. Processing errors are related to the content of the data or the processing logic, such as format incompatibility or script execution failures. System errors, on the other hand, involve NiFi's infrastructure, including network failures, resource limitations, or external system unavailability.

- Processing errors

- System errors

To manage these errors, Apache NiFi offers several mechanisms:

Data Provenance: NiFi provides a comprehensive data provenance tool that allows users to track the flow of data through the system. By leveraging this tool, users can identify where an error occurred in the data pipeline, significantly simplifying the debugging process.

Connection Queues: NiFi uses queues to manage data between processors. Each connection queue can be configured with backpressure settings and prioritization schemes to mitigate the impact of errors. For example, if a processor fails to process FlowFiles correctly, backpressure can stop the flow of incoming data until the issue is resolved, preventing a system overload.

Retry Mechanisms: Some processors in NiFi are equipped with built-in retry mechanisms. These can be configured to automatically attempt to process the data again, a defined number of times, before considering the operation failed. This is particularly useful for transient errors, such as temporary network failures.

The `RetryFlowFile` processor is a powerful tool for implementing custom retry logic within data flows. Below is an example of how to configure this processor to retry processing a FlowFile up to three times in case of processing failures.

```
1  <processor>
2    <type>RetryFlowFile</type>
3    <properties>
4      <property name="Maximum Retries">3</property>
5      <property name="Penalization Period">5 min</property>
6      <property name="Yield Period">30 sec</property>
7    </properties>
8  </processor>
```

RouteOnAttribute Processor: This processor routes FlowFiles based on their attributes. It can be used to direct FlowFiles that encountered errors to specific branches of a flow for error handling or analysis. By examining FlowFile attributes, such as `failure.reason`, this processor can segregate failed data for correction or notification purposes.

Bulletin Board and Alerts: NiFi's Bulletin Board provides a platform for generating alerts based on specified conditions, such as error messages or processing failures. Setting up alerts for critical errors enables timely intervention, thereby minimizing data processing disruptions.

Failure recovery in NiFi entails restoring the data flow to a known good state after an error has occurred. NiFi's design facilitates recovery through its use of atomic operations and persistent state management. Furthermore, NiFi's version-controlled flow configurations enable the rollback of data flows to previous stable versions following a failure, enhancing recovery prospects.

In cases where errors have led to data corruption or loss, NiFi facilitates recovery through its data lineage capabilities. By tracing the lineage of a FlowFile, operators can determine the point of failure and the affected data, guiding the restoration process.

Effective error handling and failure recovery within Apache NiFi data flows require a comprehensive understanding of the types of errors that can occur, coupled with strategic use of NiFi's built-in mechanisms for error detection, response, and recovery. By implementing these practices, organizations can ensure the resilience and reliability of their data pipelines, optimized for continuous data processing and analysis.

4.12 Automating Data Flow Management with Templates and Parameters

In this section, we will discuss the automation of data flow management within Apache NiFi, emphasizing the use of templates and parameters. Automation in this context refers to the ability to replicate and deploy predefined data flow configurations across different environments without requiring manual intervention for each deployment. This capability is crucial for organizations dealing with large-scale data processing across multiple environments, such as development, testing, and production.

Templates in Apache NiFi serve as blueprints for data flows. They allow for the exportation and importation of specific data flow configurations, facilitating the reuse of these configurations across different instances or environments. This not only ensures consistency in data flow management but also significantly reduces the time and effort required to set up complex data processing pipelines.

Creating a template within NiFi involves encapsulating a selected group of processors, connections, and process groups into a portable and reusable configuration. The process is straightforward:

1. Select the components of the data flow that you want to include in the template.

2. Right-click on the canvas and choose "Create Template".

3. Provide a name and an optional description for the template.

4. The template is then saved and can be exported as an XML file.

To utilize a template in another NiFi instance or environment, the template XML file is imported through the NiFi user interface. Once imported, the template can be dragged onto the canvas, instantly recreating the data flow in the new environment.

Parameters in Apache NiFi offer a level of abstraction over static values within processor properties, enabling dynamic configuration of data flow components. Parameters are defined within parameter contexts and can be associated with any number of process groups. This affords the flexibility to change values such as file paths, database connections, and API URLs dynamically across multiple processors without editing each processor's configuration individually.

A parameter context is defined as follows:

1. Navigate to the NiFi settings and select "Parameter Contexts".

2. Create a new parameter context and specify a name for it.

3. Add parameters to the context, providing a name and value for each.

Process groups are then linked to parameter contexts, allowing the processors within those groups to reference parameters by their names. This mechanism significantly streamlines the process of configuring and maintaining processors, especially in complex data flows or when migrating data flows across environments with different configurations.

The combination of templates and parameters in Apache NiFi facilitates a highly efficient, automated approach to data flow management. Templates enable the rapid deployment and replication of data flows, while parameters provide the flexibility needed to customize these flows for different environments or use cases without altering the underlying process logic. Together, they form a powerful toolset for managing complex data pipelines, reducing manual oversight, and enhancing the overall reliability and scalability of data-processing activities.

By leveraging templates and parameters, organizations can achieve a more agile and responsive data infrastructure, capable of adapting to changing requirements and environments with minimal effort. This automation capability aligns closely with the principles of DevOps and continuous integration/continuous deployment (CI/CD) pipelines, further integrating data flow management into the broader landscape of IT operations and development practices.

Chapter 5

NiFi Expression Language and Attributes

The NiFi Expression Language provides a powerful means for manipulating and transforming data attributes within flows. It allows for dynamic adjustments to flow behavior by accessing and modifying the metadata (attributes) of FlowFiles as they move through the system. This feature enables users to create more flexible and adaptable data processing pipelines, where decisions about routing, processing, and data manipulation can be made on-the-fly based on the attributes of the data being processed. Mastering the NiFi Expression Language and understanding the role of attributes are essential for taking full advantage of Apache NiFi's capabilities to automate and optimize data flows.

5.1   Introduction to NiFi Expression Language

Apache NiFi's Expression Language (EL) underpins the flexibility and dynamic nature of data flow design within the NiFi ecosystem. By facilitating the interrogation and manipulation of FlowFile attributes, EL enables the design of highly customizable and adaptable data processing pipelines. This section will discuss the foundational aspects of NiFi Expression Language, highlighting its syntax, capabilities, and the role of attributes in data flow configurations.

NiFi Expression Language allows users to dynamically adjust Flow-Files within a data flow. Unlike static data processing configurations, which operate in a predetermined manner, EL employs dynamic expressions that can evaluate and modify FlowFile attributes in real time. This dynamism is critical for conditions where data processing logic needs to adapt to the varying nature of incoming data.

At the core of NiFi's EL are expressions, built from literals, operators, and functions, which can access various scopes of data, including FlowFile attributes, system properties, and external sources. The syntax of NiFi EL is concise yet powerful, designed to maximally leverage the metadata attached to each FlowFile for decision-making processes.

```
1   ${attributeName}
```

The above example demonstrates the basic structure of an EL expression, where `attributeName` would be replaced by the name of the specific FlowFile attribute you wish to access. This form of direct attribute reference forms the basis upon which more complex expressions are constructed.

NiFi EL provides a wide array of operators for manipulating and comparing attribute values. These include arithmetic operators, string concatenation, logical operators, and more, allowing for complex decision-making and data manipulation directly within the flow. For instance, to concatenate two attributes, one might use an expression resembling the following:

```
1   ${attributeOne:add(${attributeTwo})}
```

Moreover, EL features a broad spectrum of functions that further extend its capability to process and transform attribute data. Functions can perform tasks ranging from format conversion, mathematical computation, to conditional logic execution, enabling a depth of flow control that is both powerful and efficient.

One of the most significant advantages of NiFi Expression Language is its ability to facilitate dynamic property setting. Properties of NiFi processors, controllers, and even the flow itself can be set dynamically using EL, based on the attributes of FlowFiles in real time. This capability enables a level of adaptability that ensures data flows can efficiently handle diverse and changing data characteristics, without the need for manual reconfiguration.

The NiFi Expression Language is a versatile tool for data flow design, offering the ability to dynamically manipulate and route data based on real-time attributes. Its functionality is built upon the handling of attributes—key-value metadata associated with FlowFiles—allowing for complex decision-making and processing logic that adapts as the data itself changes. Mastery of EL syntax, operations, and functions is imperative for leveraging the full potential of Apache NiFi in automating and optimizing data flows. As we progress, subsequent sections will delve deeper into leveraging this powerful language for specific use cases, including routing, filtering, and even external system interactions.

5.2 Understanding Attributes in NiFi

Attributes in Apache NiFi are key-value pairs associated with a piece of data that moves through the system, known as a FlowFile. Attributes play a vital role in the operation of NiFi, as they store metadata about the FlowFiles. This metadata can include information such as the file name, file size, MIME type, or any custom data that a developer chooses to associate with a FlowFile. Understanding the nature and functionality of attributes is essential for effectively manipulating and utilizing data within NiFi workflows.

Each FlowFile has two main components: the content, which is the data payload itself, and the attributes, the metadata describing the payload. When FlowFiles are processed by NiFi processors, while the content may be transformed, filtered, or routed based on its content, it is the attributes that often provide the necessary context or directives for these operations. For instance, attributes can dictate how a processor routes a FlowFile, can be used within NiFi Expression Language to dynamically alter processor behavior, or to enrich the data passing through the system with additional metadata.

Attributes are mutable and can be modified as a FlowFile progresses through a dataflow. This is a powerful feature that allows for dynamic adjustments to how data is processed based on its associated metadata. Processors such as UpdateAttribute and AttributeExtractor can be used to modify or add to the attributes of a FlowFile. For example, one might use an UpdateAttribute processor to add a timestamp attribute indicating when a FlowFile was processed or to modify an existing attribute to reflect some processing logic.

Attributes can also be initially populated by processors that ingest data into a NiFi flow, such as GetFile, ListenHTTP, or ConsumeKafka. These processors often populate a set of standard attributes such as `filename`, path, and `uuid`, and may also add source-specific attributes such as HTTP headers or Kafka topic names.

The utilization of attributes extends beyond controlling processor behavior or content modification. Attributes are instrumental in logging and auditing processes within NiFi, allowing for detailed tracking of how data is manipulated as it moves through the system. Logging can be configured to include specific attributes, thus providing context to the data as it flows and is processed, thereby enabling more effective debugging and auditing of data pipelines.

NiFi's Expression Language further extends the power of attributes. Through it, attributes can be accessed and manipulated within expressions to dynamically adjust processor properties, route FlowFiles, or transform content based on the attributes' values. This capability allows for the creation of highly adaptable and responsive dataflows that can adjust in real-time to changes in the data or its context, as defined by its attributes.

In designing NiFi dataflows, understanding the lifecycle and scope of attributes is crucial. When a FlowFile splits into multiple FlowFiles, the original attributes are typically inherited by the resulting Flow-Files. This behavior ensures that essential context is preserved as data is branched and processed in parallel. Conversely, when multiple FlowFiles are merged, conflict resolution strategies may be necessary to handle attributes that may differ across the merged FlowFiles.

In summary, attributes in NiFi serve as a critical mechanism for annotating FlowFiles with metadata that provides context, directs the flow of data, and enables dynamic and flexible data pipeline designs. Mastery of how to effectively leverage attributes, including their manipulation and exploitation within NiFi's Expression Language, is fundamental for any developer seeking to optimize and enhance their dataflows in Apache NiFi.

5.3 Basic Syntax and Functions of NiFi Expression Language

The NiFi Expression Language enables the dynamic processing of FlowFiles by utilizing their attributes. This section will discuss the syntax and fundamental functions within the NiFi Expression Language, which are critical for manipulating attributes and influencing flow behavior effectively.

The syntax of the NiFi Expression Language is designed to be straightforward and accessible. Expressions are typically enclosed within two sets of curly braces. Inside the braces, attributes are referenced by name, prefixed with a dollar sign and curly braces: ${attributeName}. This basic construct allows users to access the value of any attribute present in a FlowFile.

Let us consider an example to illustrate the access of an attribute named filename:

```
1  ${filename}
```

In this case, the expression simply returns the value of the filename attribute of the FlowFile being processed. The real power of the NiFi Expression Language lies in its functions, which can be applied to the values accessed by such expressions.

Functions in the NiFi Expression Language follow a straightforward notation. They are applied to an attribute's value by appending a colon followed by the function name directly after the attribute name within the braces. If the function requires arguments, these are enclosed in parentheses and follow the function name.

Consider the following example, where the toUpper function is applied to convert the value of the filename attribute to uppercase:

```
1  ${filename:toUpper()}
```

This expression will take the value of the filename attribute, convert all characters to uppercase, and return the resulting string.

Functions can also be chained together to perform more complex manipulations. For instance, if one wishes to replace a part of the filename and then convert it to uppercase, the expression would look something like this:

```
1  ${filename:replace('data', 'log'):toUpper()}
```

Here, the replace function first replaces occurrences of the substring "data" with "log" in the filename's value, and then the toUpper function converts the resulting string to uppercase.

The NiFi Expression Language supports a wide range of functions that can be used to perform operations on strings, numbers, dates, and also to make logical decisions within expressions. Some of the key functions include:

- `toUpper()` and `toLower()` for case conversion.

- `substring(startIndex, endIndex)` for extracting substrings.

- `equals(string)` and `equalsIgnoreCase(string)` for string comparison.

- `isNull()` and `isNotNull()` for null checking.

- `format()` for date formatting.

- `matches(regex)` for regular expression matching.

It is essential to note that while the NiFi Expression Language offers substantial functionality through its syntax and functions, expressions are evaluated against the attributes of a single FlowFile at a time. Thus, the context in which an expression is used within a flow is crucial for achieving the desired data manipulation or routing logic.

The basic syntax and functions of the NiFi Expression Language provide a foundation on which more complex data transformations and routing logic can be built. By effectively leveraging these tools, one can harness the full potential of Apache NiFi to automate and optimize data flows based on dynamic conditions and data attributes.

5.4 Dynamic Property Setting Using Expression Language

Dynamic property setting using NiFi's Expression Language plays a crucial role in the customization and flexibility of data processing workflows. This capability allows properties of processors, controllers, and other components within a NiFi flow to be set or modified at runtime, based on the attributes of FlowFiles or external factors. This dynamic modification significantly enhances the adaptability of data pipelines to changing data or environmental conditions.

To utilize dynamic property setting, it is important to understand the basic syntax of the Expression Language and how it interacts with

FlowFile attributes. The Expression Language syntax for referencing an attribute is ${attributeName}, where attributeName is the name of the FlowFile attribute you wish to access.

For instance, consider a scenario where it is necessary to route a FlowFile based on its MIME type, which is stored in an attribute named mime.type. The property for routing can be dynamically set using an Expression Language statement like ${mime.type:equals('text/plain')}. This evaluates to true if the mime.type attribute equals 'text/plain', allowing for conditional routing based on the content type of the FlowFile.

Another common use case is the dynamic setting of file paths or names. For example, when storing FlowFiles to a file system, you might want to organize them based on the year, month, and day attributes present in each FlowFile. This can be achieved by setting the directory path property to ${year}/${month}/${day}, which will be evaluated and replaced with the corresponding attribute values at runtime, ensuring that FlowFiles are stored in the correct directory structure.

```
1  // Example of dynamic directory setting
2  DirectoryPath = $\{year\}/$\{month\}/$\{day\}
```

Dynamic property setting is not limited to FlowFile attributes alone. NiFi's Expression Language also supports the use of functions and operators to manipulate attribute values or to reference system properties and environment variables. This provides a powerful mechanism for adjusting flow behavior in response to the broader context in which the data flow is operating.

For instance, incorporating external configuration through the use of environment variables can be especially useful in deploying NiFi flows across different environments (e.g., development, testing, production) without the need to manually adjust properties for each environment.

```
1  // Example of accessing environment variable in NiFi Expression Language
2  DatabaseConnectionURL = $\{env('DB_CONNECTION')\}
```

The Expression Language also offers support for logical conditions and functions that can perform string manipulations, numerical calculations, and other transformations, enabling complex dynamic property settings. For example, adjusting a property value based on the size of a FlowFile might involve a conditional expression that checks if the file size exceeds a certain threshold, and if so, applies a different setting or routing path.

111

```
// Conditional dynamic property setting based on file size
If ($\{fileSize:toNumber()\} > 1048576) UseHighCapacityRoute = true
Else UseHighCapacityRoute = false
```

When implementing dynamic property setting, it's imperative to be mindful of performance considerations. The evaluation of Expression Language statements, especially complex expressions or those requiring external system calls, can introduce latency into the data flow. As such, optimizing expressions for efficiency and minimizing their usage where a static property would suffice is recommended.

The ability to dynamically set properties using NiFi's Expression Language profoundly increases the flexibility and efficiency of data flows, allowing them to adapt seamlessly to varying data attributes and environmental conditions. By mastering dynamic property setting, developers and data engineers can construct more adaptable, efficient, and sophisticated data processing workflows within Apache NiFi, tailored precisely to the requirements of each unique data processing scenario.

5.5 Manipulating Attributes with Expression Language

Manipulating attributes with the NiFi Expression Language enables dynamic data processing within Apache NiFi pipelines. This capability is fundamental for customizing flow behaviors based on the metadata, or attributes, of FlowFiles. To effectively manipulate attributes, one must understand the basic syntax and functions of the NiFi Expression Language, as well as how to apply these within the context of data flows.

The primary manner in which attributes are modified and leveraged within NiFi involves the use of Expression Language statements within Processor properties. These statements can perform a range of operations from simple attribute value replacements to complex conditional processing.

For example, to replace an attribute value with a new string, an expression might appear as follows:

```
1   ${attributeName:replace('oldValue', 'newValue')}
```

This syntax utilizes the 'replace' function to change 'oldValue' to 'new-Value' within the value of 'attributeName'. It's a straightforward example of how Expression Language can directly manipulate string values of attributes.

In more complex scenarios, conditional logic might be necessary to determine the flow path of a FlowFile based on its attributes. For instance, to route FlowFiles differently based on the presence of a specific attribute, the following expression could be utilized within a RouteOnAttribute Processor:

```
1  ${filename:contains('data'):ifElse(true, false)}
```

This expression checks if the 'filename' attribute contains the substring 'data'. If true, it returns true; otherwise, it returns false. The 'ifElse' function in this context demonstrates the use of Expression Language to perform routing decisions based on dynamic criteria derived from FlowFile attributes.

To further enhance the manipulation of attributes, NiFi provides functions for date and time manipulation. The next example demonstrates how to adjust a FlowFile's attribute to the current timestamp:

```
1  ${now():format('yyyy-MM-dd HH:mm:ss')}
```

Here, 'now()' fetches the current date and time, and 'format' applies a specific formatting pattern to it. Such temporal adjustments are crucial for timestamping data as it flows through the system, allowing for precise tracking and scheduling of data processing tasks.

Manipulation is not limited to altering existing attributes. The Expression Language also supports the creation of new attributes by setting Processor properties to Expression Language statements that define the new attribute's value. For example, creating a new attribute that combines two existing ones might look like the following:

```
1  ${attribute1:append(${attribute2})}
```

In this case, 'append' concatenates the values of 'attribute1' and 'attribute2', demonstrating how new data points can be synthesized from existing metadata.

While the examples above provide insights into the mechanics of attribute manipulation, applying these techniques effectively demands familiarity with the full range of NiFi Expression Language functions. This library of functions addresses string manipulation, conditional logic, mathematical operations, and date/time handling, each contributing to the versatile toolkit for data flow customization.

In practice, the manipulation of attributes using Expression Language is a powerful method for directing the behavior of dataflows. It allows flow developers to construct adaptable, context-aware systems capable of sophisticated decision-making processes. As data attributes evolve throughout a flow, the dynamic nature of these manipulations ensures that data processing logic remains both relevant and responsive to the changing data landscape.

Beyond the mechanics of manipulation, understanding the impact of dynamic attribute changes on flow performance and behavior is critical. Each Expression Language statement incurs computational overhead. Efficient expression design and strategic attribute manipulation are essential for maintaining optimal flow performance. Furthermore, the predictability of data flow behavior relies on a clear understanding of how Expressions evaluate and modify attributes, underscoring the importance of thorough testing and debugging practices.

In summary, the ability to manipulate attributes with NiFi Expression Language is at the core of creating flexible and intelligent data processing pipelines in Apache NiFi. Mastery over this aspect of NiFi enables developers to architect flows that can dynamically adapt to the intricacies of the data they manage, unlocking the full potential of data-driven automation.

5.6   Using Expression Language for Routing and Filtering

Routing and filtering data in Apache NiFi pipelines are vital operations that enable the creation of complex data flow patterns. These patterns are designed to segregate, redirect, and selectively process FlowFiles based on their attributes and content. Through the use of the NiFi Expression Language, dynamic routing and filtering conditions can be created, making these operations both powerful and flexible.

The foundation for routing and filtering with the NiFi Expression Language lies in its ability to evaluate expressions against FlowFile attributes. This capability allows for the dynamic determination of flow paths and processing requirements. The expression language supports a wide range of functions that can be used to construct logical conditions for these purposes.

Let us delve into an example that demonstrates the use of the NiFi Expression Language for routing FlowFiles based on a specific attribute. Imagine a scenario where FlowFiles contain a metadata attribute named sourceType, and the goal is to route these files to different processing groups based on the value of this attribute.

```
1  <property>
2    <name>RouteOnAttribute</name>
3    <value>
4      ${sourceType:equals('sensorData')}
5    </value>
6  </property>
```

In the above configuration, the RouteOnAttribute processor is used with a custom property set to a NiFi Expression Language statement. This statement evaluates whether the sourceType attribute of a FlowFile equals the string 'sensorData'. If the condition is true, the FlowFile is routed to a corresponding output queue for sensor data processing.

This example encapsulates the essence of dynamic routing - evaluating FlowFile attributes and making routing decisions based on their values. The process becomes increasingly powerful when combined with other NiFi features such as regular expressions and string manipulation functions.

```
1  <property>
2    <name>RouteToMultiplePaths</name>
3    <value>
4      ${filename:matches('(?i).*\\.txt$'):ifElse('TextFiles', 'BinaryFiles')}
5    </value>
6  </property>
```

In this instance, the routing condition checks if the filename ends with '.txt' (case insensitive), employing a regular expression within the expression language. Depending on the evaluation, FlowFiles are tagged correspondingly as either 'TextFiles' or 'BinaryFiles', which can then be used to route them to different paths.

Filtering involves selectively passing through FlowFiles that meet specific criteria while discarding others. This can be effectively achieved using the NiFi Expression Language to evaluate FlowFile attributes and content, applying conditions to determine whether each FlowFile should be processed further or filtered out.

```
1  <property>
2    <name>FilterOutEmptyFiles</name>
3    <value>
```

```
4      ${fileSize:gt(0)}
5      </value>
6    </property>
```

The above configuration demonstrates a filtering condition where only FlowFiles with a size greater than 0 bytes are passed through. Such conditions ensure that empty files, which may not need processing, are automatically removed from the flow.

The use of the NiFi Expression Language for routing and filtering embodies a significant shift towards more dynamic and adaptable data flows. It grants developers the flexibility to create nuanced data processing pipelines that respond intelligently to the characteristics of the data itself.

To maximize the performance and maintainability of data flows utilizing expression language for routing and filtering, it is crucial to understand the computational cost of expressions and to design expressions that are both efficient and easy to debug. Optimizing these expressions involves minimizing complexity, reusing expressions where possible, and leveraging NiFi's caching mechanisms to avoid redundant evaluations.

The NiFi Expression Language serves as a powerful tool for configuring routing and filtering logic in Apache NiFi. By harnessing the full potential of this language, developers can design highly responsive and adaptable data pipelines capable of handling a wide array of processing scenarios with finesse and efficiency.

5.7 Date and Time Handling in Expression Language

Date and time manipulation is a fundamental requirement in data processing pipelines, given its necessity for timestamping, scheduling, data partitioning, and expiration of data. Apache NiFi's Expression Language provides robust support for handling date and time values, enabling dynamic adjustments and decisions based on temporal information within FlowFiles. This section will discuss the syntax, functions, and practical applications of date and time handling in the NiFi Expression Language.

NiFi's Expression Language offers a range of functions to extract and manipulate date and time information from attributes. The most commonly used function for obtaining the current date and time is now(). This function returns the current date and time in milliseconds since January 1, 1970, UTC. The now() function is often used in combination with formatting functions to convert the current time into human-readable formats.

To work with formatted date and time strings, the format() function is applied. It accepts a date, time, or timestamp and a SimpleDateFormat pattern to produce a string representation of the date and time. For example, to format the current timestamp into a readable format such as 'YYYY-MM-dd HH:mm:ss', the expression would be structured as follows:

```
1  ${now():format("YYYY-MM-dd HH:mm:ss")}
```

Conversely, the toDate() function is utilized to parse a string into a date object according to a specified format. This function is essential when one needs to convert a string attribute containing a date and time into a format that can be used for date arithmetic or further date formatting. An example use case is converting a string to a date object:

```
1  ${'2023-01-01 13:00:00':toDate("YYYY-MM-dd HH:mm:ss")}
```

NiFi Expression Language also supports date arithmetic which enables adding or subtracting time units from a date. This functionality is crucial for generating dynamic time-based queries or creating time windows for data processing. Date arithmetic is accomplished using the adjust() function. For example, adding 5 days to the current date is achieved through:

```
1  ${now():adjust("5 days")}
```

Another powerful aspect of date and time handling within NiFi's Expression Language is the ability to work with epoch time. Epoch time, or Unix time, is the number of milliseconds that have elapsed since January 1, 1970, UTC. Converting between human-readable date formats and epoch time is straightforward using the toNumber() function on a formatted date, or by formatting an epoch timestamp using the format() function.

```
1  // Convert a formatted date to epoch time
2  ${'2023-01-01 13:00:00':toDate("YYYY-MM-dd HH:mm:ss"):toNumber()}
3
4  // Convert epoch time to a formatted date
5  ${1609459200000:format("YYYY-MM-dd HH:mm:ss")}
```

For handling time zones, the Expression Language allows specifying the time zone in the formatting and parsing functions. Handling time zones is critical for applications that process data from multiple geographical locations, ensuring that time calculations are accurate and consistent across different locales. The time zone can be incorporated into the format() and toDate() functions by appending the time zone ID to the pattern:

```
1   ${now():format("YYYY-MM-dd HH:mm:ss z", "GMT")}
```

Effective date and time manipulation in data flows enables precise control over timing aspects of data processing, allowing for temporal logic to be embedded directly into the flow design. From scheduling and partitioning to timestamping and time-based filtering, mastering date and time handling in NiFi's Expression Language is indispensable for building efficient and adaptable data pipelines.

5.8   Accessing External Properties and Environment Variables

In the context of designing and implementing data flows using Apache NiFi, the ability to interact with external properties and environment variables extends the versatility and adaptability of your data pipelines. This flexibility is crucial for creating flows that are both dynamic and sensitive to the execution environment, allowing for configurations that can vary between development, testing, and production environments without altering the flow definitions. This section will discuss how the NiFi Expression Language supports accessing these external parameters and the implications for flow design.

NiFi's Expression Language (EL) offers the capability to reference external properties and environment variables directly within expressions. This is accomplished through the use of specific functions designed for this purpose. The primary method for accessing these values is the ${env:VARIABLE_NAME} syntax for environment variables and the ${propertyName} syntax for custom properties defined in NiFi.

- To access an environment variable, the NiFi Expression Language provides the env function. For instance, to access an environment variable named PATH, the expression would be written as ${env:PATH}. This technique enables the flow to dynamically adapt based on the environment it's running in, useful for paths or configuration settings that differ between environments.

- Accessing custom properties requires first defining these properties within NiFi. Once defined, these can be accessed similar to environment variables but without the env prefix. If a custom property named inputDirectory was defined, it could be accessed with ${inputDirectory}. Custom properties enhance the flexibility of NiFi flows by allowing external configuration of parameters that can influence flow behavior.

It is important to note that when referencing environment variables or custom properties, if the referenced variable or property does not exist, the expression will resolve to an empty string. This behavior should be carefully considered during the design of your flows to ensure that missing configurations do not lead to unexpected behaviors.

For more complex scenarios, NiFi also allows the combination of these references within a single expression. For example, if an external property defines a directory path and you want to use an environment variable to determine the filename, the expression might look like ${inputDirectory}/${env:FILENAME}. Such expressions enable high degrees of customization and dynamic behavior, making your data flow designs more robust and adaptable.

```
1  // Example of combining environment variable and custom property
2  // Assuming `inputDirectory` is a custom property
3  // and `FILENAME` is an environment variable
4  \${inputDirectory}/\${env:FILENAME}
```

This access to external configurations not only facilitates the creation of more dynamic NiFi flows but also promotes best practices in software engineering, such as externalization of configurations. By leveraging environment variables and external properties, sensitive or environment-specific configurations can be kept out of the flow definitions, enhancing security and simplifying the migration of flows across different environments.

However, when utilizing these features, it is essential to maintain discipline in how these external configurations are managed. Misuse or over-reliance on overly complex configurations can make the flow harder to understand and maintain. Therefore, it is advisable to keep the usage of external properties and environment variables clear and justified within the context of each application.

Accessing external properties and environment variables through NiFi's Expression Language significantly enhances the capability to create adaptable, environment-aware data flows. By understanding and applying these techniques judiciously, you can develop NiFi flows that are both flexible and maintainable, tailored to the specific requirements of various operational environments.

5.9 Advanced Techniques: Regular Expressions in Expression Language

Regular expressions are a fundamental aspect of text processing, allowing for the search, match, and manipulation of strings based on defined patterns. In Apache NiFi, the integration of regular expressions with the NiFi Expression Language offers powerful capabilities for manipulating FlowFile attributes. This section will discuss how to leverage regular expressions within NiFi Expression Language to enhance the flexibility and efficiency of data processing pipelines.

NiFi Expression Language supports regular expressions through several functions, enabling users to perform pattern matching, substitution, and extraction on FlowFile attributes. These functions include 'matches', 'replaceAll', and 'find', among others. Understanding how to apply these functions effectively can significantly improve the capability to process and route FlowFiles dynamically based on content-specific criteria.

An example use case is conditional processing based on the presence or absence of specific patterns in the data attributes. For instance, using the 'matches' function allows for the evaluation of whether a FlowFile attribute adheres to a specified pattern. The syntax for this operation within a NiFi Expression Language statement is illustrated below:

```
1   ${attributeName:matches('regex')}
```

In this example, 'attributeName' represents the name of the attribute to be evaluated, and 'regex' is the regular expression pattern. This function returns true if the attribute value matches the regular expression pattern, enabling conditional logic to be built around this result.

Another common requirement is modifying attribute values by replacing parts of the text that match a regular expression. The 'replaceAll' function serves this purpose by substituting all occurrences of the matched pattern with a specified replacement string. The following demonstrates this function's usage:

```
1   ${attributeName:replaceAll('regex', 'replacement')}
```

Here, 'regex' is the pattern to match within the attribute value, and 'replacement' is the text to substitute for each match. This function is particularly useful for sanitizing or normalizing data attributes.

Extracting subsets of strings based on regular expression groups is another powerful technique facilitated by NiFi Expression Language. The 'find' function can capture specific parts of an attribute value, which match the given pattern. Consider the scenario where an attribute contains a formatted date, and there is a requirement to extract the year. The following example illustrates how to achieve this:

```
1   ${attributeName:find('(\d{4})').group(1)}
```

The 'find' function searches the attribute value for occurrences of the specified regular expression, where '(4)' is a regex group matching a sequence of four digits, typically representing a year. The 'group' function is used to extract the part of the string matched by this specific group. In this case, 'group(1)' refers to the first capturing group of the regex.

When leveraging regular expressions in NiFi Expression Language, it is vital to adhere to the syntax and constraints of the Java regular expression engine, as this is the underlying mechanism NiFi uses for regex operations. Additionally, considering the performance implications of using complex regular expressions is crucial, as overly complicated patterns can significantly impact the processing time of data flows.

To summarize, integrating regular expressions with NiFi Expression Language enhances data manipulation capabilities within Apache NiFi. By mastering the use of regex-based functions such as 'matches', 'replaceAll', and 'find', users can implement more sophisticated attribute manipulations, enriching the overall data processing workflow. As with any advanced technique, careful application and testing are recommended to ensure optimal performance and accuracy of data flow configurations.

5.10 Debugging and Troubleshooting Expression Language Expressions

Debugging and troubleshooting expression language expressions in Apache NiFi can be challenging, given the dynamic nature of data flows and the transformations applied to FlowFiles. Fortunately, there are effective strategies and tools within NiFi that aid in identifying and resolving issues in expression language statements.

The first step in debugging expression language expressions is to ensure the syntax is correct. Expression language syntax errors often lead to the processor failing to operate as expected. Common syntax errors include missing braces, incorrect function names, and improper use of operators. To verify syntax, review the expression carefully, paying close attention to the structure and ensuring it matches the syntax outlined in the NiFi documentation.

When syntax is correct but the expression does not produce the expected outcome, it is essential to examine the attributes of the FlowFiles being processed. This can be achieved by using the `LogAttribute` processor, which logs all current attributes of a FlowFile to the NiFi logs. This processor is invaluable for understanding the state of a FlowFile's attributes at a given point in the data flow.

```
2023-03-15 10:23:45,678 INFO [NiFi logging thread] o.a.n.p.standard.LogAttribute
LogAttribute[id=12345]
Attributes of FlowFile 12345
key1: value1
key2: value2
```

Often, issues arise due to unexpected or missing attributes, leading to expression language statements not executing as intended. This discrepancy can be especially true in complex flows where multiple processors modify the attributes. By examining the logs, developers can gain insight into the attribute values at the time of expression evaluation and adjust their expressions accordingly.

In addition to logging attributes, leveraging the `EvaluateExpressionLanguage` processor can significantly aid in debugging. This processor evaluates expression language statements without changing the FlowFile, allowing developers to test their expressions dynamically. The processor can be configured with a test expression, and the evaluation result will be added as an attribute to the FlowFile, making it easy to inspect and troubleshoot expressions.

```
1    ${filename:equals('data.txt')}
```

```
Evaluation result: true
```

For more intricate issues where the above methods do not suffice, NiFi offers the ability to access detailed logs. Adjusting the log level for the `org.apache.nifi.processors` package to DEBUG or TRACE in the `logback.xml` configuration file can unveil more in-depth information about how expressions are evaluated and processed. While this approach can generate a significant volume of log data, it is particularly useful when tracking down elusive issues in complex expressions.

- Ensure that logging levels are set back to their original levels after debugging to avoid overwhelming the log files with verbose output.

- Utilize comments within the expression language to isolate sections of the expression. Commenting out parts of the expression can help identify the segment causing the issue.

- Practice incremental development. Gradually build up expressions from simple to complex, verifying each step along the way. This approach can prevent complicated debugging scenarios and help identify problems early in the development process.

Finally, when expressions involve regular expressions, using external tools to test and validate the regular expressions before implementing them in NiFi can save time and reduce debugging efforts. Tools such as regex101.com provide a real-time environment to test regular expressions against sample inputs, ensuring they perform as expected prior to integration into NiFi expressions.

In sum, debugging and troubleshooting expression language expressions in Apache NiFi requires a methodical approach, starting with syntax verification and attribute inspection, followed by incremental testing and detailed logging. By leveraging built-in NiFi processors and tools, developers can efficiently identify and resolve issues, ensuring their data flows operate correctly and efficiently.

5.11 Performance Considerations When Using Expression Language

Apache NiFi's Expression Language allows for dynamic and flexible manipulation of FlowFile attributes, enabling sophisticated control over data flows. However, the extensive use of NiFi's Expression Language can have implications for system performance. When designing and implementing data flow strategies, it is crucial to understand these performance considerations to maintain an efficient and responsive system.

Firstly, the complexity and number of expressions executed in a flow directly impact the CPU utilization of the NiFi instance. Expressions are evaluated at runtime, which involves parsing the expression, accessing the necessary attributes, performing the specified operations, and generating the result. This process consumes computational resources, particularly when expressions are complex or must be evaluated against a large number of FlowFiles.

To mitigate the impact on CPU utilization, it is advisable to optimize expression language usage by:

- Minimizing the complexity of expressions wherever possible. Simple expressions are faster to evaluate.

- Reducing the number of expressions executed in a flow. Consolidating or simplifying flow logic can help achieve this.

- Using caching strategies for frequently accessed data. If an expression retrieves information from an external source (e.g., database, API), consider caching this information if it does not change frequently.

Secondly, the evaluation of expressions can lead to increased memory usage. Each evaluation potentially generates intermediate objects in memory, and when processing a high volume of FlowFiles, this can accumulate quickly. Efficient expression design can help in reducing memory footprint; however, monitoring and appropriately sizing the NiFi instance's heap memory is also important to ensure there is sufficient memory available to handle the workload.

Thirdly, the execution time of expressions affects the overall throughput of the processing system. Expressions that involve complex calculations, external system calls, or iterative operations over large sets of attributes can significantly increase the time taken to process each FlowFile. This, in turn, can lead to backpressure and reduced data throughput. To enhance system throughput, consider the following practices:

- Evaluate the necessity of each expression. If the same outcome can be achieved through simpler means or fewer expressions, revise the flow design accordingly.

- For operations that require processing large amounts of data or complex calculations, consider pre-processing this information outside of NiFi or using NiFi's built-in processors that are optimized for such tasks.

- In cases where expressions must call external systems or services, ensure those systems are adequately scaled and responsive. Timeouts and retries should be configured appropriately to handle failures without causing undue delay.

Furthermore, the debugging and optimization of expressions pose their own challenges. Unlike static code analysis, the dynamic nature of expression evaluation means that understanding the performance characteristics of an expression requires observing its behavior over time, under varying conditions of load and data characteristics. Utilizing NiFi's provenance data and logs can aid in identifying expressions that are significant contributors to processing delays or resource consumption.

While the NiFi Expression Language is a powerful tool for dynamic data flow manipulation, it is essential to employ it judiciously, keeping in mind the potential performance impacts. Through careful design, optimization of expressions, and appropriate system scaling, it is possible to build highly efficient and responsive data processing flows that leverage the full capabilities of Apache NiFi.

5.12 Real-world Use Cases for Expression Language

Expression Language (EL) within Apache NiFi presents a flexible toolset for addressing a variety of real-world data flow and transformation challenges. By allowing dynamic interactions with FlowFile attributes, EL enables the creation of adaptable and efficient data pipelines suited to diverse operational requirements. This section illustrates concrete use cases highlighting the practical applications of EL in real-world scenarios.

Dynamic Routing Based on Content and Metadata: In many instances, data needs to be routed to different paths in a workflow based on its content or associated metadata. NiFi's Expression Language can be used to implement such conditional logic, examining FlowFile attributes to make routing decisions dynamically. For example, a FlowFile containing transaction data could be routed based on attributes such as transaction amount, type, or geographic location.

```
1  <property name="RoutingStrategy">
2    ${attribute:type} == 'sale' ? 'SalesPath' :
3    ${attribute:type} == 'refund' ? 'RefundPath' : 'Other'
4  </property>
```

This snippet demonstrates how EL can direct FlowFiles to different processing queues based on the 'type' attribute, ensuring that data is handled by the appropriate parts of the system.

Customizing File Names During Data Ingestion: When ingesting data into a NiFi flow, it is often necessary to rename files in a way that reflects their content or the context of their generation. Using EL, filenames can be dynamically constructed using attributes such as timestamps, source identifiers, or any custom metadata added during previous processing steps.

```
1  <property name="FileName">
2    ${'filename':replace('.txt','.processed'):prepend(${now():format('yyyyMMddHHmmss_
     ')})}
3  </property>
```

This code sample demonstrates generating a new filename by appending a timestamp and changing the file extension, facilitating traceability and preventing name collisions.

Conditional Processing Based on Thresholds: Data flows often require conditional logic to process items differently based on specific criteria, such as thresholds in data value. For instance, a flow might check if a sensor reading exceeds a certain value and only then perform additional processing or alerting operations.

```
1  <property name="ShouldAlert">
2    ${attribute:sensorValue} > 100
3  </property>
```

By evaluating whether the 'sensorValue' attribute exceeds a threshold, EL allows for straightforward implementation of condition-based processing routes.

Data Masking and Redaction: In situations requiring compliance with data protection regulations, sensitive information within a dataset may need to be obscured or removed. Through EL, specific patterns in data attributes can be identified and manipulated accordingly, enabling the redaction of sensitive data without impeding the flow's overall processing.

```
1  <property name="RedactedMessage">
2    ${attribute:message}:replaceAll('(?<=\\bSSN:\\s)\\d{3}-?\\d{2}-?\\d{4}','REDACTED
       ')
3  </property>
```

This example utilizes a regular expression to find and redact Social Security numbers within a message attribute, showcasing EL's capability to address complex data sanitization requirements.

Aggregating and Formatting Data for Reporting: Often, data collected in a flow needs to be aggregated, formatted, or transformed for reporting or further analysis. EL can manipulate values, perform arithmetic, and format data into structures suitable for consumption by reporting tools or downstream systems.

```
1  <property name="FormattedReport">
2    ${attribute:transactionDate:format('yyyy-MM')},${attribute:customerId},${
       attribute:salesAmount}
3  </property>
```

Here, transaction attributes are formatted into a CSV line suitable for monthly sales reporting, illustrating how EL facilitates data aggregation and preparation tasks.

In summary, the NiFi Expression Language offers a broad spectrum of possibilities for dynamically manipulating data as it moves through processing pipelines. From routing based on complex conditions to sensitive data handling and beyond, EL equips developers and data engineers with the means to implement tailored, efficient data flows capable of addressing a wide range of real-world data processing challenges.

Chapter 6

Advanced NiFi Techniques and Best Practices

This chapter delves into the specialized techniques and best practices that enable advanced usage of Apache NiFi, enhancing the efficiency, reliability, and scalability of data flows. It covers a broad spectrum of strategies, from optimizing performance for high-volume data processing to securing sensitive information and ensuring data integrity across distributed systems. Additionally, the chapter addresses custom processor development, effective error handling, and the use of scripting to extend NiFi's functionality. Adopting these advanced techniques and practices allows users to fully leverage NiFi's powerful framework for complex data integration tasks, ensuring robust and efficient data pipelines.

6.1   Advanced Data Flow Design Patterns

In this section we will discuss various advanced data flow design patterns that are instrumental in building robust, efficient, and scalable data pipelines in Apache NiFi. These design patterns are not only best practices distilled from extensive use of NiFi across different scenarios but also serve as a guided approach to solving complex data integration problems. The patterns covered here will provide insights into designing data flows that are easy to manage, monitor, and optimize.

Dataflow Segmentation: Segmenting data flows into logical units of functionality is crucial for managing complexity and enhancing the readability of the workflow. This approach involves breaking down a data pipeline into smaller, manageable segments where each segment performs a distinct function. For instance, a complex pipeline can be divided into segments such as data ingestion, data transformation, and data delivery. This pattern not only facilitates easier maintenance but also allows for parallel development and testing of individual segments.

- It promotes modularity and reusability of segments.

- Enhances the maintainability and scalability of data flows.

Backpressure and Load Balancing: Efficient management of data flow is paramount in handling high-volume data processing. NiFi provides mechanisms for backpressure and load balancing to ensure that data processing resources are not overwhelmed. Backpressure prevents upstream processors from forwarding data to the next processor in the flow if certain thresholds are reached. Load balancing, on the other hand, distributes incoming data across a cluster to optimize resource utilization.

```
1  <property name="Backpressure Data Size Threshold">1 GB</property>
2  <property name="Backpressure Object Threshold">10000</property>
```

These configurations help maintain the stability and performance of NiFi data flows under heavy load conditions.

Use of Controller Services: Controller Services in NiFi are shared services that can be utilized by processors across the application. Leveraging controller services for common tasks such as database connections, SSL contexts, or credential stores promotes reusability and consistency across the dataflow. For example, a single DBCPConnectionPool can be shared among several processors that require database connectivity, thereby simplifying configuration and management.

```
1  <controllerService>
2     <id>dbcp_service_id</id>
3     <name>DBCPConnectionPool</name>
4     </controllerService>
```

This pattern reduces redundancy and facilitates centralized configuration management of shared resources.

Error Handling and Retry Mechanisms: Implementing robust error handling and retry mechanisms is essential to ensure the reliability

130

of the data pipeline. NiFi offers several processors and routing capabilities that allow for sophisticated error handling strategies. Processors such as `RetryFlowFile` and `RouteOnFailure` can be employed to handle errors gracefully and reroute or retry processing based on configurable criteria.

```
1   <processor>
2       <name>RetryFlowFile</name>
3       <class>org.apache.nifi.processors.standard.RetryFlowFile</class>
4   </processor>
```

Effective error handling ensures minimal data loss and maintains the integrity of the data flow even in the face of intermittent failures.

Data Buffering and Caching: In scenarios where real-time data processing is not critical, data buffering and caching can significantly enhance performance by reducing IO operations. NiFi's content repository acts as a buffer for incoming data, enabling processors to operate on this buffered data without immediate persistence to the final destination. Moreover, utilizing caching strategies for frequently accessed resources can minimize expensive processing and retrieval operations, thus improving the overall efficiency of the data pipeline.

FlowFile Attributes for Control and Metadata Management: The use of FlowFile attributes for controlling flow behavior and managing metadata is a powerful feature in NiFi. By enriching FlowFiles with custom attributes, processors can make dynamic routing decisions, perform conditional processing, and preserve essential metadata throughout the flow. This pattern promotes flexibility and adaptability of the data pipeline to changing requirements and data characteristics.

```
1   <updateAttribute>
2       <name>addAttributes</name>
3       <class>org.apache.nifi.processors.attributes.UpdateAttribute</class>
4       <property name="newAttribute">value</property>
5   </updateAttribute>
```

In summary, adopting these advanced data flow design patterns in Apache NiFi enhances not only the efficiency and reliability of data pipelines but also their scalability and maintainability. Implementing these patterns judiciously in the design phase can lead to significant improvements in the performance and functionality of data integration tasks, thereby fully leveraging NiFi's capabilities to meet complex data processing needs.

6.2   Optimizing NiFi for Large Data Volumes

Optimizing Apache NiFi for handling large data volumes is critical for the performance and efficiency of data pipelines. This optimization involves various strategies, including proper resource allocation, efficient data routing, and employing effective data processing techniques, among others. This section will discuss how to tailor NiFi's performance to deal with extensive amounts of data seamlessly.

Effective resource allocation is fundamental to optimizing NiFi's performance. This means configuring the NiFi instances to utilize the available system resources adequately. The bootstrap.conf file provides several configuration options that can be adjusted to optimize resource utilization. Setting the java.arg.2 property to adjust the Java Virtual Machine (JVM) memory is one such example:

```
1   java.arg.2=-Xms1024m -Xmx4096m
```

This setting increases the initial heap size to 1024MB and the maximum heap size to 4096MB, allowing NiFi to allocate more memory and handle larger data sets more effectively.

Data routing in NiFi plays a crucial role in handling large volumes of data. Employing a partitioning strategy can significantly improve data processing efficiency. By dividing the data into smaller, manageable segments, NiFi can process data in a distributed manner, reducing the load on any single process. The PartitionRecord processor can be configured to partition data based on specific fields, thus optimizing the flow of large datasets.

```
1   <processor>
2     <id>PartitionRecord_Example</id>
3     <name>PartitionRecord</name>
4     <class>org.apache.nifi.processors.standard.PartitionRecord</class>
5     <property name="Partitioning Strategy">Record Hash</property>
6     <property name="Hash Field Names">id</property>
7   </processor>
```

In addition, employing back pressure settings and prioritizing queues effectively manage data flow, preventing any single component from becoming overwhelmed with data. These settings can be adjusted from NiFi's interface by navigating to the connection settings between processors.

Efficient data processing techniques are essential when dealing with large data volumes. Utilizing record-based processors, such as

QueryRecord and UpdateRecord, allows for more efficient data filtering, transformation, and aggregation without having to write extensive custom code. These processors perform operations on a per-record basis, making them highly suitable for high-volume data processing.

```
1  <processor>
2    <id>QueryRecord_Example</id>
3    <name>QueryRecord</name>
4    <class>org.apache.nifi.processors.standard.QueryRecord</class>
5    <property name="SQL Statement">SELECT * FROM FLOWFILE WHERE amount > 1000</
        property>
6  </processor>
```

Leveraging compression within NiFi flows can significantly reduce the volume of data being transmitted and stored, enhancing system performance. The CompressContent processor can compress data streams, minimizing network and storage resource utilization.

```
1  <processor>
2    <id>CompressContent_Example</id>
3    <name>CompressContent</name>
4    <class>org.apache.nifi.processors.standard.CompressContent</class>
5    <property name="Compression Format">GZIP</property>
6  </processor>
```

To monitor and adjust the performance of NiFi in handling large data volumes, a thorough understanding of NiFi's reporting tasks is beneficial. Configuring reporting tasks for monitoring JVM memory, system load, and dataflow throughput provides visibility into the system's performance. This information allows for informed adjustments to NiFi configurations, ensuring optimal performance.

Optimizing Apache NiFi for large data volumes involves strategic configuration of NiFi instances, effective data routing through partitioning and prioritizing, employing efficient data processing techniques, and leveraging data compression. Following these strategies ensures NiFi's performance remains robust and efficient, even when processing large volumes of data. Through careful monitoring and continuous adjustments based on performance metrics, NiFi administrators can maintain high-performance data pipelines capable of handling extensive datasets.

6.3 Securing Sensitive Data within Flows

Securing sensitive data within data flows is paramount in maintaining privacy, ensuring compliance with legal and regulatory requirements,

133

and preventing unauthorized access or data breaches. Apache NiFi provides several mechanisms and configurations to secure sensitive information from the moment it enters the pipeline, throughout its processing, and until it's stored or transmitted out of the system.

Firstly, the use of encrypted provenance repositories and content repositories is essential. NiFi supports encryption in both of these repositories which ensures that any data, whether in-flight within the system or stored for provenance purposes, is encrypted using strong cryptographic algorithms. The configuration involves specifying the encryption key in `nifi.properties` and selecting the appropriate cryptographic algorithms. Care must be taken to securely manage these encryption keys, as access to these can compromise the security of the encrypted data.

```
1  nifi.provenance.repository.encryption.key.provider.implementation=org.apache.nifi.
      provenance.AESProvenanceRepositoryEncryptor
2  nifi.provenance.repository.encryption.key.id=KeyID
3  nifi.provenance.repository.encryption.key=Base64EncodedKey
```

Access control and authentication mechanisms enforce who can access NiFi and what actions they are permitted to perform. Utilizing NiFi's integration with LDAP, Kerberos, or OIDC for authentication ensures that only authenticated users can access the system. Once authenticated, NiFi's authorization policies can be finely tuned to control access to data flows, processors, and even specific pieces of data within the flow based on user roles and groups.

An important feature in NiFi that aids in securing sensitive data is the use of the Record processors with sensitive property detection and encryption/decryption services. For instance, the `UpdateRecord` processor can be configured to replace or mask sensitive fields as the data passes through the flow. When combined with the `EncryptContent` processor, it's possible to encrypt fields within a flow, ensuring that sensitive data is never exposed in plain text.

```
1  <property name="Replacement Value Strategy">Literal Value</property>
2  <property name="Fields">social_security_number</property>
3  <property name="Replacement Value">****-****</property>
```

Moreover, NiFi supports the configuration of an SSL/TLS context to secure data in transit. By requiring processors that transmit data outside of NiFi, such as `PutSFTP`, `GetHTTP`, and `InvokeHTTP`, to use SSL/TLS contexts, data in motion can be protected against interception and unauthorized access.

```
1  <sslContextService>
```

```
2    . . .
3    <property name="Keystore Type">JKS</property>
4    <property name="Keystore Password">password</property>
5    <property name="Key Password">password</property>
6    . . .
7  </sslContextService>
```

Managing sensitive properties within NiFi configuration files also presents a security concern. The `nifi.sensitive.props.key` in `nifi.properties` allows encrypting sensitive configuration settings, ensuring they are not stored in clear text. This mechanism should be employed to secure database passwords, API keys, and other sensitive configuration parameters.

```
nifi.sensitive.props.key=changeme
```

Adopting these techniques to secure sensitive data within NiFi flows not only ensures compliance with security policies and regulations but also builds trust in the system's ability to protect valuable and sensitive data assets. It's imperative that as data flows evolve and expand, continuous attention is given to effectively securing sensitive information against new threats and vulnerabilities, following the principle of least privilege and employing encryption judiciously to protect data at rest, in use, and in transit.

6.4 Leveraging Scripting Processors for Custom Logic

Apache NiFi's robust and flexible framework offers the capability to extend its out-of-the-box functionality through the use of scripting processors. These processors, including ExecuteScript and InvokeScriptedProcessor, provide a powerful tool for injecting custom logic directly into NiFi data flows. This allows for the development of tailored solutions that can handle specific data processing needs, which are not natively supported by existing processors.

Scripting processors in NiFi support a variety of scripting languages such as Groovy, JavaScript, Python, and Lua. This flexibility enables developers to leverage their existing programming skills and quickly implement custom logic within NiFi's data flow pipelines. The primary advantage of using scripting processors is their ability to perform complex transformations, dynamic routing, and even interact with external systems or APIs, all within the streamlined context of a NiFi flow.

To effectively utilize scripting processors, one must understand the NiFi scripting API and the interaction between scripts and NiFi Flow-File objects. A FlowFile in NiFi represents a single piece of data moving through the system, encapsulating the data itself along with metadata and attributes. Scripting processors operate on these FlowFiles, allowing the script to read and modify both the content and attributes of the FlowFiles as they pass through the processor.

Consider the following example where Groovy is used to filter and modify FlowFiles based on their attributes in an ExecuteScript processor:

```
1   import org.apache.nifi.processor.io.StreamCallback
2   import org.apache.nifi.stream.io.StreamUtils
3
4   flowFile = session.get()
5   if(!flowFile) return
6
7   flowFile = session.write(flowFile, new StreamCallback() {
8       @Override
9       void process(InputStream inputStream, OutputStream outputStream) throws
            IOException {
10          String inputContent = new BufferedReader(new InputStreamReader(inputStream)).
                readLine()
11          String outputContent = inputContent.replaceAll("oldString", "newString")
12          outputStream.write(outputContent.getBytes(StandardCharsets.UTF_8))
13      }
14  })
15  session.transfer(flowFile, REL_SUCCESS)
```

In the above script, the `session.get()` method is used to fetch a Flow-File from NiFi's incoming queue. The `session.write()` method is then utilized to modify the content of the FlowFile, specifically replacing occurrences of "oldString" with "newString" within the data. Finally, the modified FlowFile is transferred to the processor's success relationship using the `session.transfer()` method.

When implementing custom logic through scripting, it is essential to keep in mind the potential impact on NiFi's performance. Scripted operations, especially complex ones, can consume significant CPU and memory resources. Therefore, testing and optimization are crucial steps in ensuring that the addition of scripted logic does not negatively affect the overall performance of the data flow.

Moreover, thorough error handling within scripts is vital to maintain the robustness and reliability of the data flow. Scripts should be designed to gracefully handle unexpected conditions, such as malformed input data or external system failures. This includes proper logging of errors and, if necessary, routing FlowFiles to failure relationships for further inspection or recovery actions.

Leveraging scripting processors in Apache NiFi offers an expansive avenue for incorporating custom logic into data flow processes, far beyond the capabilities of pre-built processors. By adhering to best practices in scripting, including performance optimization and error handling, developers can enhance the flexibility and functionality of their NiFi data pipelines, enabling more sophisticated data processing scenarios with precision and efficiency.

6.5 Integration with Big Data Tools and Systems

Integration of Apache NiFi with big data tools and systems is a crucial capability for organizations aiming to harness the power of real-time data processing within their big data ecosystems. This integration facilitates seamless data flow between NiFi and various big data platforms, enabling the efficient ingestion, processing, and distribution of large datasets across systems. The focus of this section is on elucidating the strategies and configurations necessary for integrating NiFi with prominent big data tools such as Hadoop, Spark, Kafka, and others, ensuring optimal performance and scalability.

Apache NiFi provides a wide array of processors explicitly designed for interaction with big data systems. These processors are optimized to handle the connectivity, data exchange, and operational requirements specific to each system. To achieve successful integration, a comprehensive understanding of these processors alongside the configuration nuances of the target big data system is essential.

Hadoop Ecosystem Integration: Apache Hadoop, a framework that allows for the distributed processing of large data sets across clusters of computers, is a common integration point for NiFi. The integration is facilitated by processors such as PutHDFS, GetHDFS, FetchHDFS, ListHDFS, and DeleteHDFS. These processors are responsible for reading from and writing to HDFS, providing a bridge between NiFi and the Hadoop ecosystem. Configuring these processors involves specifying the Hadoop Configuration Resources property, which requires the path to the Hadoop configuration XML files (e.g., core-site.xml, hdfs-site.xml).

Apache Kafka Integration: Kafka, a distributed streaming platform, is another critical system for which NiFi offers robust integration capabilities. Processors such as PublishKafka, ConsumeKafka, and FetchKafka enable NiFi to publish, consume, and fetch data from Kafka topics, respectively. Configuring these processors involves specifying the Kafka broker details, topic name, and potentially the security protocol if the Kafka cluster is secured. The integration enables the creation of real-time streaming data pipelines that can ingest data from various sources, process it in NiFi, and then publish processed data to Kafka for consumption by other applications.

Apache Spark Integration: While NiFi and Apache Spark perform distinctly different roles within a data ecosystem, integrating the two can significantly enhance real-time and batch processing capabilities. NiFi can ingest and preprocess data, serving it to Spark for complex analytics and machine learning workloads. Integration is typically achieved through the use of Spark's data source API, enabling Spark applications to read from and write to dataflows managed by NiFi.

Custom Integration Techniques: In cases where direct integration with big data tools and systems is not supported out-of-the-box by NiFi processors, leveraging NiFi's scripting processors can offer a flexible alternative. Processors such as `ExecuteScript` and `InvokeScriptedProcessor` allow the execution of custom scripts written in languages such as Groovy, Python, or JavaScript. These scripts can implement custom logic for interacting with APIs or libraries specific to a big data tool, providing a means to extend NiFi's integration capabilities.

Optimizing Performance: When integrating NiFi with big data tools and systems, performance optimization is a pivotal aspect. This involves tuning NiFi's process groups and processors, as well as the configuration of the external systems to handle the volume and velocity of data accurately. Practices such as partitioning data intelligently across the cluster, leveraging data locality, and optimizing serialization and deserialization processes can significantly impact the efficiency and throughput of data flows.

Integration with big data tools and systems extends NiFi's utility as a data integration platform, bridging the gap between data collection and big data processing. It allows organizations to build more cohesive, responsive, and scalable data architectures capable of handling the complexities of modern data ecosystems. Through careful planning, configuration, and performance tuning, NiFi can be an invaluable component of any big data strategy, facilitating real-time insights and actions based on vast datasets.

6.6 Automating NiFi Processes with REST API

Automating Apache NiFi processes is a critical capability for managing large-scale data pipelines efficiently. The NiFi REST API provides a way to automate these processes, enabling users to control NiFi without accessing the user interface directly. This section will discuss utilizing the REST API for creating, deploying, and managing data flows programmatically.

NiFi's REST API endpoints can be leveraged to perform various tasks such as deploying new flows, starting/stopping processors, updating processor configurations, and monitoring system status. It is an essential tool for developers seeking to integrate NiFi with continuous integration/continuous deployment (CI/CD) pipelines or automated deployment systems.

Let's start with the basics of interacting with NiFi's REST API.

To invoke the REST API, one must first authenticate with NiFi. NiFi supports multiple authentication mechanisms, including username/-password, LDAP, and Kerberos. Authentication ensures that only authorized users can perform operations via the API.

```
1   curl -k -u username:password https://nifi.example.com/nifi-api/process-groups/root
```

This command fetches information about the root process group, assuming a basic authentication mechanism. The "-k" option is used to ignore SSL certificate validation, useful in development environments but should be avoided in production.

Once authenticated, users can create or modify processors by sending POST or PUT requests to the appropriate API endpoints. For instance, to create a new processor:

```
1   curl -k -X POST -H "Content-Type: application/json" -d @newProcessor.json -u
        username:password https://nifi.example.com/nifi-api/process-groups/{
        processGroupId}/processors
```

Here, newProcessor.json contains the JSON representation of the processor configuration. This JSON typically includes the processor type, name, and configuration properties. The {processGroupId} should be replaced with the ID of the process group where the processor will be created.

To update an existing processor's configuration, a PUT request can be sent:

```
1   curl -k -X PUT -H "Content-Type: application/json" -d @processorConfig.json -u
        username:password https://nifi.example.com/nifi-api/processors/{processorId}
```

In this command, `processorConfig.json` is a JSON file containing the new configuration for the processor, and `{processorId}` is the ID of the processor to be updated.

For automating data flow deployments, one can use the API to upload and instantiate a template:

```
1   curl -k -X POST -F template=@myDataFlowTemplate.xml -u username:password https://
        nifi.example.com/nifi-api/process-groups/{processGroupId}/templates/upload
```

After uploading, the template can be instantiated by another API call, which places the components of the template onto the canvas.

Monitoring is another critical aspect of automated NiFi processes. The REST API can retrieve status information about processors, connections, process groups, the NiFi system, and more. To get the status of a processor:

```
1   curl -k -u username:password https://nifi.example.com/nifi-api/processors/{
        processorId}/status
```

The output is a JSON object detailing the processor's status, including whether it is running, stopped, or invalid, and various statistics about its performance.

The NiFi REST API is a powerful tool for automating the operational aspects of NiFi processes. It enables automated workflows that can deploy, configure, and monitor data flows programmatically, making it an essential component for scalable and efficient data pipeline management. The flexibility offered by the REST API accelerates the integration of NiFi within larger IT ecosystems, empowering organizations to maintain sophisticated data flows with minimal manual intervention.

6.7 Version Control and Deployment Strategies

Version control and deployment strategies are crucial for the efficient management of Apache NiFi flows, particularly as data pipelines become increasingly complex and involve multiple stakeholders. These practices not only facilitate smooth and consistent changes across different environments but also enhance collaboration among developers. This section will discuss the fundamental concepts of version control in the context of NiFi, the importance of deployment strategies, and best practices for implementing these concepts effectively.

Apache NiFi supports version control through its integration with the NiFi Registry, a sub-project designed specifically for this purpose. The NiFi Registry allows users to version control flow definitions (dataflows), which can be saved as snapshots and efficiently managed over time. The integration facilitates deployment across different environments, such as from development to test to production, ensuring that changes can be tracked, reviewed, and rolled back if necessary.

Versioned Flow Snapshots form the core of NiFi's version control system. These snapshots capture the state of a dataflow at a given point in time and are stored in the NiFi Registry. When a flow is versioned for the first time, it is given a unique ID and an initial version number. Subsequent changes to the flow result in new snapshots being created, each with a higher version number. This approach allows developers to easily revert to previous versions of a flow in case of errors or to compare different versions to understand the changes made over time.

Deployment strategies in NiFi revolve around promoting flow changes from one environment to another while minimizing disruptions and maintaining data integrity. A commonly used strategy involves having separate NiFi instances for development, testing, and production environments. This separation ensures that changes can be thoroughly tested before being deployed to production, reducing the likelihood of unexpected issues affecting live dataflows.

Example of promoting a NiFi flow from test to production

```
1   <flowSnapshot>
2     <snapshotMetadata>
3       <groupId>com.example.nifi</groupId>
4       <artifactId>DataIngestionFlow</artifactId>
5       <version>1.2.0</version>
6     </snapshotMetadata>
7   </flowSnapshot>
```

The above XML snippet illustrates a simplified flow snapshot metadata example. This information is crucial when promoting a flow from one environment to another, as it uniquely identifies the flow and its version.

Deployment can be automated using the NiFi REST API, which offers endpoints for uploading flow snapshots to the NiFi Registry and deploying them to NiFi instances. Automation significantly streamlines the deployment process, making it faster and more reliable.

```
HTTP/1.1 200 OK
Content-Type: application/json

{
  "snapshotMetadata": {
    "groupId": "com.example.nifi",
    "artifactId": "DataIngestionFlow",
    "version": "1.2.0"
  },
  "flowContents": {...}
}
```

The JSON response from the NiFi REST API, as shown above, confirms the successful deployment of a flow version. Such automated deployments are critical for maintaining version consistency across different stages of the development lifecycle.

Furthermore, it is important to establish guidelines for managing changes to flow designs, such as implementing a peer review process and maintaining documentation for each version. These practices ensure that all changes are deliberate, well-understood, and traceable.

Version control and deployment strategies are foundational elements for managing Apache NiFi projects. Effective implementation of these practices enables organizations to manage their dataflows more efficiently, ensuring that pipelines are reliable, consistent, and maintainable over time. By leveraging the NiFi Registry, adhering to structured deployment processes, and automating where possible, teams can achieve seamless progression from development through to production, thereby minimizing the risk and maximizing the effectiveness of their data integration efforts.

6.8 Cluster-Wide Configuration and Management

Cluster-wide configuration and management in Apache NiFi are pivotal for ensuring consistent and efficient operations across all nodes in a NiFi cluster. This process involves synchronizing configuration settings, effectively managing resources, and monitoring cluster health to maintain optimal performance and reliability. This section will discuss strategies for managing configurations, the implications of such configurations on the cluster's operations, and best practices for cluster management.

To initiate, understanding NiFi's architecture is imperative. A NiFi cluster comprises a series of nodes that are managed by a Cluster Coordinator and primary nodes that are responsible for handling cluster-wide operations like starting, stopping, and managing the flow of data across the cluster. Each node in the cluster runs an instance of NiFi that executes data flows. Consistent configuration across these nodes is crucial to prevent data processing inconsistencies and potential data loss.

One of the foundational steps in managing a cluster-wide configuration is to utilize the `flow.xml.gz` file, which contains all configurations related to data flows. Ensuring that this file is synchronized across all nodes is crucial. This can be achieved through manual synchronization methods or by using NiFi's built-in cluster management capabilities, which automatically synchronize flow configurations across nodes.

```
1  # Example of manual synchronization command
2  scp /path/to/local/flow.xml.gz nifi@node2:/path/to/nifi/conf/
```

```
# Expected output indicates successful transfer
flow.xml.gz                              100%   15KB 3.3MB/s   00:00
```

However, for more dynamic configuration management, leveraging NiFi's Zero-Master Clustering (ZMC) paradigm is recommended. In ZMC, the Cluster Coordinator dynamically manages the distribution of flow configurations, ensuring that all nodes in the cluster have up-to-date configurations without requiring manual intervention.

Regarding resource management, Apache NiFi allows for the configuration of specific controller services and reporting tasks at the cluster level. These configurations are critically important for managing shared resources such as databases, API connections, or external services. It is advisable to configure these resources centrally to ensure uniform access and prevent resource contention across the cluster.

```
1  # Example of a centrally managed controller service configuration
2  <controllerService>
3    <identifier>dbConnectionPool</identifier>
4    <name>Database Connection Pooling Service</name>
5    <class>org.apache.nifi.dbcp.DBCPConnectionPool</class>
6    <properties>
7      <property name="Database Connection URL">jdbc:mysql://dbserver:3306/nifi_db
         </property>
```

143

```
8        <property name="Database Driver Class Name">com.mysql.jdbc.Driver</property>
9        <property name="Database User">nifi_user</property>
10       <property name="Password">[password]</property>
11     </properties>
12   </controllerService>
```

For monitoring cluster health and operations, deploying a NiFi Reporting Task at the cluster level is effective. The Reporting Task can be configured to collect and report metrics on each node's health, data flow status, and system performance.

```
1    # Example configuration of a cluster-wide reporting task
2    <reportingTask>
3      <identifier>clusterMetricsReporter</identifier>
4      <name>Cluster Metrics Reporting Task</name>
5      <class>org.apache.nifi.reporting.ambari.AmbariReportingTask</class>
6      <properties>
7        <property name="Ambari Metrics Collector Host">ambari.server.host</property>
8        <property name="Application Id">nifi</property>
9      </properties>
10   </reportingTask>
```

Finally, for sustainable cluster-wide management, adopting version control for flow configurations is highly recommended. Tools such as NiFi Registry provide capabilities for tracking changes, enabling rollback to previous configurations, and simplifying the deployment of configurations across environments.

Effective cluster-wide configuration and management in Apache NiFi are foundational for maintaining the integrity, performance, and reliability of data flows across large-scale distributed systems. By leveraging NiFi's built-in tools for synchronization, resource management, and version control, administrators can ensure that NiFi clusters operate seamlessly and efficiently, even in complex data processing scenarios.

6.9 Troubleshooting Complex Flows

Troubleshooting complex flows in Apache NiFi involves a systematic approach to diagnose and resolve issues that may arise during the design, development, and execution of data flows. Given the dynamic and distributed nature of NiFi, challenges such as performance bottlenecks, data loss, or unexpected behavior can often occur. This section will discuss strategies to identify and address these issues, ensuring the stability and efficiency of your data pipelines.

The first step in troubleshooting is to enable detailed logging on NiFi components. NiFi provides configurable logging that can be adjusted to meet the needs of troubleshooting without overwhelming the system with irrelevant information. By increasing the log level of processors or connectors that are suspected to be at the root of an issue, one can gain valuable insights into the internal workings and any errors that may not be immediately visible through the NiFi user interface.

```
1   <logger name="org.apache.nifi" level="DEBUG"/>
```

Once detailed logging is enabled, it is crucial to monitor the NiFi logs for any signs of errors or unusual activity. The `nifi-app.log` file is particularly useful for this purpose, as it records a comprehensive log of all activities and events occurring within NiFi. Checking this file periodically or in response to specific issues can help quickly isolate problems.

```
2023-01-01 12:00:00,123 ERROR [Timer-Driven Process Thread-1] o.a.n.p.myProcessor
MyProcessor[id=12345678-1234-1234-1234-123456789abc] Failed to process session due
to org.apache.nifi.processor.exception.ProcessException: My custom error message;
rolling back session: org.apache.nifi.processor.exception.ProcessException: My
custom error message
```

When examining logs, look for common issues such as out of memory errors, connection timeouts, or processing exceptions. These are indicative of deeper problems within the flow and may require adjustments to configurations, such as increasing heap size, modifying connection timeouts, or reviewing the logic within custom processors.

Another effective tool for troubleshooting is the use of data provenance. NiFi's data provenance feature allows users to track the flow of data through the system, providing visibility into the lifecycle of each piece of data. By examining provenance events, one can identify where data is getting stuck, duplicated, or lost.

```
1   ProvenanceEventRecord UUID=12345678-1234-1234-1234-123456789abc,
2   EventType=RECEIVE, FlowFileUUID=abcd1234-1234-1234-abcd-123456789abc,
3   FileSize=1024 bytes, Duration=500 ms
```

Should a data bottleneck be identified, the next step would be to analyze the configuration of the implicated processors or connections. Often, increasing the concurrent tasks for a processor or adjusting the back-pressure settings for connections can alleviate throughput issues. These adjustments should be made cautiously and monitored closely to avoid introducing new performance bottlenecks elsewhere in the flow.

```
1   <property name="Maximum Concurrent Tasks">4</property>
```

2 | `<property name="Back Pressure Data Size Threshold">1 GB</property>`

For particularly stubborn or complex issues, splitting the flow into smaller, more manageable segments can help isolate the problem. By redirecting the output of each segment to a debug queue or file, one can methodically verify the operation of each part of the flow. This divide-and-conquer strategy is especially useful when dealing with large and intricate flows, where issues may stem from multiple sources.

In addition to the techniques mentioned above, leveraging the NiFi community and resources can be invaluable during troubleshooting. The Apache NiFi mailing lists, forums, and issue trackers can provide insights and solutions from other users who may have encountered similar problems.

- Monitoring resource utilization (CPU, memory, disk I/O) to identify bottlenecks.

- Verifying external systems (databases, APIs, file systems) are accessible and performing as expected.

- Testing flow components in isolation to ensure each performs its intended function correctly.

Troubleshooting complex NiFi flows requires a blend of technical proficiency, systematic investigation, and sometimes, creativity. By following a structured approach and leveraging NiFi's extensive toolset for monitoring and debugging, one can effectively identify and resolve issues, ensuring the smooth and efficient operation of data pipelines.

6.10 Monitoring NiFi Performance and Health

Monitoring the performance and health of Apache NiFi is critical for ensuring the reliability, efficiency, and uptime of data pipelines. This involves observing various metrics and indicators that can inform administrators about the current state of the system, potential bottlenecks, and points of failure. Effective monitoring strategies enable proactive adjustments and optimizations, thus minimizing disruptions and operational risks. This section will discuss the key aspects of monitoring NiFi, including the utilization of built-in tools, external monitoring solutions, and the interpretation of important metrics.

Apache NiFi provides a set of built-in tools and features designed to facilitate system monitoring and performance analysis. The NiFi User Interface (UI) offers real-time visualization of data flow, including specific metrics like flow file counts, data sizes, and processing times for each processor. Additionally, the UI displays system health indicators such as heap memory usage, content repository storage availability, and processor load. These metrics are essential for identifying underperforming components and diagnosing issues related to resource allocation and throughput.

```
1  # Example of accessing processor metrics via NiFi REST API
2  curl -X GET http://nifi-host:8080/nifi-api/processors/{processor-id}/status
```

```
{
  "processorStatus": {
    "id": "processor-id",
    "name": "Sample Processor",
    "flowFilesReceived": 100,
    "bytesReceived": 102400,
    "flowFilesSent": 100,
    "bytesSent": 102400,
    "flowFilesQueued": 0,
    "bytesQueued": 0,
    "input": "1 MB",
    "output": "1 MB",
    "taskCount": 10,
    "tasksDurationNanos": 500000000
  }
}
```

For more comprehensive and customizable monitoring, integrating Apache NiFi with external monitoring systems such as Grafana, Prometheus, or Elasticsearch is highly beneficial. These platforms can consume metrics exposed by NiFi's REST API or via reporting tasks such as MonitorMemory, SiteToSiteStatusReportingTask, and AmbariReportingTask to aggregate, visualize, and analyze data flow health and performance over time. Configuring such integrations typically involves setting up data collectors or agents that periodically fetch metrics from NiFi and transmit them to the monitoring solution.

```
1  # Configuration snippet for a Prometheus exporter
2  <reportingTask>
3    ...
4    <class>org.apache.nifi.reporting.prometheus.PrometheusReportingTask</class>
5    ...
6  </reportingTask>
```

Effective monitoring extends beyond merely collecting metrics; it also involves setting up alerts based on thresholds for specific indicators such as CPU usage, memory pressure, or backpressure conditions.

Alerting mechanisms can be configured within external monitoring tools or through NiFi's built-in notification services, enabling timely responses to potential issues or system failures before they escalate into more significant problems.

In addition to real-time monitoring, it is crucial to analyze historical performance data to identify trends, patterns, and anomalies. This historical analysis aids in capacity planning, understanding seasonal impacts on data flows, and tuning NiFi configurations for optimal performance. Establishing a baseline of normal operation metrics allows for more accurate anomaly detection and more effective troubleshooting.

Lastly, it's worth noting the importance of custom metrics tailored to specific data flows or business requirements. Apache NiFi allows for the development of custom processors and reporting tasks, enabling the capture and reporting of bespoke metrics. This is particularly useful for complex data pipelines where standard metrics may not adequately represent the health or efficiency of the flow.

```
1   # Skeleton for a custom reporting task
2   public class CustomMetricsReportingTask extends AbstractReportingTask {
3       @Override
4       public void onTrigger(final ReportingContext context) {
5           // Implementation for custom metrics collection
6       }
7   }
```

Monitoring Apache NiFi's performance and health is a multifaceted endeavor that involves leveraging both built-in and external tools, understanding key metrics, and interpreting data for proactive management of data pipelines. Adopting a robust monitoring strategy ensures that NiFi deployments remain efficient, reliable, and able to support the evolving demands of data-driven applications.

6.11 NiFi Extensions: Custom Processors and Controller Services

Apache NiFi's flexibility and extensibility lies in part in its ability to be customized through the development of custom processors and controller services. Extensions in NiFi allow for the addition of new functionalities that are not provided out of the box. This section will discuss the creation of custom processors and controller services, their importance, and guidelines for development.

Custom processors in NiFi are Java classes that operate on the flowfile(s) within a NiFi data flow. They are the workhorses of NiFi, designed to perform specific tasks that are not covered by the standard processors. The development of a custom processor involves implementing interfaces provided by the NiFi framework. A well-designed custom processor encapsulates logic for a specific task, such as interacting with a new external system, transforming data in a unique way, or implementing custom routing and decision-making.

The development of a custom processor typically involves several key steps:

- Implementing the `Processor` interface, which requires overriding methods such as `onTrigger` to define the processor's behavior when executed.

- Defining processor properties and relationships. Properties allow users to configure the processor, while relationships define how flowfiles are routed after processing.

- Handling flowfiles within the `onTrigger` method, using the ProcessSession for reading, writing, and manipulating flowfiles.

A simple custom processor might look like this in code:

```
1   public class MyCustomProcessor extends AbstractProcessor {
2
3       public static final Relationship SUCCESS_RELATIONSHIP = new Relationship.
            Builder()
4           .name("SUCCESS")
5           .description("All successfully processed flowfiles go here.")
6           .build();
7
8       @Override
9       public void onTrigger(ProcessContext context, ProcessSession session) throws
            ProcessException {
10          FlowFile flowFile = session.get();
11          if (flowFile == null) {
12              return;
13          }
14          // Custom logic here
15          session.transfer(flowFile, SUCCESS_RELATIONSHIP);
16      }
17  }
```

Controller services in NiFi provide shared functionality or resources to processors, such as database connections or clients for external services. Similar to processors, they are Java classes that implement specific interfaces from the NiFi API, but are designed to be reusable across multiple processors.

Developing a controller service involves:

- Implementing the ControllerService interface or extending an existing base class that implements this interface.

- Defining configurable properties specific to the service.

- Implementing the lifecycle methods to manage resource initialization and cleanup.

The use of controller services can greatly reduce duplication of code and effort when multiple processors need to interact with the same external resource or share common processing logic.

An example controller service for managing a simple resource might look like this:

```
1   public class MyResourceControllerService extends AbstractControllerService
        implements MyServiceInterface {
2
3       @Override
4       public void onEnabled(final ConfigurationContext context) {
5           // Initialize your resource here
6       }
7
8       @Override
9       public void onDisabled() {
10          // Cleanup resource here
11      }
12  }
```

Custom processors and controller services are powerful mechanisms for extending Apache NiFi's capabilities. They allow developers to tailor NiFi to their specific needs, integrating new data sources, custom algorithms, or external services into their data flows. Effective use of these extensions can significantly enhance the efficiency, functionality, and maintainability of NiFi implementations.

6.12   Best Practices for Scalability and Maintenance

Apache NiFi's architecture is designed for flexibility and scalability, enabling it to handle anything from a few files to millions of records per second. However, maximizing these capabilities while ensuring the maintainability of your NiFi deployments requires adherence to several best practices. This section will discuss practices designed to enhance scalability and ease the maintenance of NiFi data flows.

First and foremost, effective resource management is pivotal. Allocating sufficient resources (CPU, memory, disk I/O, and network bandwidth) in accordance with your processing needs ensures that NiFi operates efficiently. It is equally important to monitor these resources to anticipate and mitigate bottlenecks. In a cluster setup, ensuring that resources are balanced across the cluster can prevent nodes from becoming overwhelmed, hence improving overall throughput.

- Design dataflows with performance in mind. Use processors judiciously and prefer built-in processors over custom scripting for common tasks to minimize the computational overhead.

- Leverage backpressure settings and prioritize queue management to regulate data flow and prevent system overload. Adjust the queue's backpressure settings based on throughput and processing demands.

- Partition dataflows when possible. Utilize NiFi's capability to segment high volume flows into manageable parts using partitioning techniques such as RouteOnAttribute or PartitionRecord processors.

- Optimize content repository usage by cleaning up unnecessary data promptly and adjusting the repository's size based on your retention policy and throughput requirements.

Regarding scalability, constructing NiFi data flows that can be dynamically scaled up or down in response to load changes is crucial. In clustered environments, use NiFi's Zero-Master Clustering mechanism to distribute loads evenly and ensure no single point of failure. Implement auto-scaling in cloud environments by monitoring performance metrics and programmatically adjusting the number of nodes in the NiFi cluster based on demand.

To maintain high availability and fault tolerance, replicate critical components across multiple nodes in the cluster and employ persistent data stores that support replication and failover. In case of failures, ensuring quick recovery with minimal data loss is imperative. Techniques such as storing state in external systems (e.g., distributed caches or state management services) allow for faster recovery by decoupling state from individual NiFi instances.

151

Security considerations are also paramount, especially when scaling NiFi deployments. Implement fine-grained access control to data flows and resources, encrypt sensitive data both in transit and at rest, and monitor audit logs for unauthorized access. Utilizing NiFi's built-in support for secure protocols and integrating with external security services (e.g., LDAP, Kerberos) can significantly bolster your data pipeline's security posture.

For ongoing maintenance, version control of data flows plays a critical role. Leverage NiFi's Versioned Flows feature to track changes, enable collaboration among team members, and facilitate a smooth roll-out of updates or roll-back in case of issues. Additionally, automate deployment processes using NiFi's REST API or tools like Apache NiFi Registry for more efficient updates and scaling operations.

Finally, regular monitoring and performance tuning are essential for maintaining optimal operation. Utilize NiFi's built-in monitoring tools (e.g., Bulletin Board, Data Provenance) and integrate with external monitoring solutions for a comprehensive view of system health. Adjust configurations based on performance data and continuously look for optimization opportunities.

```
Versioned Flows in NiFi Registry:
- Facilitates collaboration
- Simplifies deployment
- Aids in rollback procedures
```

In summary, scalability and maintenance in Apache NiFi environments hinge on effective resource management, thoughtful data flow design, robust security practices, and diligent monitoring and performance tuning. By adhering to these best practices, organizations can ensure that their NiFi-based data pipelines are both scalable and maintainable, ready to meet current and future data processing challenges.

Chapter 7

Securing Data Flows in Apache NiFi

Securing data flows is a critical aspect of managing sensitive information within Apache NiFi. This chapter provides comprehensive insights into the mechanisms and configurations necessary to protect data at rest and in transit through encryption, access control, and authentication techniques. It emphasizes the importance of implementing robust security policies, managing user permissions, and employing best practices for securing data flows against unauthorized access and potential breaches. Understanding these security measures is fundamental for organizations to ensure compliance with data protection regulations and maintain the confidentiality, integrity, and availability of their data within NiFi environments.

7.1 Understanding Security in Apache NiFi

Apache NiFi is a powerful, scalable software solution designed for data routing, transformation, and system mediation. As data moves through the pipelines created in NiFi, securing this data becomes paramount, especially when dealing with sensitive or personal information. Security in Apache NiFi extends beyond the mere prevention of unauthorized access; it encompasses the protection of data at rest and in transit, ensuring data integrity and availability while maintaining confidentiality.

Data flow in Apache NiFi can be secured using various mechanisms and configurations, tailored to safeguard against threats and vulnerabilities intrinsic to data processing environments. The fundamental aspects of NiFi security include encryption, both at rest and in transit, authentication and authorization of user actions, and the management of sensitive properties through encryption keys.

Encryption is a critical component in securing data flows. Apache NiFi supports SSL/TLS encryption to protect data as it moves between NiFi and external systems. This ensures that data in transit cannot be easily intercepted or tampered with. For data at rest, NiFi can be configured to encrypt sensitive property values using various encryption algorithms, thereby securing configuration details such as passwords and keys.

Authentication in Apache NiFi is facilitated through pluggable authentication mechanisms. These mechanisms can range from simple username/password credentials to more complex setups involving external identity providers and multi-factor authentication processes. Once authenticated, users' interactions with NiFi are subject to authorization.

Authorization, the process of determining the resources a user can access and the actions they can perform, is governed in NiFi through policies and user groups. NiFi's access control policies allow administrators to finely tune the level of access granted to users and groups, thus limiting potential damage from compromised accounts or insider threats.

The management of sensitive properties is another area where NiFi provides robust security features. NiFi administrators can configure the system to encrypt sensitive property values stored in the flow configuration files. This is particularly important for maintaining the confidentiality of credentials, API keys, and other sensitive information.

To implement these security measures effectively, NiFi leverages several internal components and external integrations. For encryption, NiFi utilizes the Transport Layer Security (TLS) protocol and supports various cryptographic standards for encrypting sensitive properties. For authentication and authorization, NiFi integrates with LDAP, Kerberos, and OAuth 2.0, among others, to facilitate secure user verification and resource access control.

Additionally, understanding the concept of data provenance and audit logging is crucial in the security context of Apache NiFi. Data provenance offers insights into the data lifecycle within NiFi, tracking data lineage, including where it came from, how it was processed, and where it was delivered. This, combined with comprehensive audit logging, allows administrators to perform security audits, identify unauthorized access attempts, and ensure compliance with regulatory standards.

To encapsulate, securing data flows within Apache NiFi requires a multifaceted approach. From stringent encryption protocols to detailed access control mechanisms and beyond, each layer of security serves to protect the integrity, confidentiality, and availability of data. For organizations relying on NiFi to process their data, understanding and implementing these security features is not just a recommendation—it is essential for safeguarding sensitive information against unauthorized access, ensuring regulatory compliance, and maintaining the trust of stakeholders involved in the data's lifecycle.

7.2 Configuring SSL/TLS for Secure Data Transfer

Ensuring the confidentiality and integrity of data as it moves through Apache NiFi pipelines is quintessential for maintaining trust in data processing activities. To achieve this, Secure Sockets Layer (SSL) and its successor, Transport Layer Security (TLS), provide cryptographic protocols for securing communications over networks. This section will discuss the comprehensive steps required to configure SSL/TLS in Apache NiFi to secure data transfers.

Firstly, it is imperative to understand that SSL/TLS works by using a combination of asymmetric cryptography for key exchange, symmetric encryption for data confidentiality, and message authentication codes for message integrity. When configuring SSL/TLS for Apache NiFi, the goal is to ensure that data in transit is encrypted and only accessible by intended parties.

The configuration process starts with generating or obtaining a digital certificate. This digital certificate must be trusted by both the sender and receiver of the data. There are two approaches to obtaining a certificate: using a Certificate Authority (CA) or generating a self-signed certificate. While CA-signed certificates are preferred for production environments due to their inherent trustworthiness, self-signed certificates can be suitable for testing or internal usage.

```
1   # Generate a new key and self-signed certificate
2   keytool -genkey -keyalg RSA -alias selfsigned_nifi -keystore keystore.jks -
        storepass password -validity 360 -keysize 2048
```

After generating or acquiring the certificate, it needs to be imported into NiFi's keystore. The keystore is a secure repository containing the keys and certificates used for SSL/TLS. NiFi utilizes Java's Key-Store format (JKS) for storing these cryptographic assets. The process involves utilizing Java's keytool utility, which is included in the Java Development Kit (JDK).

Following the importation of certificates into the keystore, the next step is to configure NiFi to use the keystore and truststore. The truststore contains certificates from other parties that you expect to communicate with, or from Certificate Authorities that you trust. NiFi properties related to SSL/TLS configuration are found in the 'nifi.properties' file. Key properties include:

- `nifi.security.keystore`: Specifies the location of the keystore.

- `nifi.security.keystoreType`: Specifies the type of the keystore (e.g., JKS).

- `nifi.security.keystorePasswd`: Specifies the password for the keystore.

- `nifi.security.truststore`: Specifies the location of the truststore.

- `nifi.security.truststoreType`: Specifies the type of the truststore (e.g., JKS).

- `nifi.security.truststorePasswd`: Specifies the password for the truststore.

In addition to modifying the 'nifi.properties' file, ensuring the secure transfer involves adjusting the 'nifi.web.https.host' and 'nifi.web.https.port' properties to enable HTTPS in the NiFi UI. To further strengthen the security configuration, consider enabling client certificate authentication for NiFi. This requires clients to present a valid, trusted certificate when establishing connections, adding another layer of authentication.

```
1  # Example configurations in nifi.properties for enabling HTTPS
2  nifi.web.https.host=my.nifi.server
3  nifi.web.https.port=8443
```

Moreover, to maintain robust security, it is recommended to regularly update certificates and keys before they expire and to use strong encryption algorithms. Monitoring and auditing SSL/TLS configurations using tools like SSL Labs' SSL Test can help identify potential vulnerabilities and ensure best practices are followed.

In summary, configuring SSL/TLS for securing data transfer in Apache NiFi involves generating or obtaining a digital certificate, importing certificates into the keystore and truststore, modifying the 'nifi.properties' file to utilize these cryptographic assets, and enabling HTTPS for the NiFi UI. By following these steps, organizations can safeguard their data pipelines against eavesdropping and tampering, ensuring the confidentiality, integrity, and availability of their data in transit.

7.3 User Authentication and Authorization Mechanisms

Ensuring the security of data flows within Apache NiFi involves not only securing the data itself but also ensuring that access to the data is tightly controlled. This is achieved through a comprehensive system of user authentication and authorization mechanisms. Authentication verifies the identity of a user requesting access to the system, whereas authorization determines the level of access or permissions granted to the authenticated user. Apache NiFi offers multiple strategies for both authentication and authorization, catering to various security needs and deployment scenarios.

Authentication Mechanisms in Apache NiFi:

Apache NiFi supports various authentication mechanisms, allowing administrators to select the most appropriate method based on their security requirements and infrastructure.

- *Username/Password Authentication*: The simplest form of authentication, it requires users to provide a username and a password. Apache NiFi stores and manages these credentials securely.

- *LDAP Authentication*: This method uses the Lightweight Directory Access Protocol (LDAP) for authenticating users against an existing directory service, enabling centralized management of user credentials.

- *Kerberos Authentication*: For environments requiring more stringent security measures, Apache NiFi supports Kerberos authentication, which uses tickets rather than passwords to prove the identity of users.

- *OAuth*: NiFi can be configured to use OAuth2 for authentication, allowing integration with modern identity providers and enabling Single Sign-On (SSO) capabilities.

- *Client Certificate Authentication*: In this approach, users present a client certificate as their identity proof. This is commonly used in conjunction with SSL/TLS for both authentication and encryption.

Each of these authentication methods can be configured within NiFi's security settings, and it's possible to employ multiple methods concurrently to accommodate diverse user needs.

Authorization Mechanisms in Apache NiFi:

After users are authenticated, NiFi employs authorization mechanisms to enforce access controls. Authorization in Apache NiFi is managed through policies that define what actions authenticated users or groups can perform. These policies can be as granular as necessary, from controlling access to specific data flows up to administrative actions within the NiFi ecosystem.

- *User Group Based Authorization*: Administrators can define user groups and assign specific rights and permissions to each group. This simplifies the management of permissions as users can be added to or removed from groups without the need to alter individual access settings.

- *Access Policies*: Apache NiFi allows the creation of detailed access policies for data processors, controller services, and reporting tasks. These policies can specify, for instance, who can start or stop a processor, view its properties, or modify its configuration.

- *Multi-tenant Authorization*: In multi-tenant environments, NiFi supports the isolation of resources between different tenants. Administrators can set up authorization policies that restrict users from one tenant accessing resources allocated to another.

Implementing Secure Authentication and Authorization:

Implementing secure authentication and authorization in Apache NiFi requires careful planning. It begins with a thorough assessment of the organization's security policies and compliance requirements. Based on these requirements, administrators can choose the most appropriate authentication mechanism(s) and design a suitable authorization model. This process involves mapping out all the resources within the NiFi environment and deciding on the level of access required for different user roles or groups.

Effective management of NiFi's authentication and authorization capabilities also includes monitoring and auditing access patterns. Apache NiFi provides extensive logging and auditing features, which administrators should leverage to track authentication attempts, changes to access policies, and other security-related events. This not only aids in detecting potential security breaches but also facilitates compliance with various regulatory standards.

Apache NiFi offers a flexible and robust framework for securing access to data flows through multiple authentication and authorization mechanisms. By carefully selecting and configuring these mechanisms, and by continuously monitoring access patterns, organizations can significantly enhance the security of their NiFi environments, ensuring that sensitive data is protected against unauthorized access.

7.4 Managing Sensitive Properties and Passwords

Managing sensitive properties and passwords is a crucial aspect of securing data flows in Apache NiFi. It involves safeguarding critical configuration settings and credentials that control access to data sources, external systems, and various components of a NiFi deployment. This section will discuss the methods and best practices for managing these sensitive pieces of information, focusing primarily on the tools and functionalities provided by NiFi to enhance security.

Apache NiFi offers several mechanisms to encrypt sensitive properties, including passwords, keys, and other confidential configuration parameters. The NiFi EncryptConfig tool is a standalone utility that helps administrators encrypt or decrypt sensitive properties in the nifi.properties file. This functionality is vital for protecting critical information at rest and mitigating the risks associated with exposing sensitive data.

To utilize the EncryptConfig tool, administrators must first generate an encryption key. This can be achieved using the ./nifi.sh encrypt-config command. The syntax for generating an encryption key is straightforward and requires specifying the bootstrap.conf file as an argument. Once the encryption key is generated, it is stored securely in the bootstrap.conf file, and the sensitive properties in the nifi.properties file can be encrypted.

```
1   ./nifi.sh encrypt-config --bootstrapConf=./conf/bootstrap.conf
```

After executing this command, the sensitive properties within the nifi.properties file are encrypted, rendering them unreadable without the appropriate decryption key.

In addition to encrypting properties in the nifi.properties file, Apache NiFi also supports the use of encrypted property values for components within a data flow. This capability is particularly useful for protecting credentials or other sensitive information that is used by processors, controllers, and services. NiFi uses a pluggable encryption module that allows the specification of encrypted values directly within the processor's configuration UI. When a processor or service is configured with an encrypted property value, NiFi automatically decrypts the value at runtime, ensuring that sensitive information is kept secure.

To specify an encrypted property value, administrators can use the NiFi Expression Language in conjunction with the 'encrypt' function. For example:

```
1   ${encrypt('password', 'AES')}
```

This approach enables NiFi to dynamically decrypt property values, ensuring that sensitive data remains protected both at rest and in transit.

- Ensure encryption keys and passwords are stored securely and are accessible only to authorized personnel.

- Regularly rotate encryption keys and passwords to mitigate the risk of compromise.

- Audit access to sensitive properties and monitor for unauthorized access attempts.

Furthermore, managing sensitive properties and passwords extends beyond encryption. It encompasses best practices for access control, such as defining strict permissions for users who can edit or view sensitive properties. This can be achieved by configuring user groups and policies within the NiFi interface, ensuring that only authorized individuals have the ability to access or modify encrypted properties.

Lastly, incorporation of external credentials stores, such as HashiCorp Vault or the AWS Secrets Manager, into the NiFi ecosystem allows for centralized management of secrets and sensitive properties. This integration empowers administrators to separate the management of sensitive values from the NiFi configuration files, thereby enhancing security by abstracting sensitive information away from the NiFi deployment.

Effective management of sensitive properties and passwords within Apache NiFi is essential for maintaining the security and integrity of data flows. Through the application of encryption, access control mechanisms, and integration with external secrets management solutions, organizations can significantly reduce the risk of sensitive data exposure and ensure compliance with industry standards and regulations for data protection.

7.5 Data Encryption Techniques within NiFi

Data encryption within Apache NiFi plays a pivotal role in enhancing the security of sensitive information as it flows through the data pipelines. Encryption is the process of converting data from a readable format into an encoded format that can only be read or processed after it has been decrypted. This section will discuss the key concepts, methods, and configurations for implementing encryption to secure data in transit and at rest in a NiFi environment.

At the core of NiFi's encryption strategy are two primary types: encryption of data at rest and encryption of data in transit.

Encryption of Data at Rest: NiFi provides mechanisms to encrypt sensitive information stored on disk, such as flow configuration files and content repositories. This is crucial for protecting data against unauthorized access when stored. NiFi uses the Advanced Encryption Standard (AES) for this purpose, a widely recognized encryption algorithm known for its strength and efficiency. Configuring encryption for data at rest in NiFi involves generating or specifying an encryption key and updating the NiFi properties file to use this key for encrypting stored data.

```
1  nifi.sensitive.props.key=<encryption_key>
2  nifi.sensitive.props.algorithm=AES/GCM/NoPadding
3  nifi.sensitive.props.provider=BC
```

The above configuration specifies the encryption key and algorithm used by NiFi to encrypt sensitive properties.

Encryption of Data in Transit: Securing data in transit involves encrypting data as it moves between NiFi and other systems or within NiFi components. NiFi supports Transport Layer Security (TLS) and its predecessor, Secure Sockets Layer (SSL), to encrypt data in transit. Configuring TLS/SSL requires generating a keystore and truststore, importing the necessary certificates, and configuring NiFi to use these cryptographic materials.

```
1  nifi.security.keystore=./conf/keystore.jks
2  nifi.security.keystoreType=JKS
3  nifi.security.keystorePasswd=<keystore_password>
4  nifi.security.truststore=./conf/truststore.jks
5  nifi.security.truststoreType=JKS
6  nifi.security.truststorePasswd=<truststore_password>
```

This setup ensures that all data transmitted to or from NiFi is encrypted, safeguarding against interception and unauthorized disclosure.

Apart from securing data in transit and at rest, NiFi also offers a unique feature for encrypting individual dataflows. This is achieved through processors such as `EncryptContent` and `DecryptContent`. These processors allow for the encryption and decryption of flow files using various algorithms, providing fine-grained control over the encryption of specific dataflows.

```
1  EncryptContent
2  -Algorithm: AES/GCM/NoPadding
3  -Password: <encryption_password>
4  -Key Derivation Function: PBKDF2WithHmacSHA256
```

The EncryptContent processor can be configured with the desired algorithm, password, and key derivation function to encrypt data as it flows through NiFi. Similarly, the DecryptContent processor is used to decrypt the data using a similar configuration.

Ensuring the secure configuration of these encryption techniques necessitates a thorough understanding of cryptography principles and adherence to best practices. This includes the proper management of encryption keys, using strong algorithms and key lengths, and regularly updating cryptographic materials.

In summary, implementing data encryption within NiFi encompasses securing data at rest and data in transit, alongside providing capabilities for encrypting specific data flows. By leveraging these techniques, organizations can significantly enhance the security posture of their data pipelines, ensuring that sensitive information is protected against unauthorized access and breaches.

7.6 Using Access Policies for Securing Data Flains in Apache NiFi

Access Policies in Apache NiFi provide a granular level of security by defining who can do what within the system. These policies are essential in restricting access to sensitive data and ensuring that only authorized users can perform specific actions. This section will discuss how to configure and manage access policies to secure data flows effectively.

Apache NiFi employs a role-based access control (RBAC) model, which allows administrators to assign roles to users and groups. These roles are associated with a set of permissions that dictate the actions users can perform. Access policies in NiFi are based on this principle, enabling administrators to control access to data flows, components, and system resources.

To begin configuring access policies, administrators must first ensure that the NiFi instance is running in secure mode, with user authentication and authorization mechanisms properly set up. This setup is a prerequisite as access policies will link to authenticated users or groups.

The configuration of access policies starts with accessing the NiFi User Interface (UI) and navigating to the Policies section under the settings tab. Here, administrators can view, add, and modify policies related to the system, data, and access control. The process involves specifying the resource for which the policy is being created, such as a processor, input/output port, or system resource like provenance data. Next, administrators specify the action (e.g., read, write, execute) and the user or group that the policy applies to.

Consider an example where an administrator wants to restrict access to a sensitive processor. The following steps would be taken:

1. Navigate to the `Policies` section in the NiFi UI.

2. Click on `Add` to create a new policy.

3. Specify the resource (e.g., the ID of the sensitive processor).

4. Choose the action (e.g., 'read' or 'write').

5. Select the user or group that should have the specified access.

6. Save the policy.

Once the policy is created, only the designated users or groups will have the specified access to the processor. All other users will be denied access, thus securing the sensitive processor from unauthorized access.

In addition to UI-based policy management, Apache NiFi supports the automation of access policy configuration through its REST API. This capability is particularly useful in large-scale environments or when integrating NiFi with external security systems. By using the REST API, administrators can programmatically create, update, and delete access policies, streamlining the security configuration process.

Access policies in Apache NiFi also extend to data provenance. Administrators can control who has the ability to view and query data provenance information. This control is crucial for protecting sensitive data from unauthorized access, as data provenance logs can contain details about the data flow and processing actions. By restricting access to provenance information, organizations can further ensure the confidentiality and integrity of their data.

To effectively manage access policies, it is recommended that administrators regularly review and update policies to reflect changes in user roles and responsibilities. This practice helps maintain a secure NiFi environment by ensuring that access permissions align with current organizational policies and user roles.

Access policies in Apache NiFi are a powerful tool for securing data flows by providing fine-grained access control. By carefully configuring access policies for different components and system resources, administrators can protect sensitive data and ensure that only authorized users can perform certain actions. Regular review and management of these policies ensure that the NiFi environment remains secure and compliant with organizational security policies.

7.7 Audit Logging and Data Provenance for Security

In this section, we will discuss the importance of audit logging and data provenance in securing Apache NiFi data flows. Audit logs are vital for tracking user activities and system events, thus providing visibility into the operations within a NiFi ecosystem. Data provenance, on the other hand, concerns recording the history of data as it moves through the system, detailing how data has been modified, accessed, and transported.

Audit logging in Apache NiFi captures a detailed record of events that include, but are not limited to, login attempts, configuration changes, and flow modifications. These logs are crucial for security analysis and forensic investigations, enabling administrators to detect anomalies, potential breaches, and unauthorized activities. It is through audit logs that security teams can reconstruct events after a security incident to understand the extent of a compromise and to develop strategies to prevent future occurrences.

To facilitate comprehensive audit logging, Apache NiFi provides several configurable parameters that determine the breadth and depth of the logs. These configurations allow the adjustment of log levels and the specification of events that should be logged. For instance, setting up audit logging to capture all failed login attempts can be instrumental in identifying brute-force attacks.

```
1  # Example of configuring logback for more detailed audit logs
2  <logger name="org.apache.nifi" level="INFO"/>
3  <logger name="org.apache.nifi.processors" level="WARN"/>
4  <logger name="org.apache.nifi.controllers" level="WARN"/>
5  <logger name="org.apache.nifi.logging.ComponentLog" level="DEBUG"/>
6  <logger name="org.apache.nifi.web.security" level="INFO"/>
7  <logger name="org.apache.nifi.web.api.config" level="INFO"/>
```

Audit logs should be stored securely and monitored regularly. Storing logs in a centralized log management solution can offer better protection and facilitate more effortless monitoring and analysis.

Next, we explore data provenance which provides granular details about data's lifecycle within NiFi. Data provenance tracks the origin of data, its movements, transformations, and every interaction with the data. This level of insight is critical for validating the integrity and security of the data flows.

Apache NiFi's provenance repository is a dedicated component that records and stores provenance events. These events can be accessed via the NiFi UI or programmatically through NiFi's APIs. For high-volume data flows, managing the size of the provenance repository becomes crucial to avoid performance degradation. NiFi allows for configurations that manage the data aging policy, storage location, and indexing strategies to optimize performance while ensuring critical provenance information is retained.

```
1  # Example configuration for the provenance repository
2  nifi.provenance.repository.implementation=org.apache.nifi.provenance.
       PersistentProvenanceRepository
3  nifi.provenance.repository.directory.default=/var/lib/nifi/provenance_repository
4  nifi.provenance.repository.max.storage.time=24 hours
5  nifi.provenance.repository.max.storage.size=100 GB
```

The security aspect of provenance data is of utmost importance, as it contains sensitive information about the data flows. Access to provenance information should be tightly controlled through NiFi's policies and access controls to ensure that only authorized users can view or manipulate this information.

Furthermore, integrating data provenance with audit logging offers a comprehensive view of the security posture of NiFi data flows. Pairing provenance data with audit logs enables organizations to trace malicious activities back to their source, understand the scope of data alterations, and implement stringent security measures to safeguard against future threats.

Combining the strengths of audit logging and data provenance forms a foundational element in the security framework of Apache NiFi. By maintaining vigilant monitoring and in-depth analysis of these records, organizations can significantly enhance their ability to detect, respond to, and prevent security incidents, ensuring the integrity, confidentiality, and availability of data within their NiFi environments.

7.8 Securing NiFi in Multi-tenant Environments

In multi-tenant environments, where resources are shared among various users or groups, ensuring the confidentiality, integrity, and availability of data flows becomes significantly challenging. Apache NiFi's robust security model provides several features to effectively manage and isolate data flows, ensuring that tenants can only access data and resources pertinent to their operational needs. This section will discuss the mechanisms and strategies implemented in Apache NiFi to secure data in multi-tenant environments, including tenant isolation, user authentication, authorization, and the management of sensitive properties.

The first step in securing NiFi in a multi-tenant setup is to ensure tenant isolation. This is achieved by segregating resources and data flows so that they are accessible only by authorized users or groups. Apache NiFi leverages user groups and policies to control access at a granular level. Administering precise user permissions ensures that tenants cannot access or modify data flows beyond their scope of authorization.

```
1  # Example of creating a user group with specific access policies
2  nifi.sh create-group --name "Data Engineering Team"
3  nifi.sh add-user-to-group --group-name "Data Engineering Team" --user "John Doe"
4  nifi.sh set-access-policies --resource "/dataflows/financial_reports" --action READ
     --group "Data Engineering Team"
```

The configuration of Secure Sockets Layer (SSL)/Transport Layer Security (TLS) for encrypted communication is paramount in multi-tenant architectures. This ensures that data in transit between the client and server is encrypted, safeguarding against interception or unauthorized access. Configuring SSL/TLS in NiFi involves generating or importing a keystore and truststore, followed by configuring NiFi properties to use these stores for secure communication.

```
# Example output indicating successful SSL/TLS configuration
Successfully configured SSL/TLS for Apache NiFi on port 9443
```

User authentication and authorization form the cornerstone of securing NiFi in multi-tenant environments. Apache NiFi supports various authentication mechanisms, including Lightweight Directory Access Protocol (LDAP), Kerberos, and OpenID Connect. These mechanisms ensure that only authenticated users can access the system. Once authenticated, NiFi's authorization model checks the user's permissions to perform actions on NiFi resources. This model is flexible, supporting role-based access control (RBAC) to easily define and manage user roles and permissions across different tenants.

```
1   # Configuration snippet for LDAP authentication
2   nifi.security.user.login.identity.provider=ldap-provider
3   nifi.security.user.ldap.url=ldaps://ldap.example.com:636
4   nifi.security.user.ldap.user.search.base=cn=users,dc=example,dc=com
5   nifi.security.user.ldap.user.search.filter=(sAMAccountName={0})
```

Sensitive properties and passwords within NiFi, especially in multi-tenant environments, must be adequately protected. NiFi offers a tool for encrypting sensitive property values in its configuration files, ensuring that they are not stored in plain text. This mechanism prevents unauthorized users from gaining access to sensitive information, such as database passwords or API keys.

```
# Output when encrypting a property
Property nifi.database.password encrypted successfully.
```

Another critical aspect of securing NiFi in multi-tenant environments is the management of access policies. NiFi's access policy framework enables administrators to define what actions users or groups can perform on specific resources, such as processor groups, controller services, or system operations. This granular control is vital for ensuring that tenants have the necessary access to perform their duties without infringing on the security or integrity of other tenants' data.

```
1   # Example of creating an access policy for a processor group
2   nifi.sh add-access-policy --resource "/processor-groups/472e6f70-016a-1000-ffff-
        ffff99d70524" --action WRITE --group "Data Science Team"
```

Securing NiFi in multi-tenant environments necessitates a comprehensive approach that encompasses authentication, authorization, encryption, and strict access controls. By employing these strategies, administrators can ensure that their NiFi instances are well-protected, providing a secure, multi-tenant environment that upholds the principles of data protection and privacy. Effective security in multi-tenant environments not only secures data but also fosters trust among tenants, encouraging collaboration and innovation while maintaining compliance with data protection regulations.

7.9 Integrating NiFi with External Security Systems

Integrating Apache NiFi with external security systems is an essential process for enhancing the security framework of NiFi deployments, especially in complex environments where multiple systems and services must interact securely. This integration not only bolsters NiFi's innate security features but also ensures a seamless and secure interoperation with other components of the organization's technological ecosystem. Focus here is afforded to the mechanisms and considerations pivotal for integrating NiFi with LDAP (Lightweight Directory Access Protocol) for authentication and authorization, Kerberos for secure authentication, and external SSL/TLS certificates for encrypted communication.

To begin with, integration with LDAP for authentication and authorization purposes is a critical step for organizations seeking to centralize their user management. Apache NiFi supports this integration through its pluggable authentication mechanism. Configure NiFi to communicate with an LDAP server by specifying the relevant connection details in the login-identity-providers.xml file. This requires specifying the LDAP server's address, communication port, and the user query parameters. LDAP groups can also be mapped to NiFi user groups, enabling fine-grained access control based on existing organizational roles. This approach simplifies user management and ensures that access policies in NiFi are always in alignment with broader organizational policies.

```
1  <provider>
2      <identifier>ldap-provider</identifier>
3      <class>org.apache.nifi.ldap.LdapProvider</class>
4      <property name="Authentication Strategy">SIMPLE</property>
5      <property name="Manager DN">cn=Manager,dc=example,dc=com</property>
6      <property name="Manager Password">password</property>
7      ...
8  </provider>
```

Integrating NiFi with Kerberos offers another dimension of security through stronger authentication mechanisms. Kerberos, a network authentication protocol, uses tickets to allow nodes communicating over a non-secure network to prove their identity to one another in a secure manner. Configuring NiFi to use Kerberos involves specifying the Kerberos Principal and the location of the keytab file that contains the principal's credentials. NiFi's krb5.conf file must also be configured to specify the locations of the Kerberos KDC (Key Distribution Center) and the domain realm. This setup ensures that each user or process accessing NiFi is authenticated through Kerberos, significantly enhancing the security posture against unauthorized access attempts.

```
1  nifi.kerberos.krb5.file=./conf/krb5.conf
2  nifi.kerberos.service.principal=nifi/service@EXAMPLE.COM
3  nifi.kerberos.service.keytab.location=/etc/security/keytabs/nifi.service.keytab
```

Moreover, integrating NiFi with external SSL/TLS certificates is imperative for ensuring encrypted communication, both internally among NiFi components and externally with clients and third-party services. The process involves generating or importing a trusted SSL certificate and configuring NiFi to use this certificate for its web servers and internal communication channels. The keystore and truststore configurations in NiFi's nifi.properties file play a key role in this process, storing the SSL certificates and keys securely.

```
1  nifi.security.keystore=./conf/keystore.jks
2  nifi.security.keystoreType=JKS
3  nifi.security.keystorePasswd=password
4  nifi.security.keyPasswd=password
5  nifi.security.truststore=./conf/truststore.jks
6  nifi.security.truststoreType=JKS
7  nifi.security.truststorePasswd=password
```

This integration ensures that sensitive information remains encrypted during transmission, protecting against interception by unauthorized parties. Furthermore, it facilitates secure connections with external systems, particularly when exchanging data over public networks or interfaces.

Integrating Apache NiFi with external security systems necessitates a careful approach to configuration and management. Such an integration leverages the strengths of established authentication, authorization, and encryption mechanisms, improving the security of data flows. It is imperative for organizations to regularly review and update their security configurations to align with evolving security standards and threat landscapes. Proper integration not only helps in securing the NiFi environment but also complements the overall security strategy of the organization.

7.10   Securing NiFi REST API and UI

In this section, we will discuss the critical measures required to secure the Apache NiFi REST API and the User Interface (UI). Given that both the API and UI provide access to the control and management of data flows, securing these endpoints is paramount to protect against unauthorized access and potential security breaches.

Authentication and Authorization: The foundational step in securing the NiFi REST API and UI is to implement robust authentication and authorization mechanisms. Apache NiFi supports various authentication methods, including Lightweight Directory Access Protocol (LDAP), Kerberos, and JSON Web Tokens (JWT). For instance, configuring NiFi to use LDAP for authentication involves specifying the LDAP provider in the `login-identity-providers.xml` file:

```
1  <provider>
2      <identifier>ldap-provider</identifier>
3      <class>org.apache.nifi.ldap.LdapProvider</class>
4      ...
5  </provider>
```

After authentication, authorization ensures that authenticated users have appropriate permissions. NiFi employs a policy-based authorization model, where access policies control the actions users can perform. Administering these policies effectively is crucial for restricting access to sensitive parts of the UI and API.

Securing the Connection with SSL/TLS: Encrypting data in transit between clients and NiFi's REST API/UI is essential for preventing interception and eavesdropping. Configuring NiFi to use SSL/TLS encryption involves generating or obtaining a valid SSL Certificate and configuring NiFi properties to use this certificate:

```
1  nifi.web.https.port=9443
2  nifi.security.keystore=./conf/keystore.jks
3  nifi.security.keystoreType=JKS
4  nifi.security.keystorePasswd=<keystore-password>
5  nifi.security.keyPasswd=<key-password>
6  nifi.security.truststore=./conf/truststore.jks
7  nifi.security.truststoreType=JKS
8  nifi.security.truststorePasswd=<truststore-password>
```

This configuration ensures that all data transmitted to and from the NiFi UI and REST API is encrypted, safeguarding it against unauthorized access during transit.

171

API Tokens for non-interactive Access: When external systems or scripts need to interact with the NiFi REST API, employing API tokens for authentication is a secure practice. NiFi can generate access tokens that authorize API requests. Using tokens eliminates the need for external systems to store user credentials, reducing the potential attack surface.

Configuring NiFi's Access Control Policies: Fine-grained access control policies enable administrators to define specific permissions for different user groups or applications interacting with the NiFi UI or REST API. These policies dictate what resources users can access and what operations they can perform, providing a comprehensive mechanism to limit exposure to sensitive data and operations.

Monitoring and Audit Logging: Continuous monitoring and audit logging are indispensable for detecting unauthorized access attempts and ensuring the effectiveness of the security configurations. NiFi's audit logs record all user activities, including logins, requests to the REST API, and changes to flow configurations. Regularly reviewing these logs can highlight security incidents and areas for improvement in the security posture of the NiFi environment.

Securing Apache NiFi's REST API and UI encompasses implementing stringent authentication and authorization measures, encrypting data in transit, managing API tokens securely, intricately configuring access control policies, and rigorous monitoring and logging. These practices form a comprehensive security strategy that protects NiFi installations from unauthorized access and potential data breaches, ensuring that the management and orchestration of data flows occur in a secure manner.

7.11 Common Security Pitfalls and How to Avoid Them

In this section we will discuss common security pitfalls encountered in Apache NiFi and strategies to mitigate them. Apache NiFi, while robust in its capabilities to manage data flows securely, is not immune to misconfigurations and oversights that can compromise the security of data. Recognizing and avoiding these pitfalls is essential for maintaining a secure data flow environment.

One common pitfall is the inadequate encryption of sensitive data, both at rest and in transit. To mitigate this risk, it is advisable to:

- Ensure that all data in motion is encrypted using SSL/TLS by configuring NiFi's web server and client components with valid certificates.

- Encrypt sensitive properties and passwords in the NiFi properties file using the encryption tool provided by NiFi.

Another significant concern is the improper management of user permissions and access controls. Preventing unauthorized access requires:

- Implementing strict authentication mechanisms. NiFi supports LDAP, Kerberos, and OIDC among others, which should be leveraged according to the security requirements of the organization.

- Defining clear access policies that specify who can access what data and operations within NiFi. Regular audits and reviews of these policies ensure that they remain effective and relevant.

Neglecting to monitor and audit system and user activities is also a pitfall. Continuous monitoring allows for the early detection of suspicious activities that could indicate a security breach. To enhance the security posture:

- Enable audit logging in NiFi to keep a record of all user actions and changes to the system. This includes accessing, modifying, or deleting data, as well as changes to policies and permissions.

- Regularly review audit logs and use automated tools, if possible, to analyze these logs for anomalies.

Leaving default configurations unchanged upon installation is a common oversight that can lead to security vulnerabilities. To address this issue:

- Change all default passwords and usernames immediately after installation.

- Review all default configurations and adjust them to align with security best practices and organizational policies.

A lack of regular updates and patches also presents a significant security risk. Apache NiFi is actively maintained and frequently updated to address security vulnerabilities and bugs. Therefore:

- Subscribe to Apache NiFi mailing lists or other channels to stay informed about new releases and security patches.

- Promptly apply updates and patches to NiFi components to protect against known vulnerabilities.

Lastly, failing to secure the NiFi REST API can expose the system to unauthorized access and control. To safeguard the API:

- Implement HTTPS for all communications with the NiFi REST API.

- Use access tokens or certificates for authentication and ensure that API endpoints are accessible only to authorized users.

While Apache NiFi provides comprehensive features for securing data flows, the effectiveness of these features depends on their proper configuration and management. By avoiding these common pitfalls through diligent practices and regular system reviews, organizations can significantly enhance the security of their data flows within NiFi environments.

7.12   Security Best Practices for Apache NiFi Deployment

In this section, we will discuss the best practices for securing Apache NiFi deployments. Implementing these practices is essential for enhancing the security posture of data flows and ensuring that sensitive information is protected against unauthorized access and potential threats. While NiFi provides robust mechanisms for data protection, the effectiveness of these features relies on their proper configuration and usage.

Use HTTPS for Web Interfaces: One of the foundational steps in securing Apache NiFi is to configure all web interfaces to use HTTPS. This practice ensures that data transmitted between clients and the NiFi server is encrypted, protecting it from eavesdropping and man-in-the-middle attacks.

```
1   # Example of configuring HTTPS in nifi.properties
2   nifi.web.https.host=<hostname>
3   nifi.web.https.port=9443
4   nifi.security.keystore=./conf/keystore.jks
5   nifi.security.keystoreType=JKS
6   nifi.security.keystorePasswd=<keystore_password>
7   nifi.security.keyPasswd=<key_password>
8   nifi.security.truststore=./conf/truststore.jks
9   nifi.security.truststoreType=JKS
10  nifi.security.truststorePasswd=<truststore_password>
```

Enforce Strong Authentication and Authorization: It is crucial to employ strong authentication mechanisms to verify the identity of users accessing the NiFi environment. Integrating with external identity providers such as LDAP or Kerberos can provide more robust authentication schemes than NiFi's built-in mechanisms. Additionally, configuring authorization policies to grant or deny permissions based on users' roles ensures that only authorized individuals can access or modify sensitive data flows.

- Implement multi-factor authentication (MFA) where possible to add an extra layer of security.

- Use access policies to restrict users' abilities to read, write, or modify data flows based on their roles.

Encrypt Sensitive Properties and Passwords: Apache NiFi supports encryption of sensitive configuration parameters, including passwords used in processors and services. Utilizing the NiFi EncryptConfig tool helps in encrypting these properties, enhancing the security of sensitive information stored in configuration files.

```
1   # Example usage of the NiFi EncryptConfig tool
2   ./nifi-toolkit-<version>/bin/encrypt-config.sh \
3      -n <nifi_properties_file_path> \
4      -s <encryption_key>
```

Segment Data Flows with Process Groups: Leveraging process groups to segment data flows can limit the blast radius of any security incident by isolating different segments of the data flow. This practice enables more granular access control and facilitates the management of permissions for groups of data flows, enhancing overall security.

Monitor and Audit Access Logs: Regular monitoring of audit logs is vital for detecting unauthorized access or abnormal activities within the NiFi environment. NiFi provides extensive auditing capabilities, logging every action taken in the system. Analysts should review these logs periodically to identify potential security incidents or breaches.

```
# Example log entry for unauthorized access attempt
2023-03-15 10:31:45,789 INFO [NiFi Web Server-23]
o.a.n.w.a.c.IllegalStateExceptionMapper
Attempted access to resource /nifi-api/processors/abcd1234/edit
for which user does not have access
```

Keep NiFi and Related Components Up to Date: Software vulnerabilities are a significant risk for any system. Regularly updating NiFi and its related components to the latest versions ensure that known security vulnerabilities are patched. It is essential to apply these updates in a timely manner to mitigate the risks associated with software flaws.

Employ Network Segmentation and Firewalls: Positioning NiFi instances within demilitarized zones (DMZs) and using firewalls to control traffic can prevent unauthorized access from external networks. Implementing network segmentation not only strengthens the security perimeter but also minimizes the potential impact of network-based attacks.

Implementing these security best practices requires careful planning and continuous effort. Organizations should perform regular security audits and assessments to ensure that these practices are correctly implemented and remain effective over time. By adhering to these guidelines, organizations can significantly enhance the security of their Apache NiFi deployments, protecting sensitive data and maintaining the trust of their stakeholders.

Chapter 8

Monitoring, Logging, and Troubleshooting NiFi

Effective monitoring, logging, and troubleshooting practices are crucial for maintaining the health and performance of Apache NiFi data flows. This chapter explores the tools and techniques available within NiFi for observing system behavior, diagnosing issues, and ensuring operational stability. It covers the configuration of logging levels, the use of NiFi's built-in reporting tasks, and strategies for monitoring data flow performance and system health. Additionally, the chapter provides guidance on troubleshooting common problems, enabling users to rapidly identify and resolve issues to minimize downtime and maintain continuous data processing.

8.1   Overview of NiFi Monitoring Capabilities

Apache NiFi's architecture is designed with robust monitoring capabilities to ensure that data flows operate efficiently and reliably. Monitoring in NiFi encompasses a wide range of functionalities that provide visibility into the system's performance, health, and activity. These capabilities are integral for administrators and users to not only observe but also manage the behavior of data flows and the NiFi environment itself.

At the core of NiFi's monitoring capabilities is the Status History, which collects and displays metrics about the system and its components over time. This includes metrics on flow file processing, system health, and performance statistics. The Status History is accessible via the NiFi UI, offering a graphical representation of these metrics at both the processor and process group levels. This immediate visual feedback is critical for diagnosing performance bottlenecks and optimizing the data flow design.

NiFi also features a customizable logging framework that allows for detailed examination of operational events. The logging system is based on the Logback library, providing extensive configuration options to adjust the verbosity and format of log entries. Users can modify logging levels on the fly via the NiFi UI or by directly editing the logback.xml file, tailoring the log output to suit specific monitoring requirements.

Another key aspect of NiFi's monitoring capabilities is the integration of Provenance Data. Provenance tracking records a comprehensive history of each data flow, capturing details such as file origin, transformations applied, and final destination. This historical data is invaluable for audit purposes and for tracking down the root cause of issues within the data flow.

NiFi's built-in Reporting Tasks provide a means to regularly report on various system metrics and statuses. These tasks can be configured to run at specified intervals, generating reports that can be forwarded to external systems for further analysis or alerting. Common reporting tasks include the MonitorMemory, BulletinReportingTask, and Site-ToSiteStatusReportingTask, each serving different monitoring objectives from tracking memory usage to reporting operational bulletins and flow status.

To complement these built-in capabilities, NiFi offers Support for External Monitoring Tools through its Site-to-Site protocol and REST API. These interfaces allow third-party monitoring solutions to collect NiFi metrics, thereby enabling more comprehensive system health monitoring and performance analysis alongside other components within a larger data infrastructure.

In practice, effective monitoring in NiFi requires a combination of leveraging its built-in tools and integrating with external monitoring solutions. Administrators should configure NiFi's logging and reporting tasks to provide the necessary insights suited to their operational requirements. Meanwhile, regular reviews of Provenance data and

Status History are essential for maintaining a high-performance and reliable data flow environment.

Apache NiFi's monitoring capabilities are extensive, designed to provide administrators and developers with the necessary tools to ensure operational stability and efficiency. By effectively utilizing these tools, users can maintain high levels of visibility into NiFi's performance and health, enabling proactive management and optimization of data flows.

8.2   Configuring and Reading NiFi Logs

Configuring and reading logs in Apache NiFi is a critical aspect of monitoring and troubleshooting data flows. NiFi utilizes logback for logging, which allows for highly customizable logging configurations. This section will discuss the steps to configure logging levels in NiFi, understand the structure of NiFi logs, and interpret common log messages for efficient troubleshooting.

To modify the logging levels in NiFi, users must edit the `logback.xml` file located in the `conf` directory of the NiFi installation. This XML file defines the logging behavior, including the levels of logging for different components of the application. The primary logging levels used in NiFi, ordered from the least to the most verbose, are ERROR, WARN, INFO, DEBUG, and TRACE. By adjusting the logging level, users can control the verbosity of the logs generated by NiFi, enabling more detailed logging when troubleshooting and less verbose logging during normal operation.

```
1   <logger name="org.apache.nifi" level="INFO"/>
```

The above line from `logback.xml` sets the logging level for all classes in the `org.apache.nifi` package to INFO. To change the logging level, replace "INFO" with the desired level.

NiFi logs are stored in the `logs` directory, with `nifi-app.log` being the primary log file that contains most of the operational logging. This log file includes information about the system's status, processor-specific messages, and errors or warnings. Reading and interpreting these logs is key to understanding NiFi's behavior and diagnosing issues.

179

The structure of a log message in `nifi-app.log` typically includes a timestamp, logging level, thread, class raising the log, and the message itself. For instance:

```
2023-01-01 12:34:56,789 INFO [Timer-Driven Process Thread-1] o.a.n.c.s.
TimerDrivenSchedulingAgent Runnable component Processor[id=12345]
successfully completed and will be registered to run again in 10000 milliseconds
```

This log entry indicates that a processor with the ID 12345 has successfully completed its operation and will be executed again after 10000 milliseconds. The message includes the exact time of the log, the logging level (INFO), and the thread that generated the log message.

Common issues, such as processor failures or flow configuration errors, are often logged with the WARN or ERROR levels, making them more visible for troubleshooting. For example:

```
2023-01-02 13:14:15,678 ERROR [Timer-Driven Process Thread-2] o.a.n.p.m.MergeContent
MergeContent[id=67890]
failed to process session due to org.apache.nifi.processor.exception.ProcessException:
 Unable to merge content;
rolling back session: org.apache.nifi.processor.exception.ProcessException: Unable to
 merge content
```

This log message indicates a failure in the MergeContent processor due to an inability to merge content, highlighting the importance of reviewing ERROR logs for quick identification of issues.

When troubleshooting with NiFi logs, it is advisable to start with the ERROR and WARN logs to identify any evident problems. If the issue is not clear, increasing the logging level to DEBUG or TRACE for the relevant components can provide more detailed information to diagnose the problem.

In summary, configuring and reading NiFi logs are pivotal for monitoring the health and performance of NiFi data flows. By understanding how to adjust logging levels and interpret the logs, users can efficiently troubleshoot and resolve issues, ensuring the stability and reliability of their data processing pipelines.

8.3 Monitoring NiFi Performance and Health

Monitoring Apache NiFi's performance and health is a critical aspect of managing data flow operations efficiently. It entails observing various system metrics to ensure that the data processing environment is operating within its optimal parameters. This vigilance helps in preempting potential issues that could lead to system downtimes or performance bottlenecks.

Apache NiFi provides a comprehensive set of tools and features designed to facilitate effective monitoring of both its performance and health status. The NiFi user interface (UI) is a primary tool for real-time monitoring. It displays key metrics including flow file counts, data sizes in queues, component status, and system diagnostics. For a more granular level of monitoring, NiFi also exposes these metrics through REST APIs, allowing for the integration with external monitoring tools such as Grafana or Prometheus.

System Diagnostics in the NiFi UI is a crucial monitoring tool that offers deep insights into the JVM's memory usage, processor load, and overall system health. It provides a snapshot of the resources available to NiFi and how they are being utilized. Regularly checking system diagnostics can help in identifying memory leaks, excessive processor load, or other anomalies that may impede NiFi performance.

Another important feature for monitoring NiFi's performance and health is the Status History. This feature tracks the historical values of specific metrics over time, providing a graphical representation of these metrics through the NiFi UI. By observing trends in these graphs, operators can identify patterns that may indicate performance issues or bottlenecks. For example, a steady increase in flow file queue length might suggest a need for optimizing processors or connections in the flow.

To complement the UI-based tools, NiFi integrates with external monitoring systems via its Reporting Tasks. The MonitorMemory and BulletinReportingTask are just a few examples of built-in tasks that can be configured to periodically check the health and performance of NiFi. These tasks can be set to trigger alerts or perform specific actions when certain thresholds are met, providing an automated layer of monitoring that can aid in proactive system management.

For advanced monitoring needs, custom scripts can also be employed. These scripts can leverage NiFi's APIs to fetch metrics and analyze them according to customized business logic. Such scripts can be scheduled externally or executed within NiFi using the ExecuteScript processor, enabling a high degree of flexibility in monitoring strategies.

It is also important to monitor the content repository and the FlowFile repository's disk space usage. NiFi provides warnings and automatically pauses dataflows if the disk usage goes beyond configurable thresholds. This mechanism ensures that NiFi does not exhaust disk space, which could lead to data loss or severe system failures.

Below is an example of using NiFi's REST API with a simple `curl` command to fetch the status of a processor:

```
1   curl -X GET http://nifi.example.com:8080/nifi-api/processors/{processor-id}/status
```

This command returns JSON data that includes various metrics about the processor, such as bytes read and written, the number of tasks that have completed, and the average runtime of the tasks.

```
{
  "processorStatus": {
    "id": "12345678-1234-1234-1234-123456789abc",
    "name": "MyProcessor",
    "bytesRead": 0,
    "bytesWritten": 0,
    "runStatus": "Running",
    ...
  }
}
```

Maintaining an effective monitoring regime for Apache NiFi involves a mix of using built-in tools, configuring reporting tasks, and leveraging external monitoring systems. By staying vigilant and responsive to the insights provided by these tools, NiFi administrators can ensure that their data pipelines remain performant, resilient, and healthy.

To conclude, monitoring the performance and health of Apache NiFi is an essential practice that encompasses a comprehensive approach combining real-time metrics observation, historical data analysis, and automated alerting systems. Doing so not only safeguards against potential issues but also ensures that NiFi operates at its highest efficiency, contributing to the overall success of data flow management in organizations.

8.4   Utilizing NiFi's Built-in Reporting Tasks

Apache NiFi offers a suite of built-in reporting tasks designed to provide insights into the NiFi environment, making monitoring an integral component of system maintenance and optimization. These reporting tasks can be configured to gather, aggregate, and present data concerning various aspects of NiFi's operation, such as system health, data flow performance, and processor statistics. This section will discuss the configuration and deployment of NiFi's reporting tasks, highlighting their features and explaining how they contribute to effective system monitoring and troubleshooting.

NiFi includes several reporting tasks out-of-the-box, among them the `BulletinReportingTask`, `LogStatusMetrics`, `MonitorDiskUsage`, and `SiteToSiteStatusReportingTask`. Each of these tasks serves a unique purpose and can be configured according to specific monitoring requirements.

To configure a reporting task in NiFi, navigate to the Controller Settings in the NiFi UI. Under the Reporting Tasks tab, an operator can add a new reporting task by selecting the desired type from a dropdown menu. Once added, the task's properties and scheduling period can be configured. It is essential to adjust these settings to balance the granularity of the reported data with the overhead introduced to the system.

- `BulletinReportingTask` captures bulletin board messages generated by NiFi. These messages include warnings and errors raised by processors and controllers, providing a centralized log for identifying issues or unexpected behavior. Configuring this task to report to an external monitoring system can aid in proactive incident response.

- `LogStatusMetrics` collects metrics about the status and performance of NiFi components. This task can log processor and connection metrics, such as flowfile counts, sizes, and processing times, aiding in identifying bottlenecks or underperforming elements within the data flow.

- `MonitorDiskUsage` tracks the disk space usage of the content repository, flowfile repository, and provenance repository. Given that high disk usage can lead to NiFi performance degradation, configuring this reporting task is crucial for maintaining optimal system operation.

- `SiteToSiteStatusReportingTask` facilitates the remote monitoring of NiFi's status through site-to-site communications. This enables the consolidation of monitoring data from multiple NiFi instances, useful in clustered environments or when managing multiple standalone instances.

183

Additionally, the flexibility of these tasks allows for their customization and extension. Developers can create custom reporting tasks to address specific monitoring requirements by implementing the `ReportingTask` interface. Configuration options such as the reporting frequency, thresholds for alerts, and data destinations are customizable to suit different operational environments.

The effective use of reporting tasks in NiFi provides a comprehensive view of system health and performance, facilitating the early detection of potential issues and simplifying the troubleshooting process. By leveraging these built-in tasks, operators can ensure that their NiFi instance runs efficiently, maintaining the flow of data across their organization.

However, it is essential to note that while reporting tasks offer significant insights, they also introduce a certain level of overhead. Therefore, operators should carefully consider the balance between the depth of monitoring required and the performance impact. As best practice, start with broader, less frequent reporting and refine as necessary based on observation and requirement changes.

NiFi's built-in reporting tasks are vital tools in the arsenal of any data flow manager. They enable detailed monitoring and timely reporting on the health and performance of NiFi instances, ensuring that data pipelines are optimized and maintained effectively. Through careful configuration and strategic deployment of these tasks, operators can achieve high levels of system visibility and operational stability.

8.5   Custom Monitoring and Alerting with NiFi

For effective data pipeline management in Apache NiFi, it is essential to implement custom monitoring and alerting mechanisms that cater to the specific needs of an application or system. While NiFi provides a comprehensive set of tools and features for monitoring and logging, there might be scenarios where the built-in functionalities do not meet all the operational requirements. In such cases, developing custom solutions becomes imperative. This section will discuss the strategies and techniques for setting up custom monitoring and alerting in NiFi to ensure that data flows perform optimally and any anomalies or errors are promptly addressed.

One approach to implementing custom monitoring is to utilize NiFi's Site-to-Site Reporting Task. This feature allows transferring NiFi metrics to another NiFi instance or an external system for analysis. Metrics can include processor performance, flowfile counts, system health, and other relevant data. By sending these metrics to a centralized monitoring system, such as Elasticsearch, InfluxDB, or a custom database, users can aggregate, visualize, and analyze the data in real-time. This enables the identification of trends, potential bottlenecks, and areas for optimization.

For alerting, one effective method is to leverage NiFi's ExecuteScript processor. This processor can run custom scripts written in languages such as Groovy, Python, or JavaScript. The script can analyze specific metrics or logs and trigger alerts based on predefined criteria. For example, an alert can be sent if the processing time of a flow exceeds a certain threshold or if the error count in a processor spikes unexpectedly.

```python
# Example Python script for triggering an alert
import requests

# Placeholder function to fetch metrics from NiFi
def get_processor_status(processor_id):
    # Functionality to obtain the processor status
    return {"errors": 0, "processingTime": 100}

processor_status = get_processor_status("processor-id-example")

if processor_status["errors"] > 10:
    # Send alert
    requests.post("http://alert-system.example.com", json={"message": "Error count
        exceeded threshold"})
elif processor_status["processingTime"] > 2000:
    # Send alert
    requests.post("http://alert-system.example.com", json={"message": "Processing
        time exceeded threshold"})
```

Furthermore, NiFi's REST API provides a flexible and powerful way to monitor the state and performance of NiFi programmatically. Custom monitoring tools can be developed to call the API periodically, retrieve metrics, and evaluate the health of the system. These tools can then generate alerts or reports based on the data obtained.

Integration with external monitoring and alerting systems such as Prometheus and Grafana is also a viable strategy for achieving comprehensive observability. Prometheus can scrape metrics exposed by NiFi, store them efficiently, and provide real-time alerting capabilities based on the collected data. Grafana can be used in conjunction with

185

Prometheus for creating dashboards that visualize the metrics, offering a holistic view of the data flow performance and system health.

```
Example of Prometheus Alert Rule:

ALERT NiFiHighProcessingTime
  IF avg_over_time(processor_processing_time_ms[5m]) > 2000
  FOR 1m
  LABELS { severity="critical" }
  ANNOTATIONS {
    summary="High processing time detected in NiFi",
    description="The average processing time for a processor exceeds 2000ms over
      the last 5 minutes.",
  }
```

In addition to these techniques, custom Log Appenders can be implemented in NiFi. By extending the capabilities of the logging framework (such as Logback), it's possible to intercept log messages and perform actions such as sending an email alert, posting a message to a messaging system like Slack or Kafka, or writing critical logs to a separate file or database for further analysis.

While Apache NiFi offers robust monitoring and logging capabilities out-of-the-box, the adoption of custom monitoring and alerting mechanisms can enhance operational visibility and responsiveness. By utilizing NiFi's extensible architecture and integrating with external systems, users can tailor the monitoring solution to fit their specific requirements, ensuring that data pipelines remain healthy, performant, and reliable.

8.6   Understanding and Managing Backpressure

Backpressure in Apache NiFi refers to a mechanism used to prevent data overload in systems by controlling the flow of data between processors. It is a critical concept for maintaining the stability and performance of NiFi dataflows. Backpressure works by pausing the data flow when certain conditions are met, such as when the queue reaches a specified size or when the data processing rate decreases. This section will delve into the principles of backpressure, its configuration, and best practices for managing it effectively.

Backpressure settings are configurable on a per-connection basis within NiFi. Each connection in a dataflow can have its backpressure properties set independently, allowing for granular control over how data moves through the system. The settings include:

- Backpressure Object Threshold: Specifies the maximum number of FlowFiles allowed in a queue before backpressure is applied.

- Backpressure Data Size Threshold: Defines the maximum total size of all FlowFiles in a queue before applying backpressure.

Configuring these thresholds requires understanding the specific needs of your dataflow and the limitations of your environment. For instance, if a queue is connected to a processor that handles large files, setting a lower threshold for the Backpressure Data Size Threshold would be prudent to avoid memory issues.

To configure backpressure in NiFi, navigate to the settings of the connection you wish to modify. Inside the settings panel, you will find the backpressure settings under the 'Scheduling' tab. Here, you can adjust the Object and Data Size Thresholds according to your requirements.

```
1  <property name="Backpressure Object Threshold">10000</property>
2  <property name="Backpressure Data Size Threshold">1 GB</property>
```

The application of backpressure can significantly impact the performance and reliability of a NiFi dataflow. Effective management of backpressure ensures that no single component becomes overwhelmed with data, which could lead to processing delays or even system failure. For example, when backpressure is triggered, upstream processors will pause until the queue size decreases below the specified threshold, ensuring that downstream processors have enough time and resources to process the data efficiently.

It is also important to monitor the behavior of connections under backpressure. NiFi provides several metrics and reporting tasks that can help identify when and where backpressure is being applied. This monitoring is crucial for detecting potential bottlenecks in your dataflow and making necessary adjustments to the configuration.

One of the best practices in managing backpressure is to balance the load across the NiFi cluster. This can be achieved by distributing data evenly among nodes and ensuring that all resources are utilized optimally. Additionally, consider using NiFi's prioritization queues to control which FlowFiles are processed first when backpressure is

187

applied. This feature enables you to prioritize time-sensitive data, ensuring critical information is processed without unnecessary delays.

Understanding and managing backpressure is essential for maintaining the health and performance of NiFi dataflows. By carefully configuring backpressure settings and monitoring their effects, you can ensure that your dataflows run smoothly, even under high load conditions. Regularly revisiting these configurations and adapting them as your dataflow evolves will help in preventing processing bottlenecks and achieving optimal data processing performance.

8.7   Diagnosing Common Issues in NiFi Flows

Diagnosing common issues in Apache NiFi flows is pivotal for ensuring the stability and efficiency of data pipelines. This section will discuss strategies for identifying and resolving frequently encountered problems, including flow file backlogs, processor misconfigurations, and connectivity issues.

The first step in diagnosing issues within NiFi flows is to leverage the NiFi user interface (UI). The UI provides a comprehensive overview of the data flow, including the status of processors, queues, and connections. By observing the color coding and the status icons, operators can quickly identify components that are not functioning as expected. For instance, a processor colored in red indicates stopped or invalid status, which may be due to misconfiguration or other errors.

```
1   // Example of accessing processor status via NiFi REST API
2   curl http://nifi-host:8080/nifi-api/processors/{processor-id}
```

Flow file backlogs often occur when processors cannot handle incoming data as fast as it is received or when downstream processors are slower than upstream ones. This can be visually identified in the NiFi UI by looking for queues with a deep build-up of flow files. Utilization of the ListQueue and QueueList APIs can provide insights into the queue contents and help in understanding why flow files are not being processed.

```
Queue Identifier: 12345
Queue Size: 10000 FlowFiles
Queue Byte Size: 10GB
```

Another common issue arises from processor misconfigurations. For example, a processor may be configured with incorrect property values

188

leading to its failure to operate correctly. Operators should review processor properties in the NiFi UI or by extracting the processor configuration via NiFi's REST API. It is crucial to verify that all configurations, including file paths, API keys, and connection strings, are accurate and that the processor is compatible with the data formats it is intended to process.

Connectivity issues between NiFi and external systems (databases, APIs, remote file systems) are also prevalent. These can be diagnosed by reviewing the logs for errors related to connection timeouts, refused connections, or authentication failures. NiFi's robust logging framework allows adjusting the granularity of log messages per component, enabling detailed tracing of actions performed by processors and services.

```
1   // Changing the log level of a processor to DEBUG via NiFi REST API
2   curl -i -X PUT -H 'Content-Type: application/json' -d '{
3     "revision": {
4       "clientId": "your-client-id",
5       "version": 0
6     },
7     "component": {
8       "id": "processor-id",
9       "config": {
10        "schedulingPeriod": "10 sec",
11        "logLevel": "DEBUG"
12      }
13    }
14  }' http://nifi-host:8080/nifi-api/processors/processor-id
```

Backpressure and flow control mechanisms within NiFi ensure that systems do not become overwhelmed by excessive data volumes. However, misconfigured backpressure settings can lead to unnecessary delays in data processing. These settings should be reviewed and adjusted according to the specific requirements of the data flow and the capacities of the underlying systems.

To assist with diagnosing issues, NiFi generates bulletins for warning and error events which are accessible through the NiFi UI and REST API. Regular monitoring of these bulletins can provide early indications of issues before they escalate into significant problems.

189

NiFi Bulletin Board

Diagnosing common issues in NiFi flows involves a combination of utilizing the NiFi UI, examining processor configurations, monitoring flow file queues, troubleshooting connectivity issues, and adjusting logging levels and backpressure settings. By following these strategies, operators can quickly identify and resolve problems, ensuring the smooth operation of their data pipelines.

8.8   Troubleshooting Processor Failures

Troubleshooting processor failures in Apache NiFi involves a systematic approach to identify, diagnose, and resolve issues affecting the normal operation of processors. Processor failures can manifest in various forms, including but not limited to processing delays, data loss, or unexpected behavior in data flow. This section will discuss methods to effectively troubleshoot such failures, leveraging NiFi's instrumentation and logging capabilities to pinpoint and rectify the underlying problems.

First, it is critical to ensure that you have configured NiFi's logging appropriately to capture detailed information about processor activities and errors. The `logback.xml` file in NiFi's conf directory allows adjusting the logging level for individual processors or specific components of the system. Setting the logging level to DEBUG or TRACE for a processor that is failing can provide in-depth insights into the operations leading up to the failure. However, be cautious with these verbose logging levels in a production environment, as they can generate large volumes of log data and potentially impact system performance.

```
1   <logger name="org.apache.nifi.processors" level="DEBUG"/>
```

Upon encountering a processor failure, reviewing the NiFi app log files is the next step. These files are located in the `logs` directory within NiFi's installation folder. Specifically, the `nifi-app.log` file contains valuable information about processor execution, errors, and other runtime events. Look for exceptions or error messages that correspond to the time the processor failed. Analyzing these messages can often provide clues to the root cause of the failure.

```
2023-07-21 10:45:32,456 ERROR [Timer-Driven Process Thread-10]
o.a.n.p.standard.ExecuteSQL ExecuteSQL[id=15f4a6c5-0177-1000-ffff-ffffc0a812d5]
failed to process session due to org.apache.nifi.processor.exception.ProcessException:
java.sql.SQLException: Connection is not available; Processor Administratively
Yielded for 1 sec: {}
```

When analyzing logs, it is beneficial to correlate processor failures with specific events or conditions in the data flow. Factors to consider include sudden spikes in data volumes, changes in data format, or alterations to the flow configuration. These changes might introduce issues that a processor cannot handle without further configuration tweaks or bug fixes.

For processors that interact with external systems, such as databases or APIs, ensure that connectivity and permissions are correctly configured. Failures in these processors might not be due to issues within NiFi but rather external system availability or network connectivity problems. Tools such as telnet or ping can verify network connectivity, while external system logs can provide insights into authentication or authorization issues.

```
1  telnet example.com 3306
```

In situations where the root cause of a processor failure is not immediately apparent, consider isolating the processor in a separate data flow. This approach enables you to test the processor with sample data or simplified configurations, eliminating other variables that might obscure the root cause. Through trial and error with different configurations and inputs, you can often identify the precise conditions leading to failure.

- Validate input data formats and ensure they match processor expectations.

- Experiment with configuration settings to determine if they influence processor behavior.

191

- Monitor system resources during processor execution to identify potential bottlenecks or resource constraints.

Resolving processor failures may sometimes require updating to the latest version of NiFi or a specific processor, as bugs are continually being identified and fixed. The NiFi community is an invaluable resource for troubleshooting complex issues. Engaging with community forums or mailing lists can provide access to a wealth of knowledge from other users who may have encountered and resolved similar problems.

Troubleshooting processor failures in NiFi is a methodical process that leans heavily on detailed logging, system monitoring, and a clear understanding of the processor's function within the data flow. By combining these approaches, NiFi users can effectively diagnose and resolve processor failures, ensuring the stability and reliability of their data flows.

8.9   Recovering from Data Flow Interruptions

Recovering from interruptions in data flow is a critical aspect of managing Apache NiFi instances and ensuring the resilience and reliability of data processing activities. Data flow interruptions can arise from a variety of sources, including hardware failures, network issues, software bugs, or configuration errors. Efficient recovery strategies are paramount to minimize downtime and prevent data loss. This section will discuss recovery mechanisms within Apache NiFi, including the use of NiFi's data provenance and replay features, flow versioning, and external monitoring tools.

NiFi provides a robust data provenance tool that allows administrators and data engineers to track data through the system. Data provenance records every event related to data flow processing, including sending, receiving, transforming, and routing of flow files. In the event of a data flow interruption, these provenance records can be invaluable in diagnosing issues and determining the point at which the data flow was disrupted.

```
1  // Example of querying data provenance via NiFi REST API
2  curl -X GET http://nifi-host:8080/nifi-api/provenance/query
```

Once the point of interruption is identified, NiFi's replay feature can be used to resume data flow from the point of failure. This is particularly effective for transient errors or issues that can be quickly resolved. By replaying flow files from the failure point, data engineers can ensure minimal data loss and quickly restore normal operations.

```
1  // Example command to replay a flow file in NiFi
2  curl -X POST http://nifi-host:8080/nifi-api/provenance-events/{event-id}/replay
```

In addition to data provenance and replay, maintaining version-controlled flow configurations using NiFi's flow versioning capabilities is crucial for recovery. In scenarios where data flow interruptions are caused by configuration errors, the ability to revert to a previous, stable flow version allows for rapid restoration.

```
Flow versioning in NiFi supports rollback to previous stable versions,
ensuring quick recovery from configuration errors.
```

Beyond NiFi's built-in features, external monitoring tools play a vital role in recognizing and recovering from data flow interruptions. Monitoring tools can be configured to alert administrators to anomalies, such as sudden drops in data throughput or unresponsive processors. These alerts can trigger investigations into system health, potentially identifying interruptions before significant data loss occurs.

Implementing custom monitoring and alerting solutions may involve the following steps:

- Configuring NiFi's reporting tasks to send metrics to external systems.

- Using NiFi's REST API to programmatically monitor system and processor health.

- Integrating with third-party monitoring solutions for comprehensive oversight.

Proactive monitoring, combined with NiFi's features for data provenance, replay, and flow versioning, equips administrators with the tools necessary for rapid recovery from data flow interruptions. Ensuring data pipelines are resilient to failures not only minimizes downtime but also protects the integrity of the data being processed. By following best practices in recovery and employing robust monitoring solutions, NiFi users can maintain high reliability and performance of their data flows.

```
Alerting on critical performance metrics ensures that administrators
can rapidly respond to and recover from data flow interruptions.
```

Recovering from data flow interruptions in Apache NiFi involves leveraging built-in features such as data provenance, replay, and flow versioning, alongside external monitoring and alerting tools. By implementing these strategies, data flow interruptions can be quickly resolved, ensuring continuous and reliable data processing.

8.10   Performance Tuning for NiFi

Performance tuning in Apache NiFi is a critical process for enhancing the efficiency and throughput of data pipelines. This section will discuss the methodologies and settings that can be optimized to improve the performance of NiFi instances. It is important to approach performance tuning with a clear understanding of the goals and the current bottlenecks. Typically, performance tuning in NiFi involves adjusting the configurations related to threaded execution, content repository, and flowfile repository, among others.

To begin with, NiFi's concurrent processing capabilities allow for the parallel execution of tasks. The Concurrent Tasks setting on each processor can be adjusted to increase parallelism. However, it's crucial to balance this with the available system resources. Assigning too many concurrent tasks can lead to excessive context switching and degrade overall performance. The optimal settings vary depending on the nature of the tasks and the hardware characteristics. Monitoring system metrics such as CPU and memory usage can guide adjustments to this parameter.

Another aspect to consider is the Queue Prioritization. NiFi allows for the prioritization of flowfiles in queues. Properly configuring queue prioritization can ensure that more critical data is processed first, improving the responsiveness and performance of data flow for time-sensitive information.

The Back Pressure settings are directly related to NiFi's stability and performance. They define when NiFi starts to apply back pressure, slowing down or stopping incoming data to prevent system overload. Adjusting back pressure settings can help manage resource utilization more effectively by avoiding excessive memory use or disk I/O. This can be particularly useful in scenarios where data arrival rates are highly variable.

Customizing the Content Repository configuration is another strategy for optimizing performance. The content repository stores the actual content of the flowfiles being processed. Configuring it to use a high-performance disk or SSD can significantly reduce I/O bottlenecks. Additionally, considering the use of multiple content repository partitions across different physical disks can enhance throughput by distributing I/O operations.

Similarly, adjustments to the `FlowFile Repository` can yield performance improvements. The flowfile repository tracks the state and attributes of flowfiles within the system. Optimizing its storage configuration, including leveraging faster disks or adjusting the storage directory configuration, can reduce the latency involved in state lookup and manipulation operations.

For systems dealing with high throughput or large data sets, configuring the `Provenance Repository` is key. The provenance repository records data lineage information, which can grow rapidly. Managing its retention policy and storage strategy can help maintain a balance between operational transparency and performance.

In addition to these configuration adjustments, employing `Data Compression` techniques can significantly reduce the network and storage overhead, especially when transferring large volumes of data across the network or storing data for extended periods. Compression can be applied at various points in the data flow, including prior to long-term storage or transmission to another system.

Let's consider an example involving adjustment of concurrent tasks. In a scenario where a processor is observed to underutilize CPU resources, increasing its Concurrent Tasks setting might be beneficial:

```
1  Processor: FetchS3Object
2  Concurrent Tasks (before): 1
3  Concurrent Tasks (after): 4
```

Following this adjustment, monitoring the system's CPU and memory utilization is essential to ensure that the change does not lead to resource contention.

In summary, performance tuning in NiFi is an iterative and context-dependent process. It requires a thorough understanding of both the data flow characteristics and the underlying system infrastructure. By strategically adjusting configurations related to concurrency, prioritization, back pressure, and repository settings, one can significantly enhance the efficiency and responsiveness of NiFi data pipelines. Constant monitoring and analysis of performance metrics are vital in identifying bottlenecks and validating the effectiveness of the tuning efforts.

8.11   Using the NiFi Bulletin Board for System Messages

Apache NiFi's Bulletin Board is a key component for monitoring system messages and diagnosing issues within data flows. It serves as a centralized repository for warnings, alerts, and system notifications, making it an invaluable resource for administrators and data flow managers. This section will discuss the Bulletin Board's functionality, its integration within NiFi's user interface, and how to effectively utilize it for system monitoring and troubleshooting.

The Bulletin Board collects and displays messages from various components across the NiFi ecosystem. These messages can range from info-level notifications about process completions to error messages related to processor malfunctions or connectivity issues. Understanding the types of messages displayed and knowing how to filter and search through them are fundamental skills for efficiently managing NiFi instances.

Firstly, accessing the Bulletin Board is straightforward from the NiFi user interface. It is prominently located and can be accessed directly from the top navigation bar. Upon navigating to the Bulletin Board, users are presented with a chronological list of system messages. Each entry includes details such as the component that generated the message, the level of severity, the time of occurrence, and the message content itself.

To manage the potentially large volume of messages, NiFi provides several filtering options. Users can filter messages by severity level, allowing focus on critical errors or warnings. Additionally, filtering by component name or identifier is possible, which is particularly useful for isolating messages related to specific processors or controller services.

```
1  // Example of a simple query filter on the Bulletin Board UI
2  severity:ERROR && (componentName:"PutHDFS" || componentName:"FetchS3Object")
```

The above query example demonstrates how to use NiFi's query syntax to filter for error-level messages from two specific components: PutHDFS and FetchS3Object. This capability is fundamental when troubleshooting issues within complex data flows where pinpointing the source of a problem quickly is crucial.

Moreover, the Bulletin Board supports the configuration of automatic alerts. Administrators can define conditions based on message patterns, severity, or frequency, which trigger alerts to be sent out. This feature enables proactive monitoring of NiFi environments, allowing issues to be addressed before they escalate into more significant problems.

When dealing with large-scale NiFi deployments, the volume of messages on the Bulletin Board can become overwhelming. To address this, it is advisable to regularly review and clear messages that are no longer relevant, ensuring that the Bulletin Board remains a useful tool for current monitoring and troubleshooting activities. This can be done manually through the user interface or programmatically via NiFi's REST API.

```
Received error from ProcessGroupID=12345, ProcessorID=67890 at 2023-07-15T12:00:00Z:
"Connection timed out: no further information"
```

The above example represents a typical error message that might be encountered. It includes the identifiers for both the process group and processor where the issue occurred, along with a timestamp and the error message content.

Leveraging the NiFi Bulletin Board effectively requires a consistent approach to reviewing and responding to system messages. By utilizing filtering and alerting capabilities, administrators can maintain oversight of system health and performance, ensuring that data flows continue to operate efficiently and without interruption. Additionally, incorporating best practices for message management, such as regular review and clearance of non-critical notifications, will keep the Bulletin Board from becoming cluttered and preserve its usefulness as a diagnostic tool.

The NiFi Bulletin Board is an essential feature for real-time monitoring and troubleshooting within NiFi environments. By effectively managing and responding to system messages, administrators can enhance operational stability and prevent data processing disruptions. Acknowledging its importance and incorporating its usage into daily NiFi management practices is recommended for all users seeking to achieve optimal performance and reliability in their data flows.

8.12 Best Practices for Logging and Monitoring in NiFi

Effective logging and monitoring are essential for the operational stability and performance optimization of Apache NiFi. This section will discuss best practices that enhance the capability to observe, diagnose, and efficiently manage data flows within a NiFi environment.

Firstly, configuring log levels appropriately is critical. NiFi allows detailed configuration of log levels through the `logback.xml` file. It is imperative to set the root log level to WARN for production environments to reduce disk space usage and avoid cluttering logs with informational or debug-level messages. For troubleshooting specific issues, the log level can be temporarily set to INFO or DEBUG for the relevant classes or packages. Use the following lstlisting to adjust the log level for a specific processor:

```
1  <logger name="org.apache.nifi.processors.standard.LogAttribute" level="DEBUG"/>
```

This adjustment would increase the log output for the LogAttribute processor, aiding in detailed troubleshooting while not overwhelming the log files with debug messages from other components.

Secondly, leveraging built-in reporting tasks efficiently is highly recommended. NiFi offers several reporting tasks for monitoring system health, JVM metrics, and data flow statistics. Configuring these reporting tasks to run at appropriate intervals ensures timely insights into NiFi's performance without incurring excessive resource usage. For instance, the `MonitorMemory` reporting task can be set up to alert administrators when the available system memory falls below a certain threshold.

```
1  <property name="Reporting Task Type">MonitorMemory</property>
2  <property name="Threshold">80%</property>
```

This setup helps in proactively managing system resources, preventing out-of-memory errors that could disrupt data flow operations.

Monitoring NiFi's data flow performance and system health in real-time is another best practice. Utilizing the Data Provenance and Statistics features allows users to track data packets through the system and monitor flow rates, latency, and success rates. This real-time monitoring is essential for identifying bottlenecks and ensuring that data flows are operating at optimal efficiency.

198

Additionally, custom monitoring solutions can be employed to complement NiFi's built-in capabilities. Integrating NiFi with external monitoring tools like Grafana and Prometheus offers enhanced visualiza-
tions and historical data analysis of NiFi's performance metrics. Setting
up a custom NAR (NiFi Archive) or using the Site-to-Site reporting task
for forwarding metrics to these external systems can provide deeper
insights into operational metrics.

Understanding and managing backpressure and load balancing effectively contributes greatly to data flow stability. Adjusting backpressure
settings according to the performance characteristics of your environment ensures that NiFi can handle surges in data volume without data
loss or undue pressure on system resources. Be judicious in applying
backpressure settings, considering both queue size and data aging,
to maintain smooth flow of data through processors and across the
cluster.

Lastly, maintaining a structured approach to troubleshooting is vital.
When diagnosing issues within NiFi flows, start by examining the NiFi
logs for error messages or warnings. Using the NiFi Bulletin Board and
the provenance data can help identify the processors or connections
that are the sources of issues. Effective troubleshooting also involves
understanding the common failure modes of NiFi, including processor
misconfigurations, resource exhaustion, and networking issues. Being
familiar with these failure modes can accelerate the diagnosis and
resolution of operational problems.

In summary, adhering to these best practices for logging and monitoring in NiFi facilitates the early detection and resolution of issues,
enhances the understanding of data flow performance, and contributes
to the overall health and stability of NiFi deployments. By implementing appropriate logging levels, utilizing built-in reporting tasks
judiciously, integrating with external monitoring tools, managing backpressure effectively, and approaching troubleshooting methodically,
NiFi administrators can ensure robust and efficient data flow operations.

Chapter 9

Building Real-Time Data Pipelines with Apache NiFi

This chapter focuses on leveraging Apache NiFi to construct robust real-time data pipelines capable of processing and moving data with minimal latency. It guides readers through the end-to-end process of designing, implementing, and managing data pipelines that meet the demands of real-time data ingestion, transformation, and distribution. Emphasizing the importance of scalability, reliability, and efficiency, the chapter outlines strategies for integrating various data sources and sinks, applying transformations on-the-fly, and ensuring data quality. With practical examples and expert insights, readers will learn how to harness the full potential of NiFi to build effective real-time data pipelines that support dynamic, data-driven decision-making processes.

9.1 Introduction to Real-Time Data Pipelines

Real-time data pipelines are essential architectures designed for the swift and uninterrupted flow of data from source to destination, enabling immediate data analysis and decision-making. These pipelines support the continuous ingestion, processing, and delivery of data, differing significantly from traditional batch processing systems which handle data in discrete chunks at scheduled intervals. The core objective of real-time data pipelines is to minimize latency to such an extent that data processing and its subsequent availability for analysis appear instantaneous from an end-user perspective.

In the context of modern data-driven applications, the demand for real-time data pipelines has surged. Businesses and organizations across various industries need to process and analyze data as it arrives to promptly react to emerging trends, detect anomalies, and make data-informed decisions. This necessitates a robust framework capable of handling the volume, velocity, and variety of data characteristic of today's digital ecosystem.

Apache NiFi, a project of the Apache Software Foundation, stands out as a highly flexible and scalable tool for building real-time data pipelines. It offers a web-based user interface and supports a wide range of data sources and destinations, including several popular databases, cloud storage systems, and messaging queues. Apache NiFi's design principles emphasize ease of use, system reliability, data provenance, and security, making it an excellent choice for the construction and management of real-time data pipelines.

At the foundation of Apache NiFi's architecture is the concept of flow-based programming. In NiFi, data flows through a series of processing components, each tailored to perform specific tasks such as filtering, routing, transformation, and aggregation of data. This modular approach allows developers and data engineers to design flexible and adaptable data pipelines that can be fine-tuned to meet specific operational requirements.

The construction of a real-time data pipeline with Apache NiFi involves several key steps. First, understanding the data sources and the nature of the data is crucial for effective pipeline design. This includes considerations about data format, volume, and the frequency of data generation. Next, defining the processing requirements, such as data cleansing, transformation, and augmentation, is essential for ensuring the quality and usefulness of the data. Following this, the routing and delivery of data to appropriate destinations must be configured, with considerations for fault tolerance, load balancing, and dynamic scaling to handle varying data loads.

To ensure data quality and consistency within the pipeline, Apache NiFi provides a range of tools and mechanisms. These include data validation routines, error handling frameworks, and feedback loops for iterative improvement of data processing logic. Moreover, security features within NiFi, such as data encryption, access control, and audit logging, are integral to safeguarding sensitive information as it moves through the pipeline.

Performance monitoring and management are also critical components of operating a real-time data pipeline. Apache NiFi offers built-in tools for tracking data flow metrics, system performance, and operational status. This enables timely identification and resolution of issues, ensuring high availability and reliability of the data pipeline.

Real-time data pipelines are vital for organizations looking to leverage timely data analysis for strategic decision-making. Apache NiFi, with its comprehensive feature set and flexible architecture, provides an effective platform for building and managing complex data pipelines. Through careful design, implementation, and management, NiFi can support the demands of real-time data ingestion, processing, and distribution, thereby empowering businesses to respond swiftly to changing data landscapes.

9.2 Designing Data Pipelines with Apache NiFi

Designing data pipelines with Apache NiFi involves a series of strategic steps to ensure the seamless flow of data from source to destination, with the requisite processing applied during transit. Apache NiFi's architecture is designed to facilitate this process, offering a highly configurable environment that caters to a wide range of data processing and pipeline design needs. This section will discuss the key considerations and steps in designing effective real-time data pipelines using Apache NiFi.

The initial step in designing a data pipeline is to clearly define the data sources and destinations. Apache NiFi supports a wide range of data sources, including but not limited to, files, logs, HTTP requests, database tables, and messaging queues. Similarly, data can be routed to multiple destinations such as databases, data lakes, or other HTTP services. Understanding the nature of the data source and the intended destination is crucial for optimizing the pipeline design for performance and reliability.

Once the sources and destinations are defined, the next step involves outlining the data flow and transformations required. Apache NiFi provides a user-friendly interface to visualize the data pipeline, known as the NiFi Flow Designer. Within this interface, users drag and drop processor components that define specific tasks such as data ingestion, transformation, and routing. It is essential to map out the data flow, keeping in mind the need for flexibility to accommodate future modifications or scalability.

```
1   // Example of fetching data from an HTTP source
2   <processor>
3     <type>GetHTTP</type>
4     <properties>
5       <property name="URL" value="http://example.com/data"/>
6       <property name="Scheduling Period" value="30 sec"/>
7     </properties>
8   </processor>
```

Data transformation is a critical aspect of the pipeline design. Apache NiFi provides built-in processors for common data transformation tasks such as format conversion, data extraction, and value replacement. For instance, the 'ConvertRecord' processor can be used to transform data formats from CSV to JSON, XML to Avro, and so on. It is important to select the appropriate processor for the transformation requirements or to implement custom processors if necessary.

```
1   // Example of converting CSV data to JSON
2   <processor>
3     <type>ConvertRecord</type>
4     <properties>
5       <property name="Input Format" value="CSV"/>
6       <property name="Output Format" value="JSON"/>
7     </properties>
8   </processor>
```

Routing data to the appropriate destination based on content or context is another key consideration. Apache NiFi's 'RouteOnAttribute' processor allows for conditional routing of flowfiles based on their attributes. This capability is particularly useful for directing flowfiles to different destinations based on specific criteria or for handling errors.

```
1   // Example of routing data based on attribute
2   <processor>
3     <type>RouteOnAttribute</type>
4     <properties>
5       <property name="Routing Strategy" value="Route to Property name"/>
6       <property name="example-attribute" value="${attribute:equals('example-value')}"
           />
7     </properties>
8   </processor>
```

204

Incorporating error handling and retry mechanisms is essential for building robust pipelines. Apache NiFi supports various strategies for dealing with failures, such as retrying failed operations, redirecting flowfiles to error queues, or triggering alerts. Designing for reliability involves anticipating potential points of failure and configuring processors to handle these events gracefully.

- Utilize the 'RetryFlowFile' processor to retry operations that have failed due to transient issues.

- Configure 'Backpressure' settings on connections to prevent data loss under high volume scenarios.

- Use the 'PutEmail' processor to send alerts when errors occur, enabling rapid response to issues.

Finally, ensuring performance and scalability is critical in the design of real-time data pipelines. Apache NiFi's distributed architecture allows pipelines to scale horizontally across multiple nodes, providing the ability to process higher volumes of data. Throughput and latency can be optimized by tuning processor configurations, such as batch size and concurrent tasks, as well as by leveraging NiFi's prioritization and backpressure mechanisms.

Designing data pipelines with Apache NiFi requires a thoughtful approach, focusing on flexibility, reliability, and scalability. By carefully defining data sources and destinations, mapping out data flows and transformations, implementing conditional routing and error handling, and optimizing for performance, developers can build effective real-time data pipelines that meet the demands of diverse data processing needs.

9.3 Ingesting Data from Various Sources

Ingesting data from various sources is a fundamental step in building real-time data pipelines with Apache NiFi. This process involves acquiring data from a diverse array of sources, such as databases, log files, message queues, cloud storage, and IoT devices, and feeding it into the NiFi dataflows for further processing and analysis. The versatility in data source support underscores NiFi's capability to cater to a wide range of real-time data pipeline requirements, making it an indispensable tool for data engineers and architects.

To efficiently manage the ingestion of data, NiFi provides a comprehensive set of processors specifically designed for data acquisition. These processors can be configured to connect to different data sources, extract data in various formats, and ingest it into NiFi flows. Each processor is designed to handle specific types of data sources, thereby optimizing the ingestion process and ensuring minimal latency.

For database ingestion, NiFi offers processors like ExecuteSQL and QueryDatabaseTable. The ExecuteSQL processor executes a provided SQL query against a database connection to fetch records, which are then converted into NiFi flow files for further processing. The QueryDatabaseTable processor is particularly efficient for incremental data loading; it tracks changes in database tables and fetches only new or updated records based on customizable criteria.

```
1  <ExecuteSQL
2      Database Connection Pooling Service="DBCPConnectionPool"
3      SQL Select Query="SELECT * FROM transactions WHERE transaction_date > ?"
4      Output Format="Avro">
5  </ExecuteSQL>
```

For ingesting data from log files, NiFi's TailFile processor is designed to continuously monitor specified log files for changes, appending new content to the flow as it becomes available. This capability is essential for real-time monitoring and analysis of application logs, server logs, and system metrics.

Real-time data ingestion from message queues and streaming platforms, such as Apache Kafka and MQTT brokers, is facilitated by processors like ConsumeKafka and ConsumeMQTT. These processors connect to the respective message systems, subscribe to topics or channels, and ingest messages directly into NiFi flows for immediate processing.

```
1  <ConsumeKafka
2      Kafka Brokers="kafka-broker1:9092,kafka-broker2:9092"
3      Topic Name="sensor_data"
4      Group ID="nifi_consumers">
5  </ConsumeKafka>
```

Additionally, for ingesting data from cloud storage services like Amazon S3, Azure Blob Storage, and Google Cloud Storage, NiFi provides processors such as FetchS3Object, FetchAzureBlobStorage, and FetchGCSObject. These processors allow for seamless integration with cloud environments, enabling the construction of hybrid and cloud-native real-time data pipelines.

- `FetchS3Object` connects to an S3 bucket to retrieve specific objects, using either the object's key or a prefix to identify the target data.

- `FetchAzureBlobStorage` operates similarly for Azure Blob Storage, providing secure access to blobs using account names and access keys or SAS tokens.

- `FetchGCSObject` allows for fetching data from Google Cloud Storage, relying on service account credentials and bucket identifiers to access and ingest objects.

To manage the complexity of ingesting data from multiple sources, NiFi's design principles focus on flexibility and scalability. Processors can be configured and combined in various ways to cater to specific ingestion patterns, such as batch loading, continuous ingestion, or event-driven triggers. Moreover, NiFi's flow-based programming model enables the visual design and management of dataflows, significantly simplifying the configuration of ingestion processes, monitoring of data movement, and troubleshooting of potential issues.

In summary, the ability to ingest data from various sources with minimal latency and high reliability is a cornerstone of effective real-time data pipeline construction with Apache NiFi. By leveraging NiFi's extensive collection of processors and its flexible programming model, developers and data engineers can build scalable and efficient data ingestion pipelines that accommodate the diverse and dynamic nature of real-time data sources.

9.4 Processing and Transforming Data in Real-Time

In this section, we will discuss the critical aspects of processing and transforming data in real-time using Apache NiFi. Apache NiFi provides a flexible and scalable architecture to handle the demands of real-time data processing by allowing data to be filtered, aggregated, transformed, and routed with ease.

One of the fundamental components of NiFi that facilitates data transformation is the Processor. Processors are the building blocks of NiFi data flows, capable of performing a wide range of functions on incoming data. To effectively utilize processors for data transformation, one must understand how to configure and chain these processors to achieve the desired outcome.

```
1   // Example of a simple NiFi expression language statement used in a processor's
         configuration
2   ${file_attribute:matches('*.txt')}
```

This example uses NiFi's Expression Language in a processor's configuration to filter files based on their extension. It highlights the simplicity and power of using expressions to manipulate and make decisions about data as it flows through the system.

For more complex transformations, NiFi offers a variety of processors such as 'ConvertRecord', 'ReplaceText', and 'JoltTransformJSON'. These processors can transform data formats, modify content based on regular expressions, and transform JSON structures respectively.

```
1   // Example JSON transformation using the JoltTransformJSON processor
2   [
3     {
4       "operation": "shift",
5       "spec": {
6         "sensor_id": "sensor.id",
7         "timestamp": "sensor.timestamp",
8         "readings": {
9           "*": {
10            "temperature": "sensor.readings[&1].temperature",
11            "humidity": "sensor.readings[&1].humidity"
12          }
13        }
14      }
15    }
16  ]
```

This Jolt specification example demonstrates how to restructure a JSON document by renaming fields and reorganizing data into a nested structure, a common requirement in data processing pipelines to normalize and standardize data.

Data routing, another crucial aspect of data processing, is skillfully handled by NiFi through the use of specific processors like 'RouteOnAttribute' and 'RouteOnContent'. These processors analyze data attributes or content and route data to different paths in the pipeline based on defined criteria.

```
Example of data routing decision made by RouteOnAttribute processor:
Matched: true
Unmatched: false
```

The verbatim block simulates the outcome of a routing decision, demonstrating the binary nature of routing processes where data is either matched to a condition or not, thereby determining its subsequent path in the pipeline.

NiFi also supports integrating custom processors and scripts for specialized data processing needs. This can be particularly useful when off-the-shelf processors do not meet the specific requirements of a data processing task.

```
1  // Using ExecuteScript processor with Groovy to perform custom data transformation
2  def flowFile = session.get()
3  if (!flowFile) return
4  flowFile = session.write(flowFile, { inputStream, outputStream ->
5      // Custom Groovy logic to transform data
6      outputStream.write(inputStream.text.toUpperCase().getBytes())
7  } as StreamCallback)
8  session.transfer(flowFile, REL_SUCCESS)
```

Here, the 'ExecuteScript' processor runs a Groovy script to transform all incoming text data to uppercase, showcasing NiFi's adaptability to incorporate custom logic directly within data flows.

Processing and transforming data in real-time with Apache NiFi involves a combination of built-in processors, expression language, and the potential for custom scripting to meet diverse data processing requirements. By leveraging NiFi's comprehensive toolset, developers can build efficient, real-time data pipelines capable of handling complex transformations and routing logic, thereby unlocking the full value of their data assets.

9.5 Routing Data to Multiple Destinations

Routing data to multiple destinations is a critical component of building real-time data pipelines in Apache NiFi. This capability enables data to be sent to different systems or workflows based on specific conditions or attributes. Through dynamic routing, Apache NiFi offers a flexible framework that allows pipelines to be tailored to the diverse needs of data ingestion, transformation, and distribution processes.

Apache NiFi employs Processors such as `RouteOnAttribute`, `RouteOnContent`, and `PartitionRecord` to facilitate conditional routing. Each of these processors evaluates data based on criteria defined by the user and routes it accordingly.

Let's start with the `RouteOnAttribute` processor. This processor allows data flow to diverge based on the attributes of FlowFiles. For instance, if data needs to be routed based on the presence or absence of a certain attribute, or based on a matching pattern, `RouteOnAttribute` can be configured to achieve this goal.

```
 1  <processor>
 2    <id>RouteOnAttribute</id>
 3    <name>Route Data Based on Attribute</name>
 4    <class>org.apache.nifi.processors.standard.RouteOnAttribute</class>
 5    <property name="Routing Strategy">Route to Property Name</property>
 6    <property name="attribute-to-check">fileType</property>
 7    <property name="xml">
 8      <routingStrategy>Route to 'xml'</routingStrategy>
 9    </property>
10    <property name="json">
11      <routingStrategy>Route to 'json'</routingStrategy>
12    </property>
13  </processor>
```

In this example, data is routed based on the 'fileType' attribute. If the 'fileType' is 'xml', the FlowFile is routed to one destination; if 'json', to another.

Another powerful routing mechanism is provided by the `RouteOnContent` processor, which examines the content of FlowFiles to make routing decisions. This can be particularly useful when the routing condition depends on the data contained within the file itself rather than its attributes.

```
 1  <processor>
 2    <id>RouteOnContent</id>
 3    <name>Route Data Based on Content</name>
 4    <class>org.apache.nifi.processors.standard.RouteOnContent</class>
 5    <property name="Content Inspection Strategy">Text</property>
 6    <property name="Route Text">
 7      <expression>\{JSON\.*\}</expression>
 8      <example>Routes FlowFiles containing JSON content</example>
 9    </property>
10  </processor>
```

This configuration enables the routing of data based on its content, specifically targeting JSON structures.

Additionally, the `PartitionRecord` processor divides data into partitions based on user-defined criteria, which can then be routed or processed separately.

```
 1  <processor>
 2    <id>PartitionRecord</id>
 3    <name>Partition Data for Separate Processing</name>
 4    <class>org.apache.nifi.processors.standard.PartitionRecord</class>
 5    <property name="Record Reader">JsonPathReader</property>
 6    <property name="Record Writer">JsonRecordSetWriter</property>
```

```
7    <property name="Partitioning Strategy">Record Path</property>
8    <property name="Partition Record Path">/department</property>
9  </processor>
```

In the example above, the data is partitioned by the department field, which could aid in handling data differently based on departmental needs.

To ensure data flows to its intended destination without issues, Apache NiFi provides a comprehensive logging mechanism. These logs facilitate troubleshooting and validation of data routing logic:

```
INFO [Timer-Driven Process Thread-10]
o.a.n.p.standard.RouteOnAttribute Route Data Based on Attribute
routed 100 FlowFiles to xml, 150 FlowFiles to json.
```

The logging output above indicates successful routing of FlowFiles based on their attributes.

Implementing routing in Apache NiFi requires understanding the data, the criteria for its routing, and the destinations. By leveraging NiFi's routing processors effectively, developers can create dynamic and adaptable real-time data pipelines that meet complex processing requirements.

9.6 Integrating with External Systems and Databases

Integrating with external systems and databases is a critical aspect of building real-time data pipelines with Apache NiFi. This process involves establishing connections to various data sources and sinks, ensuring the seamless ingestion, processing, and export of data. Apache NiFi facilitates these integrations through its extensive library of processors and connectors that are designed to interact with a wide range of external systems, including relational databases, NoSQL databases, file systems, web services, and messaging systems.

To initiate the integration, the first step is to identify the external systems or databases with which the data pipeline will interact. Once identified, the appropriate NiFi processors can be selected and configured to establish connections to these systems. For example, to connect to a relational database, processors such as ExecuteSQL, QueryDatabaseTable, or PutSQL might be used. Similarly, to interact

211

with a NoSQL database, processors like `GetMongo` or `PutMongo` could be utilized.

The configuration of these processors typically involves specifying connection details such as the hostname, port, database name, credentials, and other parameters necessary for authentication and communication. It is crucial to ensure that the connection configurations are secure and comply with the best practices for data protection.

Additionally, integrating with external systems and databases often requires the transformation of data to match the schema or format expected by the target system. NiFi provides processors such as `TransformXML`, `ConvertJSONtoSQL`, and `ConvertAvroToORC` to facilitate these transformations. The ability to dynamically adjust the data format allows NiFi pipelines to be flexible and adaptable to various integration requirements.

When dealing with large volumes of data or complex transformations, performance considerations become paramount. Apache NiFi supports techniques such as partitioning, batching, and parallel processing to enhance the throughput and efficiency of data integrations. Processors like `SplitText`, `MergeContent`, and `PartitionRecord` can be leveraged to implement these techniques, thereby optimizing the performance of data pipelines.

Error handling and retry mechanisms are also integral to the successful integration with external systems and databases. NiFi's routing capabilities enable the separation of successful transactions from failed ones, allowing for the implementation of custom error handling and recovery strategies. Processors such as `RouteOnAttribute` and `HandleHttpResponse` are useful in managing different outcomes of data processing and integration activities.

In summary, integrating with external systems and databases in Apache NiFi involves selecting and configuring the appropriate processors, transforming data as needed, optimizing performance, and handling errors effectively. By following these guidelines, real-time data pipelines can be constructed to reliably connect and interact with a diverse range of external data sources and sinks, paving the way for efficient data movement and processing.

Example of configuring a database connection:

```
1  # Database connection configuration
2  nifi.db.connection.host=database.example.com
3  nifi.db.connection.port=3306
4  nifi.db.connection.user=username
```

```
5  nifi.db.connection.password=password
6  nifi.db.connection.database=mydatabase
```

This configuration snippet demonstrates how to specify the connection details for integrating with a relational database. It includes parameters for the database host, port, user credentials, and the database name. These parameters are essential for establishing a secure and functional connection between Apache NiFi and the external database.

9.7 Ensuring Data Quality and Consistency

Ensuring data quality and consistency is paramount for reliable realtime data pipelines. Apache NiFi provides a comprehensive suite of tools and strategies designed to address these critical concerns. In this section, we will discuss methodologies and components within NiFi that help maintain high data quality and consistency across even the most complex data flows.

Data validation is the first step in ensuring data quality. NiFi's ValidateRecord processor can be employed to verify the format and schema of incoming data. This processor checks each field against a predefined schema, allowing data that does not conform to be redirected to an error queue for further inspection or correction.

```
1  <ValidateRecord name="Validate CSV Data" schemaName="UserRecordsAvroSchema" />
```

Data standardization is another essential aspect of data quality. NiFi's UpdateRecord processor can modify data into a standard format, ensuring consistency across the data flow. For instance, date fields coming from different sources might be in various formats. UpdateRecord can be configured to transform these into a unified format.

```
1  <UpdateRecord name="Standardize Date Format" dateFormat="yyyy-MM-dd" />
```

De-duplication ensures that the data pipeline does not process duplicate data. The DetectDuplicate processor can keep track of data that has already been processed, using a cache to identify and eliminate duplicates.

```
1  <DetectDuplicate name="Remove Duplicates" cacheSize="1000000" />
```

Data enrichment can enhance the value of the data as it moves through the pipeline. Using processors such as LookupRecord, data can be

213

augmented with information from external sources or databases. This is crucial for ensuring that the data is as informative and up-to-date as possible.

```
1   <LookupRecord name="Enrich Data" lookupService="MySQLDatabase" />
```

Ensuring data consistency involves the synchronization of data across different systems. NiFi's `MergeContent` processor can aggregate data from multiple sources, ensuring uniformity before the data is sent to its final destination.

```
1   <MergeContent name="Consolidate Records" strategy="Bin-Packing Algorithm" />
```

In addition to these processors, NiFi's built-in data provenance and logging capabilities offer visibility into the data flow, helping identify and troubleshoot issues related to data quality and consistency. Provenance data can be accessed via NiFi's user interface or through its REST API, providing a detailed history of each data piece throughout its journey in the pipeline.

```
Provenance Event ID: 5e2fbd64-17b3-4c2c-8e5d-d8a8e8b4a4d2
Event Type: CONTENT_MODIFIED
FlowFile UUID: 2aef0a99-4e5e-4ae3-97d0-d6f03d5f45ce
Component ID: 029dbfb8-3b01-4b96-a8d9-6c478a4f2abd
Component Type: MergeContent
```

To further enhance data quality, integrating with external systems for real-time data validation and cleansing can be achieved through NiFi's extensive REST API support. This enables dynamic interaction with external validation services, ensuring data integrity and accuracy are maintained throughout the data flow process.

Data consistency can be preserved through the implementation of exactly-once processing semantics within NiFi. Configuring processors to utilize NiFi's state management capabilities ensures that data is processed in a fault-tolerant manner, with checkpoints and state recovery mechanisms in place to prevent data duplication or loss during processing.

Ensuring data quality and consistency in real-time data pipelines built with Apache NiFi involves a multifaceted approach. By leveraging data validation, standardization, de-duplication, enrichment, and consistency mechanisms, pipelines can be designed to deliver high-quality, consistent data that meets the evolving needs of data-driven organizations. Through the application of these strategies, developers can harness the full potential of NiFi to create robust, efficient, and reliable data pipelines.

9.8 Scaling NiFi for High Volume Data Processing

Scaling Apache NiFi to handle high volume data processing is critical for building real-time data pipelines that can efficiently manage the increasing amount of data generated by various sources. This section discusses strategies and considerations for scaling NiFi instances to ensure robust performance and reliability under high load conditions.

One fundamental aspect of scaling NiFi involves understanding its architecture, which consists of the Flow Controller, Processors, Connectors, and FlowFiles. To effectively scale a NiFi deployment, it is essential to distribute these components across multiple nodes in a cluster, thereby leveraging parallel processing and achieving redundancy.

Cluster Setup: Initiating a NiFi cluster involves deploying multiple NiFi nodes that work together to process data flows. A NiFi cluster is managed by a Cluster Coordinator and one or more Primary Nodes, responsible for distributing tasks and managing state across the cluster. To configure a NiFi cluster, the following steps are essential:

- Ensuring all nodes have identical NiFi versions and configurations.

- Configuring each node's `zookeeper.properties` and `nifi.properties` to enable communication with a shared ZooKeeper instance, which manages cluster coordination.

- Designating one node as the Cluster Coordinator through the NiFi user interface or configuration files.

Once a cluster is operational, data flows designed in NiFi can be executed in parallel across multiple nodes, significantly improving processing capacity.

Load Balancing: Apache NiFi supports several load balancing strategies aimed at evenly distributing data across the cluster. These strategies include:

- Partitioning FlowFiles based on attributes or content.

- Round-robin distribution, where each node takes turns receiving data.

- Random distribution for cases where there is no need for ordered processing.

Properly configuring load balancing is vital for optimizing resource utilization and ensuring that no single node becomes a bottleneck.

Backpressure and Flow Control: NiFi provides mechanisms for managing backpressure – a state where a component slows down or stops data ingestion to prevent system overload. Configuration parameters such as `Backpressure Object Threshold` and `Backpressure Data Size Threshold` can be set on connections between processors to trigger backpressure based on the number of FlowFiles or their total size. Flow control settings ensure that NiFi operates within its resource limits, thereby enhancing system stability.

For high volume data processing, it is also advisable to pay close attention to data provenance and repository management. NiFi's Data Provenance Repository tracks the history and lineage of FlowFiles. In high volume scenarios, this repository can quickly grow in size, potentially impacting performance. Configuring data retention policies and repository storage is key to maintaining performance while preserving necessary audit trails and lineage information.

Performance Tuning: Optimizing NiFi performance for high volume data processing may also involve tuning JVM settings, adjusting processor concurrency, and optimizing the configuration of the underlying hardware and network. Strategies include:

- Increasing JVM heap size to accommodate larger data volumes.

- Adjusting the number of concurrent tasks for processors that are bottlenecks.

- Ensuring that the network infrastructure supports the required throughput.

- Using SSDs for repositories to improve I/O performance.

Moreover, monitoring NiFi's performance using built-in tools and metrics is crucial for identifying bottlenecks and understanding how different scaling strategies impact the overall throughput and efficiency of data pipelines.

Scaling Apache NiFi for high volume data processing necessitates a comprehensive approach that encompasses cluster setup, load balancing, backpressure management, and performance tuning. By adhering to best practices and continuously monitoring resource usage and system performance, organizations can ensure that their NiFi deployments are capable of handling the demands of real-time data pipelines efficiently and reliably.

9.9 Monitoring and Managing Pipeline Performance

In monitoring and managing pipeline performance within Apache NiFi, it is crucial to establish metrics that accurately reflect the health, efficiency, and reliability of data flows. The inherent complexity of real-time data pipelines demands a comprehensive approach to monitor multiple facets, including throughput, latency, error rates, and resource utilization. Apache NiFi provides several tools and features designed to facilitate detailed performance monitoring and effective management of data pipelines.

A primary consideration in pipeline performance monitoring is the accurate measurement of data throughput and latency. Throughput refers to the volume of data processed in a given time frame, typically measured in records per second or bytes per second. Latency, on the other hand, measures the time taken for a data record to travel through the pipeline from its source to destination.

```
1   nifi.status.history.step=5000ms
```

The above configuration snippet signifies an example of setting the interval at which NiFi collects and stores its performance metrics, thereby influencing how granular the monitoring data will be.

Apache NiFi's user interface provides real-time visual feedback on the performance of various components of the data pipeline. Processors, connections, and system diagnostics are displayed graphically, highlighting metrics such as flow file counts, sizes, and processing times. This immediate feedback loop enables data engineers to quickly identify bottlenecks or inefficiencies within the data pipeline.

```
Process Group A:
 - Total Bytes In: 500 MB
 - Total Bytes Out: 495 MB
```

```
- Flow Files In: 100,000
- Flow Files Out: 99,500
```

An example of the type of summary statistics provided by NiFi on per-process group basis allows for quick assessments of data flow health and performance.

Apache NiFi supports the integration of external monitoring tools through its REST API and Reporting Tasks. By leveraging the REST API, developers can automate the collection of pipeline performance metrics and integrate them with existing monitoring tools like Grafana or Prometheus. Reporting Tasks in Apache NiFi can be configured to automatically send metrics to external systems at defined intervals, supporting the centralized monitoring of large-scale deployments.

```
1  <reportingTask>
2    <type>org.apache.nifi.reporting.prometheus.PrometheusReportingTask</type>
3    <bundle>
4      <group>org.apache.nifi</group>
5      <artifact>nifi-prometheus-nar</artifact>
6      <version>1.12.1</version>
7    </bundle>
8  </reportingTask>
```

This configuration example initiates a Reporting Task in NiFi designed to export metrics to a Prometheus monitoring system, illustrating how NiFi facilitates the integration with popular monitoring platforms.

Managing pipeline performance extends beyond monitoring to include proactive adjustments and optimizations. NiFi provides several mechanisms to optimize pipeline performance, including back pressure settings and prioritization queues. Back pressure is configured on a per-connection basis, allowing operators to define the conditions under which data flow should be slowed or paused to prevent downstream overload. Similarly, prioritization queues enable the sorting of data packets based on custom criteria, ensuring that critical data is processed first.

Ensuring data quality and consistency is another aspect of managing pipeline performance. Processors such as `ValidateRecord` and `UpdateAttribute` can be employed to inspect incoming data against predefined schemas or rules and apply corrections or annotations. This not only helps in maintaining the integrity of the data but also in reducing the overhead caused by processing invalid or incomplete records.

218

To scale Apache NiFi for high volume data processing, clusters can be formed from multiple NiFi instances. Clustering increases the processing capacity of the system and enhances its fault tolerance. Monitoring a NiFi cluster involves keeping track of not only individual node performance but also the health of the cluster as a whole. Clustering introduces additional metrics, such as cluster-wide throughput and the distribution of data across nodes, which must be monitored to ensure balanced workload distribution and high availability.

- Understanding and configuring back pressure and flow prioritization.

- Integrating with external monitoring tools via REST API or Reporting Tasks.

- Employing data quality processors to maintain high data integrity.

- Scaling NiFi through clustering for enhanced processing capabilities.

Monitoring and managing pipeline performance in Apache NiFi is a multifaceted endeavor that requires a detailed understanding of both NiFi's features and the characteristics of the data pipeline being managed. By meticulously measuring performance metrics, integrating with external monitoring tools, and proactively optimizing pipeline configurations, organizations can ensure that their real-time data pipelines operate efficiently, reliably, and at scale.

9.10 Handling Failures and Ensuring Data Recovery

In this section, we discuss the critical aspects of handling failures and ensuring data recovery within Apache NiFi data pipelines. Given the importance of keeping data pipelines operational and resilient, designing for failure is not an option but a necessity. Failures in data pipelines can occur for numerous reasons, including hardware malfunctions, network issues, incorrect pipeline configurations, or external system failures. A robust Apache NiFi deployment necessitates strategic planning for such eventualities to maintain data integrity and pipeline availability.

Apache NiFi provides various mechanisms and features designed to enhance fault tolerance and enable effective data recovery. These include data provenance, connection queues, backpressure, and prioritizing queue processing. Each mechanism plays a crucial role in managing failures and ensuring the pipeline's resilience.

- **Data Provenance**: NiFi's data provenance capabilities allow for comprehensive tracking of data flow through the system. This feature is essential for diagnosing failures and understanding their impact on the data and the flow. In case of failure, data provenance can be used to trace back the point of failure and determine the recovery steps needed.

- **Connection Queues**: NiFi utilizes queues to manage data between processors. These queues act as buffers for incoming data, ensuring no data loss during transient failures. When a downstream process fails or becomes a bottleneck, data is held in the queue until the issue is resolved, thereby preventing data loss and allowing for recovery.

- **Backpressure**: This feature allows NiFi to automatically adjust the flow of data to prevent overloading any component of the pipeline. By setting thresholds on queue sizes or data rates, NiFi applies backpressure to slow down or pause incoming data, thus preventing failures due to resource overutilization.

- **Prioritizing Queue Processing**: NiFi enables prioritizing data items in queues so that critical data can be processed first. This feature is particularly useful in scenarios where not all data has the same value or urgency, allowing for recovery efforts to be focused on the highest priority data first.

Designing NiFi pipelines with failure in mind involves implementing processor groups for logical separation and encapsulation of functionalities. This approach aids in isolating failures to specific groups, making it easier to identify and rectify issues without affecting the entire pipeline. Additionally, leveraging NiFi's built-in processors such as `RetryFlowFile` and `UpdateAttribute` can programmatically manage retries and error handling pathways.

For ensuring data recovery, Apache NiFi supports configurable data retention policies. Setting up appropriate archival strategies or specifying how long data should be retained in queues before being dropped is crucial for managing storage resources effectively while also ensuring that data is recoverable within a given timeframe.

Furthermore, incorporating external storage systems as part of the NiFi pipeline configuration can offer another layer of data redundancy and recovery. Using processors to snapshot data to systems like HDFS, Amazon S3, or Azure Blob Storage ensures that, even in the event of complete pipeline failure, data is not lost but stored securely in an external system, from which it can be recovered.

```
1  <processor>
2     <class>org.apache.nifi.processors.standard.FetchS3Object</class>
3     <properties>
4        <property name="Bucket Name" value="example-bucket"/>
5        <property name="Object Key" value="\${filename}"/>
6     </properties>
7  </processor>
```

This example demonstrates how to configure a processor to fetch data from an Amazon S3 bucket, highlighting the seamless integration of external storage solutions for data recovery purposes.

Handling failures and ensuring data recovery in Apache NiFi pipelines necessitates a multi-faceted approach involving strategic configurations, proactive monitoring, and leveraging built-in features for fault tolerance. By adhering to best practices for pipeline design and configuration detailed in this section, organizations can achieve a resilient real-time data infrastructure capable of withstanding failures and ensuring data integrity and availability.

9.11 Securing Real-Time Data Pipelines

Securing real-time data pipelines is critical to protect sensitive information and ensure the integrity and confidentiality of data as it moves through various stages from source to destination. Apache NiFi, a versatile and powerful tool for data ingestion and processing, provides a comprehensive security model designed to address the multi-faceted aspects of data pipeline security. In this section, we will discuss the essential security features of Apache NiFi, including authentication, authorization, data protection in transit and at rest, and monitoring for security events.

Authentication in Apache NiFi is the process of verifying the identity of a user or system entity. NiFi supports multiple authentication mechanisms such as LDAP, Kerberos, and OAuth2, enabling integration with existing enterprise identity management systems. For instance, to configure Kerberos authentication for NiFi, one would specify the Kerberos principal and keytab file in the `nifi.properties` file. Example configuration lines might resemble:

```
1  nifi.kerberos.service.principal=HTTP/nifi.example.com@EXAMPLE.COM
2  nifi.kerberos.keytab.location=/etc/security/keytabs/nifi.service.keytab
```

Following authentication, authorization determines the access levels and permissions of the authenticated entity. NiFi uses an access policy-based model for authorization, managed through the NiFi's User Interface or REST API. For example, to grant a user access to a particular process group, an administrator would create an access policy associating the user with the desired permissions (e.g., read, write, modify).

Protecting data in transit involves encrypting data flows between NiFi components and external systems. NiFi supports TLS/SSL to secure data as it moves over the network. Configuring TLS/SSL involves generating a keystore and truststore, then specifying these in the `nifi.properties` file:

```
1  nifi.security.keystore=./conf/keystore.jks
2  nifi.security.keystoreType=JKS
3  nifi.security.keystorePasswd=password123
4  nifi.security.truststore=./conf/truststore.jks
5  nifi.security.truststoreType=JKS
6  nifi.security.truststorePasswd=password123
7  nifi.security.needClientAuth=true
```

For data at rest, NiFi provides a repository encryption feature to encrypt all data written to the FlowFile, Provenance, and Content Repositories. Configuring repository encryption involves specifying encryption keys in the `nifi.properties` file and adjusting repository configurations accordingly.

Monitoring for security events is an ongoing task in securing data pipelines. NiFi's built-in reporting tasks and bulletin mechanisms can alert administrators to potential security incidents, such as unauthorized access attempts or configuration changes. NiFi logs security-relevant events which can be integrated with external monitoring tools (e.g., ELK stack, Splunk) for advanced analysis and alerting.

```
2023-03-01 12:34:56,789 INFO [NiFi Web Server-23]
o.a.n.w.a.c.AccessDeniedExceptionMapper
Attempted access by user [jdoe] to /nifi-api/process-groups/root was denied.
```

Ensuring data quality and consistency also plays a vital role in securing data pipelines. NiFi's data lineage and provenance mechanisms provide visibility into data flow history, enabling tracking of data from source to destination and identification of undesired data tampering or inconsistencies.

Securing real-time data pipelines in Apache NiFi involves a comprehensive approach that includes robust authentication and authorization mechanisms, encryption of data both in transit and at rest, continuous monitoring for security incidents, and maintaining data quality and consistency. By leveraging NiFi's security features, organizations can protect sensitive information and ensure the secure operation of their real-time data pipelines.

9.12 Case Studies: Real-World Data Pipeline Scenarios

Let's begin by examining several real-world scenarios where Apache NiFi has been leveraged to construct and manage real-time data pipelines, demonstrating its versatility and power in various industry contexts. These case studies illustrate the practical applications of the concepts discussed in the previous sections, including data ingestion, transformation, routing, and integration with external systems.

Financial Transactions Processing: In the financial sector, a leading online payment platform utilized Apache NiFi to build a real-time data pipeline for processing millions of transactions per day. The objective was to ingest transaction data from various sources, perform validations and transformations, and route the processed data to multiple destinations, including fraud detection systems and data warehouses for analytics.

```
1  // Example of a simple NiFi processor configuration for transaction data validation
2  <processor>
3    <id>ValidateTransaction</id>
4    <class>org.apache.nifi.processors.ValidateTransactionData</class>
5    <properties>
6      <property name="validation_rules">path/to/validation/rules.json</property>
7    </properties>
8  </processor>
```

Telecommunications Network Monitoring: In the telecommunications domain, Apache NiFi was employed to monitor network traffic in real-time, enabling the proactive identification of issues and ensuring optimal network performance. The data pipeline ingested logs from network devices, applied custom parsers to extract relevant metrics, and routed this information to a monitoring dashboard and alerting system.

- Ingesting log data from network devices.

- Applying parsers to extract metrics.

- Routing data to dashboards and alerting systems.

Retail Customer Behavior Analysis: A global retail chain implemented Apache NiFi to analyze customer behavior in real-time by processing data from point-of-sale systems, online transactions, and customer feedback. This multifaceted data pipeline allowed for the transformation and enrichment of data before it was stored in a data lake for further analysis, enabling personalized marketing and improved customer service.

```
Output Example for Enriched Customer Data:
{
  "customerId": "12345",
  "transactionAmount": 250,
  "itemsPurchased": ["electronics", "clothing"],
  "feedback": "positive",
  "purchaseChannel": "online"
}
```

Smart City Infrastructure Management: In a smart city initiative, Apache NiFi was used to integrate data from various IoT devices and sensors deployed across the city for monitoring infrastructure, traffic, and environmental conditions. The data pipeline facilitated the real-time analysis of data streams, ensuring efficient management of city resources and quick response to emergent situations.

IoT Data Ingestion

Real-Time Analysis

Decision Making

Healthcare Patient Monitoring System: In the healthcare industry, a hospital network implemented a real-time data pipeline using Apache

NiFi to monitor patient vitals and other health indicators. The system ingests data from medical devices, applies transformations to normalize the data formats, and routes the information to the appropriate healthcare personnel and systems for timely interventions.

Algorithm 1: Pseudocode for Patient Monitoring and Alerting

Data: Patient Vitals Stream
Result: Alerts for Critical Vitals
1 **while** *Data Stream is Active* **do**
2   Receive Data from Device;
3   Validate Data Integrity;
4   **if** *Vital Signs Outside Normal Range* **then**
5   Generate Alert;
6   Route to Health Personnel;

These case studies underscore the adaptability and efficiency of Apache NiFi in handling diverse data streaming and processing requirements across different sectors. By leveraging NiFi's capabilities, organizations can achieve real-time data processing and analytics, resulting in informed decision-making and operational improvements. The ability to ingest, process, and route data in a scalable, reliable manner underpins the development of dynamic, data-driven solutions that cater to specific organizational needs.

Chapter 10

NiFi Cluster Configuration and Management

The configuration and management of Apache NiFi clusters are critical for achieving scalability and high availability in processing large volumes or high-velocity data streams. This chapter provides a detailed examination of best practices and methodologies for setting up, configuring, and managing NiFi clusters to ensure efficient data flow across distributed environments. It addresses key aspects such as cluster architecture, node management, load balancing, and data synchronization, offering insights into achieving fault tolerance and seamless operation. By understanding these principles and techniques, readers will be equipped to optimize their NiFi deployments for enhanced performance and reliability in handling complex, large-scale data integration tasks.

10.1 Introduction to NiFi Clustering

Let's start with an understanding of what NiFi clustering entails. Apache NiFi, a robust, scalable data processing and distribution system, is designed to automate the flow of data between systems. A NiFi cluster comprises multiple NiFi nodes that work together to process data, providing both fault tolerance and high availability. This collaborative environment ensures that, should any node in the cluster fail, the processing tasks it was handling can be picked up by other nodes, thus minimizing data loss and processing downtime.

At the core of NiFi's clustering capabilities is the concept of a distributed flow. This entails the division of data flows across the cluster to leverage parallel processing, thus enhancing the overall throughput and efficiency of data management tasks. NiFi employs a zero-master shared-nothing architecture where each node in the cluster performs its tasks independently while coordinating their state across the cluster. This means there is no single point of failure in a NiFi cluster, contributing significantly to its robust fault-tolerance mechanism.

Clustering NiFi also involves setting up a Cluster Coordinator and Node Coordinators. The Cluster Coordinator is responsible for managing the cluster, deciding which nodes are part of the cluster, and distributing tasks amongst them. On the other hand, Node Coordinators are responsible for the actual execution of tasks. They handle the processing of data flows, acting on directives from the Cluster Coordinator.

For effective clustering, NiFi uses the concepts of primary nodes. A primary node is a cluster node with special roles, especially in scenarios requiring a single action to process data across the cluster, such as in the case of controllers, reporting tasks, and managing processors that are not designed to run in a cluster.

Load balancing within NiFi clusters ensures efficient distribution of data across the nodes. This is critical in preventing nodes from becoming overwhelmed with processing tasks. NiFi achieves load balancing through several mechanisms, including data partitioning based on attributes and round-robin distribution. This ensures that all nodes in the cluster contribute equally to data processing, thus optimizing the utilization of resources.

Data synchronization is another vital aspect of NiFi clustering. It ensures that all nodes in the cluster have a consistent view of the data flow, which is essential for maintaining the integrity of processing tasks. Data synchronization is achieved through the use of a shared content repository and a shared FlowFile repository. These repositories ensure that all nodes access the same set of data and state information, providing a unified processing environment.

In summary, NiFi clustering is a powerful feature that enhances the fault tolerance, scalability, and efficiency of data flow processing. By leveraging multiple nodes to distribute processing tasks, NiFi ensures high availability and optimal performance in data management operations. Understanding the fundamentals of NiFi clustering, from its architectural principles to node coordination and data synchronization, is crucial for anyone looking to deploy a robust and efficient data processing environment.

10.2 Setting Up a NiFi Cluster

Setting up a NiFi cluster is a fundamental step in deploying a scalable and fault-tolerant data flow system. This endeavor involves the installation of Apache NiFi on multiple nodes, configuration of these nodes to work together, and ensuring proper communication and management across the cluster.

The initial phase of cluster setup begins with the installation of Apache NiFi on each node designated to be part of the cluster. It is imperative that each node meets the system requirements for Apache NiFi, including sufficient processor, memory, and disk space resources, depending on the expected workload. Installation can be performed using the binary packages provided on the Apache NiFi website, following the detailed instructions specific to the operating system of the nodes.

Once NiFi is installed on each node, the next step involves configuring these individual instances to operate as a unified cluster. This configuration process is centered around the 'nifi.properties' file, located in the conf directory of the NiFi installation path. Several properties within this file must be adjusted to enable clustering, including but not limited to:

- `nifi.cluster.is.node` set to `true`, indicating that this NiFi instance should operate as part of a cluster.

- `nifi.cluster.node.address` and nifi.cluster.node. protocol.port, specifying the network address and port number for node communications.

- `nifi.zookeeper.connect.string`, which lists the ZooKeeper servers used for cluster coordination, in the format host1:port1, host2:port2, host3:port3.

- `nifi.cluster.flow.election.max.wait.time`, defining the maximum amount of time to wait for nodes to elect a primary node for cluster coordination.

In a NiFi cluster, ZooKeeper is utilized for managing the cluster state, including settings, queues, and states of all nodes. It requires setting up a separate ZooKeeper ensemble before or during the NiFi cluster configuration. The ZooKeeper ensemble should consist of an odd number of servers (at least three) to avoid split-brain scenarios and ensure high availability.

After adjusting the necessary properties in the 'nifi.properties' file, each node must be restarted for the changes to take effect. The nodes will then attempt to connect to the configured ZooKeeper servers and form a cluster.

Monitoring the logs located in the 'logs' directory of each NiFi installation is crucial during startup to identify and rectify any errors or issues in the clustering process. Messages indicating that the NiFi instance has joined the cluster successfully are signs of a properly configured environment.

The final step in establishing a NiFi cluster involves the configuration of data flow management across the cluster. This includes setting up processors, connections, input and output ports on the primary node, and ensuring that these configurations are propagated to all nodes in the cluster. The distributed nature of a NiFi cluster allows for data processing tasks to be evenly distributed across the cluster nodes, enhancing the scalability and fault tolerance of the system.

By meticulously following these steps and validating the configuration at each stage, a robust NiFi cluster can be established. Such a cluster will be capable of scalable, high-performance data flow management, capable of handling large volumes or high-velocity data streams efficiently.

10.3   NiFi Cluster Architecture and Concepts

Apache NiFi is designed to automate the flow of data between systems. In more complex scenarios, where the volume and velocity of data are considerably high, a single instance of NiFi might not suffice. This is where NiFi clustering comes into play. A NiFi cluster consists of multiple NiFi nodes (instances) connected together to form a coherent, coordinated, and distributed data processing framework. In this section, we will discuss the core architecture and concepts underlying a NiFi cluster to provide a foundation for understanding its configuration and management.

At the heart of NiFi's cluster architecture is the Zero-Master Clustering paradigm. This approach is distinct in that it does not rely on a single master node to manage the cluster. Instead, all nodes participate equally in the cluster's operation, coordinating their activities through a distributed consensus protocol. This design enhances the resilience and scalability of the cluster, as there is no single point of failure or bottleneck.

Each node within a NiFi cluster performs the same operations as a standalone NiFi instance would, such as data ingestion, processing, and data emission. However, in a cluster environment, these operations are distributed across multiple nodes, thereby providing horizontal scalability. As the volume of data or the complexity of processing requirements increases, additional nodes can be added to the cluster to distribute the load further.

The coordination amongst nodes in a NiFi cluster is achieved through the use of ZooKeeper, a centralized service for maintaining configuration information, naming, providing distributed synchronization, and providing group services. ZooKeeper holds the cluster's state, including the status of nodes and queues, ensuring consistent configuration across the cluster and facilitating the management of shared resources.

Data flow management in a NiFi cluster is orchestrated through a Cluster Coordinator and Primary Node. The Cluster Coordinator is responsible for keeping track of the nodes in the cluster and their statuses, including connectivity and roles. The Primary Node is elected from among the nodes and is responsible for tasks that should only be performed by a single node at a time, such as managing the queue of events to be processed. It's important to note that these roles are logical and are dynamically assigned by the Cluster Coordinator; thus, they do not correspond to physical distinctions between nodes.

In terms of data processing, NiFi employs a "Flow-Based Programming" model. This model treats data as a series of connected flows, enabling complex data processing pipelines to be composed of simple, reusable components. In a clustered environment, dataflows are distributed across nodes, but from a user's perspective, the cluster appears as a single, unified system. This transparency simplifies cluster management and enhances user experience, allowing users to interact with the cluster as if it were a single entity.

Load balancing is a key concept in NiFi clustering, ensuring that data is processed efficiently across nodes. NiFi supports several strategies for load balancing, including partitioning data based on attributes, round-robin distribution, and others. Effective load balancing maximizes resource utilization across the cluster and maintains high throughput, particularly in high-volume scenarios.

Lastly, data synchronization and state management are crucial for ensuring the consistency and reliability of data flows across the cluster. NiFi nodes share state information, such as processor configuration and connection status, to ensure that data is processed reliably and in the correct order, even in the event of node failure or network partitioning.

To summarize, the architecture and concepts of NiFi clustering are designed to provide a scalable, resilient, and efficient data processing framework. Understanding these principles is essential for managing a NiFi cluster, as they underpin the configuration, operation, and troubleshooting of clustered NiFi environments. By leveraging these concepts, organizations can optimize their data flows and maximize the performance and reliability of their NiFi deployments.

10.4 Configuring NiFi Nodes and Cluster Properties

Configuring NiFi nodes and their cluster properties is a fundamental step in establishing a robust data flow system that can effectively handle large volumes of data with high availability and scalability. This step is critical in ensuring that each node in the cluster operates efficiently and is properly synchronized with the rest of the system for optimal data processing and distribution. This section will discuss the practical aspects of configuring individual nodes within a NiFi cluster, as well as adjusting cluster-wide settings that affect all nodes.

NiFi nodes are individual instances of Apache NiFi that run on separate machines or virtual machines within a cluster. Each node participates in the cluster by processing data, making decisions about data flow, and communicating with other nodes to maintain cohesion and balance within the system. The configuration of these nodes involves setting various parameters that dictate how each node behaves and interacts with the cluster.

To begin, setting up a NiFi node requires the configuration of its 'nifi.properties' file. This file, located in the 'conf' directory of the

NiFi installation, contains key settings that define the node's operation within the cluster. Critical parameters in this file include:

- `nifi.cluster.is.node`: Determines whether the instance should operate as part of a cluster. Setting this to true enables clustering features.

- `nifi.cluster.node.address` and nifi.cluster.node. protocol.port: Specify the node's hostname and its cluster protocol port. These settings are vital for cluster communication.

- `nifi.web.http.host` and `nifi.web.http.port`: Defines the web interface's binding address and port, crucial for node management and monitoring.

Moreover, the 'nifi.zookeeper.connect.string' parameter must be configured to point to the ZooKeeper ensemble that manages the cluster's state coordination. This setting is vital for nodes to participate in the cluster, as ZooKeeper tracks which nodes are part of the cluster and facilitates their cooperation.

Configuring cluster-wide properties involves considerations that impact the entire cluster's performance and reliability. Such properties are primarily concerned with data synchronization, load balancing strategies, and fault tolerance measures. For instance, the 'nifi.cluster.load.balance.host' and 'nifi.cluster.load.balance.port' settings direct where nodes should send data to be evenly distributed across the cluster, ensuring that no single node becomes a bottleneck.

Ensuring consistent state management across the cluster requires configuring shared state resources. NiFi allows for the configuration of external state management providers, which can be specified in the 'nifi.state.management.configuration.file'. This enables nodes to share and sync state, such as processor configurations and cluster-wide settings, thus ensuring all nodes operate with a consistent view of the cluster's state.

Securing a NiFi cluster is another critical aspect of its configuration. Security parameters, including those for SSL/TLS configuration and user authentication, are set cluster-wide to protect data in transit and manage access control. Properties such as 'nifi.security.keystore', 'nifi.security.keystoreType', 'nifi.security.truststore', and 'nifi.security.truststoreType' are essential in defining the keystores and truststores for secure node communication.

```
1  # Example of SSL configuration in nifi.properties
2  nifi.security.keystore=./conf/keystore.jks
3  nifi.security.keystoreType=JKS
4  nifi.security.keystorePasswd=password
5  nifi.security.truststore=./conf/truststore.jks
6  nifi.security.truststoreType=JKS
7  nifi.security.truststorePasswd=password
```

Adjusting and fine-tuning these configurations is key to aligning the NiFi cluster's capabilities with the specific data flow and processing requirements of the deployment. It ensures that the cluster can handle the expected data load, provides high availability, and maintains data integrity and security throughout the data lifecycle.

Finally, it's important to mention that changes to a node's configuration or cluster-wide settings often require a node or cluster restart to take effect. Thus, planning for configuration changes and understanding their implications is crucial in minimizing downtime and ensuring the seamless operation of the NiFi cluster.

Configuring NiFi nodes and cluster properties is a meticulous task that lays the foundation for a scalable, reliable, and secure data flow system. By carefully setting node-specific and cluster-wide configurations, administrators can optimize their NiFi deployments to meet the demands of complex, high-volume data integration and processing workflows.

10.5 Load Balancing in a NiFi Cluster

Load balancing in a NiFi cluster is a vital strategy for distributing workloads evenly across the nodes in the cluster to enhance performance, prevent resource contention, and ensure high availability. This distribution mechanism targets optimal resource utilization by redirecting data flows and processing tasks in a way that no single node is overwhelmed, while others are idle or underutilized.

Connection Load Balancing: The first level of load balancing occurs at the connection level within the DataFlow. NiFi allows users to configure how data is partitioned across the cluster when queued between two processors or systems. This can be achieved through several strategies, including:

- Single Queue: All nodes share a single queue. This approach does not inherently distribute data but relies on nodes pulling data as they are able to process it.

- **Partitioned Queue**: Data is divided among nodes based on attributes or round-robin algorithms, ensuring a more equitable distribution of data across the cluster.

- **Prioritized Queue**: Data is distributed based on predefined criteria or priorities, ensuring that critical data is processed first across the cluster nodes.

Each of these strategies has its use case, depending on the nature of the data flow and the specific goals of the data processing tasks.

Site-to-Site Load Balancing: NiFi supports site-to-site (S2S) communication, enabling efficient data exchange between different NiFi instances or clusters. Implementing load balancing in S2S configurations allows for dynamic scaling of data flows across clusters, making it possible to balance traffic based on network latency, data size, or processing capabilities of target nodes.

Implementation Techniques: To configure load balancing in a NiFi cluster effectively, certain technical considerations and implementation techniques must be addressed, including:

```
1   # Configuration of load balancing properties in nifi.properties
2   nifi.cluster.load.balance.host=cluster-node-hostname
3   nifi.cluster.load.balance.port=6342
4   nifi.cluster.load.balance.connections.per.node=4
5   # Ensures that load balancing settings are correctly applied across the cluster
```

These configurations dictate how the NiFi nodes communicate for load balancing purposes, specifying the host and port for the load balancing service and the maximum number of connections per node that can be used for load balancing data flows.

Dynamic Scaling: NiFi clusters can benefit from dynamic scaling strategies, where nodes are added or removed from the cluster based on current load and processing demands. Such strategies require careful planning and monitoring to ensure that scaling actions do not disrupt ongoing data flows. Apache NiFi's in-built mechanisms facilitate the smooth transition of load as the cluster's composition changes, helping maintain a balance between throughput and resource utilization.

Monitoring and Management: Effective load balancing also demands constant monitoring and performance management. NiFi offers several tools and metrics for administrators to monitor load distribution, throughput, and processing efficiency across the cluster. These metrics provide insights into how well the load is balanced and highlight any potential bottlenecks or resource contention issues, allowing for timely adjustments.

To conclude, load balancing in a NiFi cluster is a multi-faceted process that involves careful planning, configuration, and ongoing management. By leveraging connection and site-to-site load balancing strategies, along with dynamic scaling and robust monitoring, administrators can ensure that their NiFi clusters are optimized for high performance, scalability, and reliability in processing diverse and demanding data streams.

10.6   Data Synchronization and State Management

Data synchronization and state management are foundational elements in the operation of an Apache NiFi cluster that ensure consistent and reliable data flow across its nodes. These components play a pivotal role in maintaining the integrity of data as it traverses through various processes in a distributed environment. This section will discuss the methodologies and mechanisms employed in Apache NiFi to achieve effective data synchronization and the techniques used for state management within a cluster.

Apache NiFi utilizes a shared state, also known as the cluster-wide state, to synchronize component configurations and operational states across all nodes in a cluster. This shared state ensures that any change made to a component's configuration on one node is propagated to all other nodes in the cluster, maintaining consistency and coherency of operations. This mechanism is critical for processors that maintain state, such as those tracking data provenance, ensuring data is processed in an identical manner across the cluster.

To facilitate data synchronization, NiFi implements the concept of ZooKeeper for managing the distributed coordination. ZooKeeper acts as a centralized service for maintaining configuration information, naming, providing distributed synchronization, and providing group services. All nodes in a NiFi cluster communicate with ZooKeeper to receive updates about the cluster's topology and any changes in component configurations or operational states. This approach enables NiFi clusters to dynamically adapt to changes, such as nodes joining or leaving the cluster without disrupting the data flow.

The state management in NiFi is further elaborated through two primary mechanisms: local state management and cluster state management. Local state management refers to the state maintained by individual components on a NiFi node, pertinent to their operational context. For instance, processors that perform aggregation functions may maintain local state information about the batches of records they have processed. This local state management is crucial for ensuring that upon restart or recovery, processors can resume operations without loss of data fidelity or duplication.

On the other hand, cluster state management involves maintaining state information that is shared across all nodes in the NiFi cluster. This is particularly important for processors that need to ensure unique operations across the cluster, such as generating unique identifiers for data records or maintaining counters. NiFi achieves cluster state management through the use of a distributed cache that is accessible by all nodes. This cache is utilized to store and retrieve shared state information, thereby ensuring that despite the distributed nature of operations, consistency is maintained across the cluster.

```
1   // Example of accessing shared state in a NiFi processor
2   public void onTrigger(ProcessContext context, ProcessSession session) throws
        ProcessException {
3       final StateManager stateManager = context.getStateManager();
4       final StateMap stateMap = stateManager.getState(Scope.CLUSTER);
5       // Retrieve state
6       String sharedValue = stateMap.get("sharedKey");
7       // Update state
8       Map<String, String> newState = new HashMap<>();
9       newState.put("sharedKey", "newValue");
10      stateManager.setState(newState, Scope.CLUSTER);
11  }
```

The efficient management of data synchronization and state in a NiFi cluster is instrumental in achieving high availability, fault tolerance, and seamless operation. By leveraging ZooKeeper for distributed coordination and employing robust state management practices, NiFi ensures that data flows can be scaled out across multiple nodes without compromising data integrity and operational efficiency. These mechanisms collectively contribute to NiFi's capability to facilitate reliable, large-scale data integration tasks across disparate data sources and destinations, underpinning the importance of data synchronization and state management in the context of real-time data processing and analytics.

10.7 Securing a NiFi Cluster

Securing a NiFi cluster involves implementing measures to protect the data flowing through it and the resources performing the data processing. Given the sensitivity and value of data in modern applications, ensuring confidentiality, integrity, and availability in a NiFi cluster is paramount. This section will discuss the mechanisms for securing a NiFi cluster, encompassing authentication, authorization, encryption, and system-level security.

Authentication in a NiFi cluster is the first line of defense, intended to verify the identity of users or systems requesting access. NiFi supports multiple authentication mechanisms, including username/-password credentials, LDAP (Lightweight Directory Access Protocol), Kerberos, and client certificates for SSL (Secure Sockets Layer). Configuring NiFi to use these mechanisms ensures that only authorized entities can interact with the cluster. The following code snippet demonstrates the configuration of an LDAP-based authentication in the `login-identity-providers.xml` file:

```
1   <provider>
2      <identifier>ldap-provider</identifier>
3      <class>org.apache.nifi.ldap.LdapProvider</class>
4      <property name="Authentication Strategy">LDAPS</property>
5      <property name="Manager DN">cn=Manager,dc=example,dc=com</property>
6      <property name="Manager Password">password</property>
7      <property name="TLS - Keystore">./conf/keystore.jks</property>
8      <property name="TLS - Keystore Password">password</property>
9      <property name="TLS - Truststore">./conf/truststore.jks</property>
10     <property name="TLS - Truststore Password">password</property>
11     <property name="User Search Base">ou=users,dc=example,dc=com</property>
12     <property name="User Search Filter">(uid={0})</property>
13  </provider>
```

Authorization, the process of determining the access levels and permissions of authenticated users, is managed in NiFi through the use of policies configured on user groups or individual users. NiFi employs an access policy model where resources (such as data flows, processors, and controller services) are protected by defining who can perform operations on them. This granular control over resources ensures that users can only interact with parts of the cluster necessary for their role.

Encryption is essential for protecting data at rest and in transit. NiFi supports TLS encryption for data in transit, ensuring that data flows securely between nodes in a cluster and between clients and the cluster. To configure TLS, certificates must be created and distributed to all nodes in the cluster. Additionally, NiFi provides the capability to configure encrypted provenance repositories and content repositories, safeguarding data at rest.

```
Encryption Enabled: true
Provenance Repository: EncryptedWriteAheadProvenanceRepository
Content Repository: EncryptedFileSystemRepository
```

System-level security involves securing the environment in which NiFi runs. This includes hardening the operating system, applying the principle of least privilege to NiFi processes, and ensuring network security practices are in place. Firewalls and network segmentation can be used to control access to the NiFi cluster, while system monitoring and intrusion detection systems can provide insights into unauthorized attempts to access the cluster.

Securing a NiFi cluster requires a comprehensive approach that includes authentication, authorization, encryption, and system-level security measures. By meticulously applying these security practices, organizations can significantly mitigate the risk of unauthorized access and data breaches, thereby maintaining the confidentiality, integrity, and availability of their data flows.

10.8 Monitoring and Managing Cluster Health

Monitoring and managing cluster health is essential for maintaining the robustness and efficiency of Apache NiFi clusters, enabling administrators to preemptively address issues before they escalate into major problems that impact data flow and processing. This section will discuss the mechanisms and practices for effectively observing and managing the health and performance of NiFi clusters.

The Apache NiFi user interface (UI) is a primary tool for monitoring cluster health. It provides a comprehensive overview of the cluster, displaying critical metrics such as flow file counts, queue sizes, processor statuses, and system diagnostics. Specifically, the UI offers a Cluster tab that visualizes the state of each node within the cluster, indicating whether each node is connected, disconnected, or experiencing connection issues.

To ensure a granular and continuous monitoring process, integrating NiFi with external monitoring solutions through its REST API or the

Site-to-Site (S2S) protocol is recommended. Tools such as Grafana, Prometheus, or even custom monitoring applications can consume metrics exposed by NiFi, enabling administrators to construct detailed dashboards that reflect the real-time status of the cluster. These dashboards can track metrics on a per-node basis, including processor load, throughput, heap memory usage, and garbage collection statistics.

```
1   # Example REST API call to retrieve NiFi cluster status
2   curl -X GET http://nifi-cluster-host:8080/nifi-api/flow/cluster/summary
```

```
{
  "clusterSummary": {
    "connectedNodes": "3 / 3",
    "totalNodeCount": 3,
    "connectedNodeCount": 3,
    "clustered": true,
    "connectedToCluster": true
  }
}
```

The importance of configuring alerts cannot be overstated. Threshold-based alerts can be configured to notify administrators of critical conditions, such as high CPU utilization, memory pressure, or queue backlogs exceeding predefined limits. This proactive approach enables swift response to potential issues, minimizing downtime and data processing delays.

Log files are another vital resource for monitoring cluster health. NiFi logs events and errors in detail, providing insights into the behavior of the cluster. Regularly reviewing and analyzing log files can help in identifying patterns or recurring issues that may not be immediately apparent through metrics or alerts. For efficient log management, incorporating tools like Elasticsearch, Logstash, and Kibana (the ELK stack) or similar platforms can automate log aggregation and analysis, making it easier to diagnose problems.

In managing NiFi cluster health, it is crucial to perform routine maintenance tasks. These include clearing queues that hold unnecessary flow files, reallocating or adjusting resources among different processors, and updating workflow configurations to optimize performance. Such adjustments are often necessary to adapt to changing data volumes or processing demands and can significantly affect the overall health and efficiency of the cluster.

Backup and recovery strategies form an integral part of managing cluster health. Regularly backing up NiFi configurations, including flow definitions and controller services, ensures that the cluster can be quickly restored to a known good state in the event of a failure or accidental configuration changes that disrupt data flows.

To complement these strategies, Apache NiFi provides several built-in processors and controller services designed to enhance cluster management and reliability. For instance, the SiteToSiteBulletinReportingTask processor enables the sharing of system bulletins across the cluster, facilitating the centralized collection of warnings and errors that could indicate underlying health issues.

By leveraging the Apache NiFi UI, integrating with external monitoring tools, configuring alerts, analyzing logs, performing regular maintenance, implementing backup and recovery plans, and utilizing NiFi's built-in features for cluster management, administrators can effectively monitor and manage the health of NiFi clusters. This comprehensive approach to monitoring and managing cluster health is essential for ensuring that NiFi clusters remain robust, efficient, and capable of handling large-scale data integration tasks with high reliability.

10.9 Cluster Scaling and Capacity Planning

Effective scaling and meticulous capacity planning are pivotal for the sustained performance and reliability of Apache NiFi clusters when dealing with growing or fluctuating data loads. This section delineates the framework and strategies integral to scaling and capacity planning within a NiFi ecosystem.

First, it's essential to comprehend the two primary scaling approaches: vertical scaling and horizontal scaling. Vertical scaling involves augmenting the computational power of existing nodes in the cluster (e.g., increasing CPU, memory, or storage resources), while horizontal scaling refers to adding more nodes to the cluster to expand its overall capacity. Both strategies have their merits and can be employed concurrently to meet the demands of an evolving data processing landscape.

Evaluating Cluster Performance and Identifying Bottlenecks: Before embarking on scaling efforts, one must assess the current cluster performance to identify potential bottlenecks. This process begins with monitoring key metrics such as CPU usage, memory utilization, disk I/O, and network throughput on each node, alongside an examination of NiFi-specific metrics like flow file processing time, queue sizes, and back pressure indicators. Analyzing these metrics helps in pinpointing the constraints limiting cluster performance.

Vertical Scaling Considerations: When contemplating vertical scaling, one should carefully evaluate the cost-effectiveness and potential limitations of this approach. Although it might offer a quick fix to performance issues, there are physical and economical constraints to how much a single node can be scaled. It is also prudent to consider the impact of server restarts or downtime required for hardware upgrades on data processing continuity.

Horizontal Scaling Strategy: In contrast, horizontal scaling offers a more flexible approach to capacity expansion. Adding nodes to a cluster can enhance processing power, increase redundancy, and improve fault tolerance. However, this strategy necessitates careful planning to ensure consistent data distribution and efficient load balancing across the cluster. As nodes are added, the cluster's configuration, including properties related to data flow management and inter-node communication, must be meticulously updated to maintain optimal performance.

```
1   # Example of a command to add a node to a NiFi cluster
2   nifi.sh cluster-add-node --hostname new-node-01 --port 8080
```

Automated Scaling: Embracing automation for cluster scaling can significantly enhance the cluster's ability to adapt to changing data volumes dynamically. Leveraging cloud-based infrastructure or container orchestration tools (e.g., Kubernetes) that support auto-scaling based on predefined metrics (e.g., CPU or memory utilization) can result in a highly responsive and efficient NiFi deployment. It is crucial, however, to establish appropriate scaling thresholds and policies to avoid excessive scaling operations that could lead to underutilization or cost inefficiencies.

Capacity Planning Techniques: Accurate capacity planning requires forecasting future data loads and processing requirements by analyzing historical data growth trends and projecting future needs. This foresight enables the proactive scaling of the cluster, either vertically or horizontally, to accommodate anticipated demands. Planning should also account for peak load periods, ensuring the cluster has sufficient headroom to handle sudden spikes in data volume without degradation in processing performance.

Incorporating Load Testing in the Planning Process: Conducting load testing on the NiFi cluster is a valuable practice for capacity planning.

Simulating various load scenarios can uncover how the cluster reacts to different levels of demand, providing insights into its scalability limits and the effectiveness of current scaling strategies. Iterative testing, combined with gradual scaling adjustments, contributes to developing a robust understanding of the cluster's behavior under stress, facilitating informed capacity planning decisions.

Continuous Monitoring and Adjustment: Lastly, capacity planning and cluster scaling are ongoing processes. Continuous monitoring of the cluster's performance and periodic reviews of capacity plans are imperative to ensure that the NiFi deployment remains aligned with evolving data processing needs. Adjustments to the scaling strategy should be made in response to observed changes in data patterns, infrastructure innovations, or enhancements in NiFi's capabilities.

Adhering to these principles for cluster scaling and capacity planning will equip Apache NiFi users with the strategies required to ensure that their data processing infrastructure can gracefully adjust to the demands of an ever-changing data landscape, ensuring high performance, reliability, and cost efficiency.

10.10 Troubleshooting Common Cluster Issues

Effective troubleshooting of Apache NiFi cluster issues is imperative to maintain a stable and high-performing data pipeline. This section will discuss common cluster issues and their resolution strategies to ensure the continuous operation of NiFi deployments.

One prevalent issue in NiFi cluster operation is node synchronization failures. These failures can manifest as discrepancies in data flow versions, missing or delayed data flow updates across nodes, and inconsistent processor states. The primary cause is often network connectivity issues or misconfigurations in node settings. To resolve synchronization problems, first verify the network connectivity among all cluster nodes. It is essential to check firewall rules, network interfaces, and connectivity ports specified in the NiFi configuration files, particularly `nifi.properties`, for entries related to cluster communication protocols. Additionally, ensuring time synchronization across all cluster nodes using Network Time Protocol (NTP) can prevent mismatches in time-dependent operations and logs, which could affect synchronization.

Another common challenge is load imbalances across cluster nodes, which might lead to performance bottlenecks. This scenario typically occurs when one or more nodes handle a significantly higher volume of tasks than others. NiFi provides several load balancing strategies, configurable at the connection level within data flows, to distribute data more evenly across the cluster. To configure load balancing, navigate to the connection settings in the NiFi UI, and select the desired strategy from the Load Balance Strategy drop-down menu. Options such as Round Robin, Next in Queue, and Partition by Attribute enable fine-grained control over flow distribution. Employing an appropriate strategy based on the nature of the data and flow can mitigate load imbalance issues.

Data synchronization and state management are central to the seamless operation of NiFi clusters, yet issues here can lead to data loss or duplication when not managed correctly. Utilizing the Distributed Map Cache and ZooKeeper for state management aids in maintaining consistent state information across cluster nodes. Ensuring that the ZooKeeper service is correctly configured and operational is crucial. Check the zookeeper.properties file for accurate server lists and port configurations. If ZooKeeper experiences frequent disconnections or performance issues, it may be necessary to adjust its heap size or review the network infrastructure between NiFi nodes and ZooKeeper servers.

Securing a NiFi cluster introduces its set of challenges, including certificate management and user authentication issues. If nodes fail to join the cluster due to security or certificate problems, verify the keystore and truststore configurations in nifi.properties. The certificates must be correctly issued by a trusted Certificate Authority (CA), and the truststore must include the CA's certificate used to sign the node certificates. In cases of authentication failure, reviewing the login-identity-providers.xml file for misconfigurations and ensuring alignment with the chosen identity provider's requirements are critical steps.

Monitoring and managing cluster health often reveal underlying issues not immediately visible. Regularly monitoring NiFi's logs, accessible via the logs directory, and the NiFi User Interface diagnostics can provide insights into node performance, data flow errors, and configuration problems. Setting up alert mechanisms through NiFi's reporting tasks can proactively notify administrators of potential issues before they escalate.

Addressing the common issues outlined involves a methodical approach to diagnosing and resolving cluster problems. By rigorously checking configurations, network settings, security parameters, and employing NiFi's built-in mechanisms for load balancing and state management, most cluster issues can be effectively mitigated. Keeping a NiFi cluster running smoothly requires ongoing management and attentiveness to detail, but by adhering to the strategies discussed, administrators can ensure reliable and efficient data pipeline operations.

10.11   Best Practices for Cluster Configuration and Management

Managing and configuring Apache NiFi clusters requires a comprehensive understanding of the system's intricacies to ensure optimal performance, reliability, and security. This section will discuss several best practices for NiFi cluster configuration and management, aiding in the development of robust, efficient, and scalable data flow systems.

Firstly, it is crucial to establish a consistent naming convention for all NiFi components, including nodes, connections, processors, and controller services. This convention facilitates easier identification, configuration, and troubleshooting of components within a cluster.

- Uniform naming aids in quickly locating components for configuration adjustments or issue resolution.

- Using descriptive names for processors and services enhances understanding of data flow purpose and functionality.

Secondly, optimizing the configuration of NiFi nodes for specific workloads is essential. This involves adjusting the `bootstrap.conf` and `nifi.properties` files to allocate appropriate JVM memory, specifying node roles, and enabling features such as auto-restart for enhanced resilience.

```
1   # Example of JVM memory allocation in bootstrap.conf
2   java.arg.2=-Xms4g
3   java.arg.3=-Xmx4g
4
5   # Example of node role specification in nifi.properties
6   nifi.cluster.node.protocol.port=9999
```

Load balancing is a key aspect of efficient cluster operation. Properly configured load balancing strategies ensure even distribution of data across the cluster, preventing bottlenecks and optimizing resource utilization.

- Connection-level load balancing can be configured for each data flow, offering flexibility in handling varying load patterns.

- Prioritizing connections for critical data flows ensures essential processes receive necessary resources.

Data synchronization and state management are central to maintaining consistency across the cluster. Employing a shared external state management mechanism, such as Apache ZooKeeper, facilitates synchronization of cluster-wide state, critical for processes that require consensus or coordination.

```
1  # Example ZooKeeper configuration in nifi.properties
2  nifi.zookeeper.connect.string=zk-server-1:2181,zk-server-2:2181,zk-server-3:2181
3  nifi.zookeeper.root.node=/nifi
```

Securing a NiFi cluster involves implementing authentication, authorization, and encryption mechanisms to protect data and manage access. Configuring TLS/SSL for intra-cluster communication and data ingress/egress points is a fundamental security measure.

- Leveraging NiFi's integrated user management and access control lists (ACLs) restricts access based on roles and responsibilities.

- Encrypting sensitive properties and flow content at rest adds an additional layer of security.

Monitoring cluster health and performance is essential for early detection and resolution of issues. Utilizing NiFi's built-in monitoring tools, along with external solutions like Grafana for visualizing metrics, enables comprehensive oversight of cluster status and trends.

```
# Example output from NiFi monitoring tool
[2023-03-01 12:00:00] Node 1 CPU Usage: 75%
[2023-03-01 12:00:00] Node 2 CPU Usage: 80%
```

For cluster scaling and capacity planning, adopt a proactive approach based on historical data and anticipated growth patterns. Incrementally adjusting resources and node count prevents over-provisioning while maintaining performance and fault tolerance.

Lastly, maintain a regular backup and recovery process for NiFi configurations and templates. This ensures rapid restoration in the event of failure and facilitates migration to new versions or installations with minimal downtime.

Effective NiFi cluster configuration and management are multi-faceted, requiring attention to detail across components naming, node configuration, load balancing, data synchronization, security, monitoring, scaling, and disaster recovery. Implementing these best practices allows administrators to create and maintain high-performance, secure, and resilient NiFi clusters that can handle complex, large-scale data integration tasks efficiently.

10.12   Migrating and Upgrading NiFi Clusters

Migrating and upgrading Apache NiFi clusters involves careful planning and execution to ensure data pipelines' continuity, performance, and availability. This section discusses the methodologies, precautions, and steps necessary to migrate NiFi clusters to new hardware or cloud environments and upgrade them to newer versions without disrupting ongoing data flows.

Migration Considerations

When planning the migration of a NiFi cluster, the following key considerations should guide your approach:

- **Current State Analysis:** Evaluate the current cluster configuration, including the number of nodes, their roles (primary node, node), dataflow configurations, and custom processors or extensions in use.

- **Dependency Assessment:** Identify all external dependencies, such as data sources, sink connections, and services (like databases, APIs, or external storage) that the NiFi cluster interacts with.

- **Hardware and Network Requirements:** Define the hardware and network requirements for the new environment, ensuring it meets or exceeds the current setup's specifications to maintain or enhance performance.

- **Data Migration Strategy:** Develop a strategy for migrating existing dataflows, templates, and configuration settings. Consider using NiFi's built-in export and import features for templates and versioned flows if applicable.

- **Testing Plan:** Establish a comprehensive testing plan to validate dataflows in the new environment before going live.

Upgrading NiFi Clusters

Upgrading an Apache NiFi cluster to a newer version involves several stages, from preparation to validation. Follow these steps to ensure a smooth upgrade process:

1. **Review Release Notes:** Before initiating an upgrade, review the release notes of the newer version to familiarize yourself with new features, bug fixes, and any deprecated features.

2. **Backup Existing Configuration:** Backup the existing cluster configuration, including flow definitions, custom processors, and property files. This ensures that you can restore the original state in case of an unsuccessful upgrade.

3. **Staged Roll-out:** If possible, perform the upgrade in stages. Begin with a non-production environment to validate the upgrade process and identify any issues.

4. **Upgrade Process:** Follow the recommended upgrade process, which typically involves stopping the cluster, upgrading each node sequentially, and then restarting the cluster. Pay close attention to any version-specific upgrade instructions provided in the documentation.

5. **Validate Upgrade:** Once the upgrade is complete, thoroughly test the cluster and its dataflows to ensure everything operates as expected. This might include running existing workflows, checking the integration with external systems, and monitoring cluster performance.

Post-Migration and Upgrade Tasks

After successfully migrating or upgrading a NiFi cluster, several post-migration tasks are critical to the operation and maintenance of the cluster:

- **Performance Tuning:** Depending on the new environment or version, performance tuning may be necessary to optimize resource utilization and data processing throughput.

- **Monitoring Setup:** Reconfigure monitoring tools or adjust thresholds to accommodate changes in the cluster environment or architecture. This ensures you can effectively monitor cluster health, performance, and troubleshoot issues promptly.

- **Documenting Changes:** Update internal documentation to reflect changes in the cluster configuration, including new hardware specifications, software versions, and any modifications to dataflows or processes.

- **Training and Communication:** Inform and train relevant stakeholders on any new features, improvements, or changes in operational procedures resulting from the migration or upgrade.

Migrating and upgrading NiFi clusters requires meticulous planning, thorough testing, and attention to detail. By adhering to best practices and carefully considering the unique aspects of the NiFi architecture and dataflows, organizations can ensure minimal downtime and maintain data processing capabilities throughout the process. This ensures that the NiFi cluster continues to provide robust, scalable, and efficient data management and integration capabilities needed to meet evolving data processing needs.

www.ingramcontent.com/pod-product-compliance
Lightning Source LLC
LaVergne TN
LVHW051444050326
832903LV00030BD/3238